DOS For Dummies®, 3rd Edition

Cheat Sheet

BESTSELLING BOOK SERIES

For those times when you're even too lazy to read *DOS For Dummies*, here's a quick reference to a few essential items.

Filenames

Filenames have two parts: The first part (the filename) can be from one to eight characters long. The second part (the extension) starts with a dot (period) and can be from one to three characters long.

The first part of a filename should be as descriptive as is possible with eight characters.

The second part of a filename should tell you what type of file it is: TXT for text files and DOC for documents, for example.

Filenames can contain letters and numbers and can also start with a number. Filenames cannot contain spaces. The following characters are also forbidden in a filename:

. " / \ [ ] : * | < > + = ; , ?

The ? wildcard is used to match a single character in a filename.

The * wildcard is used to match a group of characters in a filename.

The *.* wildcard matches all filenames.

Helpful info

Always quit an application when you're done with it; return to DOS, and then start your next program.

Never turn off a computer when a disk drive light is on.

Always turn off the computer when you're at a DOS prompt (C>).

`Bad command or file name` means that DOS doesn't recognize the command; check your typing, check for errant spaces, and then try again.

`File not found` means that DOS can't locate the file you've named; check your typing, check for errant spaces, and then try again.

`Abort, Retry, Ignore` means that something's amiss. If you can fix the problem, do so (such as inserting a disk into the drive), and then press R for *r*etry. If it's beyond hope, press A to *a*bort. Never press I for *i*gnore (or F for *f*ail if that option is listed).

Pathnames

The root directory on every disk is named \ (backslash).

A pathname starts with the drive letter, a colon, and then the root directory: C:\

Directory names in a pathname are separated by backslashes: C:\123\AGENDA

A pathname never ends with a backslash (see above).

A filename can be the last item in the pathname; it must be separated from the last directory by a backslash: C:\PROCOMM\

For Dummies: Bestselling Book Series for Beginners

FOR DUMMIES™

BESTSELLING
BOOK SERIES

DOS For Dummies®, 3rd Edition

Cheat Sheet

For those times when you're even too lazy to read *DOS For Dummies*,
here's a quick reference to a few essential items.

General stuff

This is the DOS prompt: C>

The DOS prompt may also look like this: C:\>

You can use upper- or lowercase letters to
type at the DOS prompt.

Press Backspace to erase.

Press Esc (Escape) to cancel.

Press F3 to repeat the last DOS command.

Press Enter to send the command to DOS.

Lost and found

Where am I?

To find your current drive and directory,
type the CD command (by itself). That
displays the full name of your current drive
and directory: C> CD C:\123\BUDGET

In this example, the CD command tells you
that you're on drive C in the \123\BUDGET
directory.

Where is it?

To find a lost file when you don't know its
name, type this DOS command: C> DIR /P

If you do know the file's name, type this
command: C> DIR \FILE1 /S

Press Enter and watch the screen for your
file (named FILE1 in this example). DOS
displays the directory in which the file is
located. You can then use the CD command
to change to that directory.

To find a lost directory, type this command:
C? DIR *.* /A:D /S | FIND "SUBDIR"

Carefully type that command and substitute
your directory's name for SUBDIR.

Sneaky DOS guide

To Do This This	Type or Press
Cancel a DOS command	Ctrl+C
Pause a long display	Ctrl+S
Turn on DOS's printer	Ctrl+P
Turn off DOS's printer	Ctrl+P
Clear the screen	CLS
Log from drive C to drive A	A:
Log from drive A to drive C	C:
Change directories to /DATA	CD DATA
Change to the root directory	CD\
List all files	DIR
List files in the wide format	DIR /W
List files with a page/pause	DIR /P
List a specific file, FILE1	DIR FILE1
Make a duplicate of a file	COPY FILE1 FILE2
Copy a file to another drive	COPY FILE1 A:
Copy a file to another directory	COPY FILE1 \ OTHER\DATA
Copy a group of files	COPY *.DOC A:
Delete a file	DEL FILE1
Delete a group of files	DEL *.DOC
Delete all files	DEL *.*
Rename a file FILEONE	REN FILE1
Rename a group of files	REN *.DOC *.BAK
Move a file (Part 1) C:\NEW	COPY FILE1
Move a file (Part 2)	DEL FILE1
Move a file (DOS 6)	MOVE FILE1 C:\
Display a file's contents	TYPE FILE1
Format a disk in drive A	FORMAT A:
Format a disk in drive B	FORMAT B:
Format a low-density 5¼-inch disk	FORMAT A:/F:360
Format a low-density 3½-inch disk	FORMAT A:/F:720

For Dummies: Bestselling Book Series for Beginners

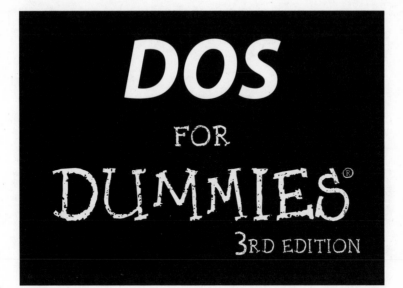

DOS
FOR
DUMMIES®
3RD EDITION

DOS FOR DUMMIES®

3RD EDITION

by Dan Gookin

author of *DOS For Dummies*®, Windows® 95 Edition;
Word 2000 For Windows® *For Dummies*®; and the
Illustrated Computer Dictionary For Dummies®

Wiley Publishing, Inc.

DOS For Dummies®, 3rd Edition

Published by
Wiley Publishing, Inc.
909 Third Avenue
New York, NY 10022
www.wiley.com

For general information on our other products and services or to obtain technical support, please contact our Customer Care Department within the U.S. at 800-762-2974, outside the U.S. at 317-572-3993, or fax 317-572-4002.

Wiley also publishes its books in a variety of electronic formats. Some content that appears in print may not be available in electronic books.

Library of Congress Cataloging-in-Publication Data:

Library of Congress Catalog Card No.: 99-66373

ISBN: 0-7645-0361-8

Manufactured in the United States of America

10

About the Author

Dan Gookin got started with computers back in the post slide rule age of computing: 1982. His first intention was to buy a computer to replace his aged and constantly breaking typewriter. Working as slave labor in a restaurant, however, Gookin was unable to afford the full "word processor" setup and settled on a computer that had a monitor, keyboard, and little else. Soon, his writing career was under way with several submissions to fiction magazines and lots of rejections.

The big break came in 1984 when he began writing about computers. Applying his flair for fiction with a self-taught knowledge of computers, Gookin was able to demystify the subject and explain technology in a relaxed and understandable voice. He even dared to add humor, which eventually won him a column in a local computer magazine.

Eventually Gookin's talents came to roost as a ghostwriter at a computer book publishing house. That was followed by an editing position at a San Diego computer magazine. During this time, he also regularly participated on a radio talk show about computers. In addition, Gookin kept writing books about computers, some of which became minor bestsellers.

In 1990, Gookin and IDG Books Worldwide, Inc., connected on an outrageous book idea: a long overdue and original idea for the computer book for the rest of us. What became *DOS For Dummies* blossomed into an international bestseller with hundreds and thousands of copies in print and many translations.

Today, Gookin still considers himself a writer and computer "guru" whose job it is to remind everyone that computers are not to be taken too seriously. His approach to computers is light and humorous yet very informative. He knows that the complex beasts are important and can help people become productive and successful. Gookin mixes his knowledge of computers with a unique, dry sense of humor that keeps everyone informed — and awake. His favorite quote is, "Computers are a notoriously dull subject, but that doesn't mean I have to write about them that way."

Gookin's titles for IDG Books Worldwide include the best-selling *DOS For Dummies*, 1st and 2nd Editions and the Windows 95 Edition; *Real Life Windows 95; Word For Windows 95 For Dummies; Microsoft MS-DOS 6.2 Upgrade For Dummies; MORE DOS For Dummies; WordPerfect For Dummies; WordPerfect 6 For Dummies; MORE WordPerfect For Dummies; PCs For Dummies*, 1st and 2nd Editions; *Word For Windows For Dummies; Word For Windows 6 For Dummies*; and all three editions of the *Illustrated Computer Dictionary For Dummies*. All told, he has written more than 30 books about computers and contributes regularly to *DOS Resource Guide, InfoWorld*, and *PC Computing* magazine. Gookin holds a degree in communications from the University of California, San Diego, and lives with his wife and three sons in the as-yet-untamed state of Idaho.

Publisher's Acknowledgments

We're proud of this book; please send us your comments through our online registration form located at www.dummies.com/register/.

Some of the people who helped bring this book to market include the following:

Acquisitions, Editorial, and Media Development

Project Editor: Rebecca Whitney

Acquisitions Manager: Michael Kelly

Technical Editor: Terrie Lynn Solomon

Editorial Manager: Mary C. Corder

Editorial Assistant: Paul E. Kuzmic

Production

Project Coordinator: E. Shawn Aylsworth

Layout and Graphics: Amy Adrian, Brian Drumm, Kelly Hardesty, Angela F. Hunckler, Kate Jenkins, Barry Offringa, Doug Rolleson, Brent Savage, Jacque Schneider, Janet Seib, Michael A. Sullivan, Mary Jo Weis, Erin Zeltner

Proofreaders: Laura Albert, John Greenough, Nancy L. Reinhardt, Marianne Santy

Indexer: Lori Lathrop

Special Help
Dwight Ramsey, Reprint Editor
Suzanne Thomas, Associate Editor/Freelance

General and Administrative

Wiley Technology Publishing Group: Richard Swadley, Vice President and Executive Group Publisher; Bob Ipsen, Vice President and Group Publisher; Joseph Wikert, Vice President and Publisher; Barry Pruett, Vice President and Publisher; Mary Bednarek, Editorial Director; Mary C. Corder, Editorial Director; Andy Cummings, Editorial Director

Wiley Manufacturing: Carol Tobin, Director of Manufacturing

Wiley Marketing: John Helmus, Assistant Vice President, Director of Marketing

Wiley Composition Services: Gerry Fahey, Vice President, Production Services; Debbie Stailey, Director of Composition Services

Contents at a Glance

Cartoons at a Glance

By Rich Tennant

page 241

page 71

"IT'S ABOUT A GROUP OF YOUNG, INEXPERIENCED GERMAN PROGRAMMERS ALL CRAMPED TOGETHER INSIDE THIS HOT, TINY COMPUTER ROOM FIGHTING THE VIRUS OF THEIR LIVES DURING THE EARLY YEARS OF NETWORK COMMUNICATIONS."

"LET ME GUESS – NO SURGE PROTECTORS...RIGHT?"

page 317

"NAAAH – HE'S NOT THAT SMART. HE WON'T BACK UP HIS HARD DISK, FORGETS TO CONSISTENTLY NAME HIS FILES, AND DROOLS ALL OVER THE KEYBOARD."

page 5

"I'M WAITING FOR MY AUTOEXEC FILE TO RUN, SO I'M GONNA GRAB A CUP OF COFFEE, MAYBE MAKE A SANDWICH, CHECK THE SPORTS PAGE, REGRIND THE BRAKE DRUMS ON MY TRUCK, BALANCE MY CHECKBOOK FOR THE PAST 12 YEARS, LEARN SWAHILI, ..."

page 155

"A CONSULTANT TOLD US THAT POLYESTER CAN CAUSE SHORTS IN THE SYSTEM, SO WE'RE TRYING AN ALL LEATHER AND LATEX DATA ENTRY DEPARTMENT."

page 289

Fax: 978-546-7747
E-mail: richtennant@the5thwave.com
World Wide Web: www.the5thwave.com

Table of Contents

Introduction

· ·

Welcome to *DOS For Dummies,* 3rd Edition, a book that wastes no time
and gets right to the point about the world's most loathsome computer operating system, DOS.

The idea here is simple: You're a smart person but a DOS dummy — and you
have absolutely no intention of ever becoming a DOS wizard. You don't want
to learn anything. You don't want to be bored by technical details or background fodder. All you need to know is that single answer to one tiny
question, and then you want to close the book and be on with your life. This
is the book you're looking for.

This book covers 100 percent of the things you do with your computer. All
the common activities, the daily chores, and the painful things that go on
with a computer are described here — in English — and in a style that I
believe you'll find engaging, informative, and, at socially correct times,
humorous.

About This Book

This book isn't meant to be read from front to back. It's more like a reference.
Each chapter is divided into sections, each of which has self-contained information about doing something in DOS. Typical sections include

Changing Disks

Typing at the Prompt

Deleting a Group of Files

"My Keyboard Beeps at Me!"

Formatting a Disk

Finding a Lost File

"Where Am I?"

You don't have to remember anything in this book. Nothing is worth memo-
rizing. You never "learn" anything here. The information is what you need to
know to get by, and nothing more. If any new terms or technical descriptions
are offered, you're alerted and told to ignore them.

How to Use This Book

This book works like a reference: You start by looking up the topic that concerns you in either the table of contents or the index. That refers you to a specific section in the book. In that section, you read about doing whatever it is you want to do. Some special terms may be defined, but usually you're directed elsewhere if you want to learn about the terms.

If you're supposed to type something, it appears in the text as follows:

```
C> TYPE THIS STUFF
```

Always press Enter after you're told to type something. In case you're baffled, a description of what you're typing usually follows (with explanations of the more difficult stuff).

Occasionally, you may have to type something specific to your system. When that happens, you're told how to type the command particular to your situation, usually by replacing the bogus filename in this book with the name of a file on your disk. Nothing is ever harder than that.

If you need more information, you're directed to that chapter and section. If anything goes wrong, you're told what to do and how to remedy the situation.

At no time does this book direct you back to the DOS manual (yuck!). If you're into learning about DOS, however, I recommend a good tutorial on the subject. Although this book helps you after the tutorial is done, the book is not meant as a substitute. (You definitely don't need to read a tutorial before using this book. Just having to breathe the same air as a computer qualifies you!)

What You're Not to Read

Several sections offer extra information and background explanations. (I just couldn't resist — after writing 20-odd books about using computers, I can't compel myself not to do this.) Those sections are clearly marked, and you can quickly skip over them, as you please. Reading them only increases your knowledge of DOS — and that's definitely not what this book is all about.

Foolish Assumptions

I'm going to make only one assumption about you: You have a PC and you "work" with it somehow. Furthermore, I assume that someone else set up your computer and may have even given you a few brief lessons. It's nice to have someone close by (or on the phone) who can help. But you know how unbalanced they can become when you ask too many questions (and don't have enough M&Ms or Doritos handy).

Icons Used in This Book

 Alerts you to nerdy technical discussions you may want to skip (or read — for that nerd in all of us).

 Any shortcuts or new insights on a topic.

 Something different or strange about using DOS with Windows 95 or later.

 A friendly reminder to do something.

 A friendly reminder *not* to do something.

Where to Go from Here

Now you're ready to use this book. Look over the table of contents and find something that interests you. Just about everything you can do with DOS is listed here. Primarily, you spend your time in what Chairman Mao called "the great struggle with the computer." Do so. Toil, toil, toil. When you hit a speed bump, look it up here. You'll have the answer and be back to work in a jiffy. (Or half a jiffy, if you're a quick reader.)

Good luck! And keep your fingers crossed.

Part I

The Absolute Basics

By Rich Tennant

"NAAAH – HE'S NOT THAT SMART. HE WON'T BACK UP HIS HARD DISK, FORGETS TO CONSISTENTLY NAME HIS FILES, AND DROOLS ALL OVER THE KEYBOARD."

In this part . . .

You know the type: The person who tells a long story? They take longer to tell the story than it took for the story to happen in the first place. Some computer books are like that. They take so much time getting around to telling you what it is that you *really* need to know — and know right now — that you could get a Ph.D. in computer science by the time they got around to it. No, no, no. You want to know the good stuff now. Up front! Very obvious! With some cheer and fun tossed in.

Welcome to the book written just for you.

Chapter 1

Getting On with It

● ●

In This Chapter

▶ Turning the computer on

▶ Examining the screen

▶ Turning the computer off

▶ Turning the computer off in Windows

▶ Leaving a computer on all the time

▶ Making the computer sleep

▶ Resetting the computer

● ●

*T*urning something on or off shouldn't be complicated. The computer is really no exception. You would think that the computer would have several On and Off switches to make it tough on you. But, no. It has just that one Big Red Switch (which is often neither big nor red) that makes the personal computer stop or go. Yet that's not such a big deal. What is a big deal is when and how to throw the switch and all the stuff that happens in between. That's what makes you chew your nails down to the nub or hop on one foot and chant a mantra while clutching your New Age Power Crystal in one hand and flipping the power switch with the other.

Fret no more. This chapter covers the basics of turning a computer on and what happens just after that and then doesn't neglect the important stuff about turning the computer off. There's much that happens as Mr. PC begins his sunshiny day. Oh — and this is definitely worth six dollars of this book's cover price — this chapter tells you the lowdown on whether you can let your computer run all day and all night without ever turning it off. (Yes, it can be done.)

Turning the Computer On

Turning a computer on is as easy as reaching for the big, red switch and flipping that switch to the On position. The switch is usually on the front of the PC, though don't be surprised if it's on the side or back.

- Most PCs made since the early 1990s have an On-Off button. You press it once to turn the computer on and again to turn the computer off.

- The On-Off switch is usually located next to a green (or yellow) "power" light. If the light is already on, so is the computer.

- Older PCs may have an On-Off switch with a bar and circle by it. Those are international symbols for a bar and circle, which also represent On and Off. The bar means On. The circle means Off. You can remember this arrangement by keeping in mind that a circle is an O and the word *off* starts with the letter O. (Then again, so does *on*. Just don't think about it.)

- If you can't see the screen, wait awhile. If nothing appears, turn the monitor on.

- If the computer doesn't turn on, check to see whether it's plugged in. If it still doesn't come on, see Chapter 20.

- If the computer does something unexpected or if you notice that it's being especially unfriendly, first panic. Then turn to Part IV of this book to figure out what went wrong.

Technical stuff to ignore

Your computer has many plug-inable items attached to it. Each one of them has its own On-Off switch. You don't have to follow any specific order when you turn any equipment on or off, though an old adage says, "Turn the computer box on last." Or is it first? I don't know. One way to save yourself from the hassle is to buy a power strip or one of the fancier computer power-control-center devices. You plug everything in to it and then turn on the whole shebang with one switch.

Look! Up on the screen!

Is it a burp? Is it a pain? No! It's text. Lots of text. Confusing and bewildering text you see every time you start your PC. Oops! There — a copyright notice flew by. Yes, it *scrolled* right up the screen and out of view. Sure hope it wasn't important.

If you're using a PC infected with any version of Windows, you see the Windows splashy graphical border displayed. Farewell, DOS! (Actually, you can still get to DOS, which is covered in Chapters 5 and 6.)

Starting the computer with the Big Red Switch is the mechanical part. What you're starting is the computer *hardware,* which is really nothing but a bunch of heavy, cold, and calculating electronic junk the cat likes to sleep on.

Eventually, DOS (or Windows), which is your computer's software part, the operating system, will come into being. It's the operating system's job to breathe the breath of life into your PC's nostrils.

Don't overly fret about all that *start-up* text. Keep in mind that it's just your computer starting and making your PC comfy-cozy for you to work. Computer scientists and the PC Wizards can fret over what it all means. Eventually, the text stops its maniacal crawl, and you're faced with a *command prompt,* some menu system, or Windows and can then get on with your work.

- ✔ If your computer starts up at the command prompt and you want to run Windows, type **WIN** at the DOS prompt.
- ✔ Working at the command prompt is covered in the next chapter.
- ✔ Yea, verily, even though the following section is titled "Turning the Computer Off," don't do it just yet. Skip ahead to another chapter in this book and read about what you can do when the computer is on and running.

Turning the Computer Off

Sure, turning the computer off is easy: Just flip the big red switch. The power goes "dink," the fan softly warbles away, and the hard drive spins to a low hum and then stops.

Attached to these easy-to-handle instructions is the following armada of rules, listed in order of importance:

- ✔ Never turn off your computer when you're in the middle of something. Always *quit to DOS* first. The only time you can safely turn off your PC is when you're at the DOS prompt. An exception to this rule is when your computer has gone totally AWOL. When that happens, see Part IV.
- ✔ If you're running a program, such as DESQview, Software Carousel, Windows 3.1, or some other menu system, see the section "Black Box Program Rules," in Chapter 15, for more information about turning off your computer.

- ✔ If you're running Windows 95 or Windows 98, you must quit your DOS programs (close their windows, which is covered in Chapter 6) and then quit Windows before you turn off your computer. See the next section.
- ✔ Don't turn off your computer when any drive light is on. Sometimes you may have quit a program but the computer is still busily storing away information on the disk. Wait for that DOS prompt, and then turn the computer off.

✔ Wait at least 30 to 40 seconds before turning the computer on again. Why? Because delicate electronic equipment gets wrecked when you rapidly flip the power switch (which is something I'm still trying to teach our 2-year-old).

✔ If possible, try not to turn off your computer more than three times a day. My advice is to leave the machine on all day and turn it off only at night. However, one school of thought recommends leaving a computer on all the time. See the section "I Want to Leave My PC on All the Time," later in this chapter.

Turning Off the PC in Windows 3.11

Turning off your computer is different if you have Windows 3.11. Because you can run several programs at once in Windows, you must first quit them all and *then* quit Windows before you turn off your PC. Okay, you don't have to close all your Windows applications; Windows can close them for you, but you do have to close any open DOS applications running in Windows. If you don't, Windows whines at you and will not quit until you do.

1. **Close all your Windows programs.**

   This is optional because Windows closes its own programs just fine. However, if you have any DOS programs running in a "window," then you must specifically quit each one before you quit Windows.

   If you fail to close a DOS program's window and try to quit Windows anyway, a warning message is displayed. Do not pass Go. Do not collect 200 shares of Microsoft. Start over.

2. **Switch to the Program Manager window.**

   In Windows 3.11, you use the Program Manager to handle many of the tasks in getting your work done, including turning off your PC. If you are not in Program Manager, press Ctrl+Esc to summon the Task List, shown in Figure 1-1. Use the up or down arrow key to highlight Program Manager and press Enter. The Task List dialog box goes away and you are switched to the Program Manager.

3. **Choose Exit Windows from the File menu.**

   Press Alt+F (for File), then X (for Exit Windows). The Exit Windows dialog box, shown in Figure 1-2, appears.

4. **Click OK.**

   You are returned to a DOS prompt.

It is now safe to turn off your computer as described earlier in this chapter.

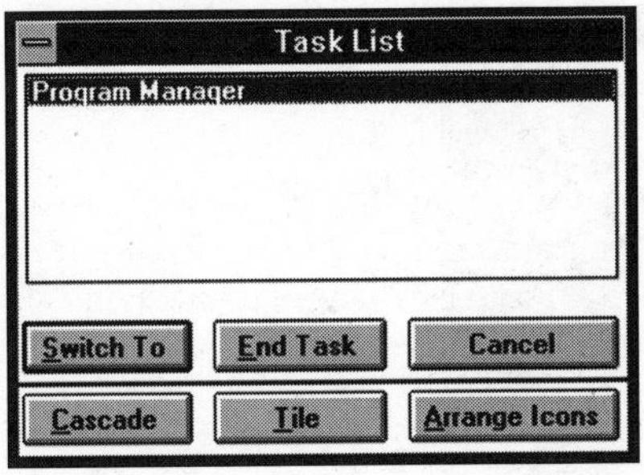

Figure 1-1:
The Task
List dialog
box.

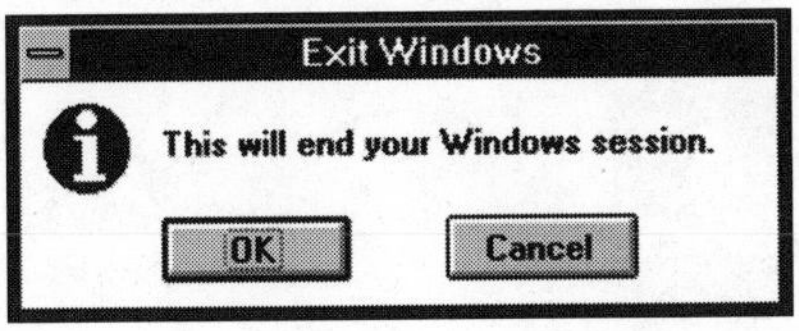

Figure 1-2:
The Exit
Windows
dialog box.

WARNING!

Turning off your computer without first exiting Windows 3.11 might result in potential PC havoc! Please, turn the PC off properly if at all possible.

Turning Off the PC in Windows 95 and Windows 98

Turning off your computer is different still if you have Windows 95 or Windows 98. You must actually tell Windows that you want to shut down your computer, as opposed to just flipping the switch. Flipping the switch still works, but — like burping out loud in a fancy restaurant — it's just not acceptable.

Because this book is about DOS, you should know how to shut down Windows 95 and Windows 98 from your keyboard. Forget that mouse stuff! Press Ctrl+Esc (or press the Windows key if your keyboard has one) to summon the Start menu, and then press **U** for the Shut Down command. Lo, the Shut Down dialog box appears. Figure 1-3 shows the Windows 95 Shut Down dialog box. Note the option to close all programs and log on as a different user. This option appears only if you are logged on to a network. Figure 1-4 shows the Windows 98 Shut Down dialog box.

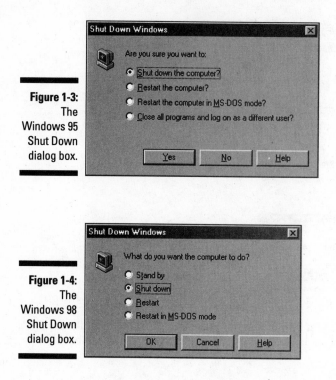

Figure 1-3:
The
Windows 95
Shut Down
dialog box.

Figure 1-4:
The
Windows 98
Shut Down
dialog box.

Press **S** to ensure that the `Shut down the computer?` or `Shut down` item is selected. Then whack the Enter key.

- Windows shuts down any application you may have been working in and prompts you to save any unsaved files.

- If you have DOS programs open, Windows cannot shut down. (Ha-ha!) Instead, a message appears, urging you to quit your DOS programs and save any unsaved stuff, and then you must shut down Windows all over again.

- When the screen says `It is now safe to turn off your computer,` you can punch the power switch. Vvvvmmmmmm, the PC powers down. Vvvmmmmmmm. . . .

- Many new computers can turn off automagically. Don't be surprised if your computer doesn't wait for you to press the power switch.

"I Want to Leave My PC on All the Time"

The great debate rages: Should you leave your computer on all the time? Well, anyone who knows anything will tell you Yes. Leave your computer on all the time, 24 hours a day, seven days a week. The only time you should really turn a system off is when it will be unused for longer than a weekend. At least that's my opinion, though many differ.

Computers like being on all the time. You leave your refrigerator on all night or when you're away on trips, so why not your PC? It doesn't raise your electrical bill either.

✔ Okay, if you want to turn your PC off, do so. It ain't no big deal.

✔ If you do leave your PC on all the time, you may consider turning the monitor off when you're away from the computer. This action helps the monitor last longer, and, besides, turning it on takes less time than turning on the whole computer.

✔ Screen-dimming programs *(screen savers)* are available to "black out" the monitor after your PC has been idle for a given amount of time. Windows comes with one of these programs that works even when DOS programs are running.

✔ If you do leave your computer on all the time, don't put it under a dust cover. The dust cover gives the computer its very own greenhouse effect and brings the temperatures inside the system way past the sweltering point.

Snooze, Computer, Snooze!

A feature of nearly every new computer is the capability to sleep. This feature isn't the same as when the computer deliberately ignores you. No, in this instance, you actually tell the computer to sleep — like a hypnotist. Don't try giving the PC suggestions, such as "crow like a chicken" or "dance like Elvis," though.

The sleep command temporarily puts your PC into a coma, suspending all operations. The monitor goes blank. The hard drive whirls down to a stop. Even the microprocessor chip switches to low gear. It's almost like the computer is off — but it's not! Touching a key, moving the mouse, or pressing a special sleep button reanimates the computer — just like turning it back on, though the computer was never really off.

If your computer is capable of sleeping, you may see a Suspend command on the Start menu in Windows 95 or a Stand by option in the Shutdown dialog box in Windows 98. Choose that command to make your PC sleep. Windows 3.11 lacks a Suspend or Stand by command.

Some PCs have a sleep button on the console. This button is usually marked with a little crescent-moon icon. Press the button to put your PC to sleep. Press it again to wake the PC up.

- ✔ Putting a PC to sleep is much better than turning it off and on all the time, and it's a wise solution if you're wary about leaving your PC on 24 hours a day.

- ✔ On some computers, it's possible to put the PC to sleep after a period of inactivity. In Windows, do this in the Control Panel with the Power icon in Windows 95 or the Power Management icon in Windows 98. I'd explain the process here, but this isn't a Windows book and (so far) the button works differently on every computer I have.

- ✔ Unlike some humans, your computer doesn't wake up grouchy after you press the sleep button.

- ✔ Pressing the Sleep button on a PC running Windows 3.11 may put your computer in a coma. You may need to reboot the computer to wake it up. If this happens to you, open a DOS window, then press the Sleep button. The computer "sleeps" (and "wakes up") just the way you expect it to.

- ✔ The sleep (or suspend) function originated on computer laptops. It was designed to save battery life by turning the power down to low when the laptop was idle.

Resetting

Resetting your computer is a way to turn it off and on again without having to actually do that (and it's healthier for the PC than kicking the power cord out of the wall, despite the full feeling that gives you). When you reset, you're restarting the computer while it's on.

You can reset a computer in two ways: If your computer has a reset switch, you can push it. Otherwise, you can press and hold the Ctrl, Alt, and Delete keys at the same time. Then release the keys. This procedure is known as the three-finger reset or Ctrl+Alt+Delete ("Control+Alt+Delete").

Now the question arises: When should you reset? Obviously, whenever you're panicked. Personally, I reset only if the keyboard is totally locked up and the program appears to have gone to the mall for some Mrs. Fields cookies and a soda. (Sometimes Ctrl+Alt+Delete doesn't work in these situations, so, if you

TECHNICAL STUFF

Trivial background fodder

A reset is often called a *warm boot*. It's like a cold boot that has been sitting in front of the furnace all night.

Try pressing Ctrl+Alt+Delete first. If that doesn't work, press your reset button. You need to press

it only once. If your system doesn't have a reset button, you have to turn off the computer, wait-wait-wait, and then turn it on again.

---

don't have a big reset button, you have to turn the computer off, wait, and then turn it on again.)

The only other time you really need to reset is just to "start over." For example, I was experimenting with a program that made my keyboard click every time I pressed a key. There was no obvious way to turn off this annoying pestilence, so I reset.

✔ As with turning a computer off, you shouldn't reset while the disk drive light is on or while you are working in an application (except when the program has flown south). Above all, do not reset to quit an application. Always quit properly to DOS before you reset or turn off your computer.

✔ Remember to remove any floppy disks from drive A before resetting. If you leave a disk in, the computer tries to start itself from that disk.

✔ A less drastic form of getting out of a tight situation is to use the DOS cancel key combination, Ctrl+C. See the section "Canceling a DOS Command," in Chapter 3.

REMEMBER

✔ Reset only when you run DOS by itself. Never reset a computer while you're running any version of Windows or a DOS program from within Windows. It just isn't right.

✔ Yeah, that could be another reason to want DOS over Windows: freedom to reset.

Chapter 2

The PC Hokey-Pokey (Or That's What It's All About)

In This Chapter

▶ Running a program

▶ Using the DIR command — and why

▶ Looking at a file

▶ Changing disks, drives, and directories

This chapter contains a quick summary of some basic computer stuff and everyday things you do on your beloved PC. These items don't collectively fit into any specific category. They're things you may be doing frequently or topics you have questions about. As with the rest of this book, everything here is cross-referenced.

Running a Program

You get work done on a computer by running a program. If you're lucky, somebody has set up your computer so that it automatically runs the program you need. Turn on the PC, and — zap! — there's your program. The only time you have a problem is when something goes wrong and the program *crashes* or doesn't turn on like it's supposed to. (Or, while you were at lunch, Petey from the mailroom came in and played games, leaving you with a C> on your screen to puzzle over.)

If you're on your own and nothing seems to happen automatically, you need to start a program yourself. Here's how:

First, you need to know the program's name. Then, you type that name at the command prompt.

For example, WordPerfect is named WP. To *run* WordPerfect, you type **WP** at the *DOS prompt* and then press Enter:

```
C> WP
```

To run Lotus 1-2-3, you type **123** at the DOS prompt and press the Enter key.

You can also run Windows programs from the DOS prompt if you are running Windows 95 or Windows 98. For example, to start the Calculator program, type **CALC** at the DOS prompt:

```
C> CALC
```

Press the Enter key, and the Calculator program pops up on-screen. (Your DOS prompt window doesn't go away; just click it with your mouse to continue using DOS.)

- ✔ If your computer is set up to run some sort of menu system, try typing **MENU** at the DOS prompt to run it.

- ✔ Other terms for running a program include *loading* a program, *launching* a program, and *starting* a program.

- ✔ DOS prompt? Command prompt? See Chapter 3 for the lowdown.

- ✔ Alas, you cannot run Windows programs from a DOS prompt in Windows 3.11. If you try, the computer informs you that the program requires Microsoft Windows.

- ✔ In Windows 95 and Windows 98, you need to start a DOS prompt "window" before you can run your DOS programs. From the Start menu, choose Programs, and then choose MS-DOS Prompt from the list that appears. (See Chapters 5 and 6 for more information about DOS in Windows.)

Background Information Worth Skipping

Programs are also known as applications, though the term *application* is more general: WordPerfect is a word-processing application. The program is WordPerfect, and its file is named WP.EXE. You type the name of the file at the DOS prompt. DOS then loads that program into memory and executes the instructions.

Under DOS, all program files are named with either a COM, an EXE, or a BAT ending (called a *filename extension*). Don't bother typing that part of the name at the DOS prompt — and you don't have to type the period that separates COM, EXE, or BAT from the file's name. See the section "Significant Filenames," in Chapter 19, for more information (worth skipping).

DIR Command

The most popular DOS command is DIR, which displays on-screen a list of files on a disk. This command is how you can find which programs and data files are located on a disk. DIR is especially helpful if you're missing something; it helps you locate that document or spreadsheet you were recently working on.

To see a list of files, type **DIR** at the DOS prompt and press Enter:

```
C> DIR
```

If the list is too long, you can type the following DIR command:

```
C> DIR /P
```

The /P makes the listing pause after each screenful of files. (Remember, "Wait for the P.")

To see a list of filenames only, type the following DIR command:

```
C> DIR /W
```

The /W means *w*ide, and it gives you a five-column, name-only list.

If you want to see the files on a floppy drive, follow the DIR command with the letter of the floppy drive:

```
C> DIR A:
```

In this example, DIR is followed by A:, indicating that the command should list files on any disk in that drive. (You should have a disk in the drive before you use that command.) If you want to find out which files are on drive B, for example, substitute B: for A:.

- ✔ You can use the DIR command to find files by name as well as to locate files in other *subdirectories* on the disk. See Chapter 17 for information about subdirectories.

- ✔ The output of the DIR command shows a list of files on your disk. The list has five columns: the file's name, the file's extension (part of the name), the file's size (in bytes or characters), the date the file was created or last modified, and the time of the last modification.

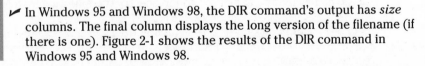

- ✔ In Windows 95 and Windows 98, the DIR command's output has *size* columns. The final column displays the long version of the filename (if there is one). Figure 2-1 shows the results of the DIR command in Windows 95 and Windows 98.

Figure 2-1:
The results
of the DIR
command
with long
filenames.

> ✔ For additional information on hunting down lost files, see the section "Name That File!" in Chapter 19. (You can find even more information on the DIR command in Chapter 19.)

Tech Tidbits to Skip

The DIR command's output may throw you. When you want to name a specific file, you glue both the file's name and extension together with a period. For example, the following is how a file may look when it's displayed by the DIR command:

```
LETTER  DOC  2,560  04-19-94  2:49p
```

However, the name of the file is really

```
LETTER.DOC
```

The DIR command spaces out the name and extension to line everything up in columns. If you don't want to see files listed in this format, try the following DIR command:

```
C> DIR /B
```

If the names fly by too fast for you to see, try the following instead:

```
C> DIR /B/P
```

Looking at Files

Two types of files are on a PC: English and Greek. You can use the TYPE command to display any file's contents. You can read the ones in English (or ASCII — see the section "Fancy-jargon section," later in this chapter). The files in Greek — they're actually in secret computer code, but it may just as well be Greek — are program files or data files or any other stuff you cannot read.

To look at a file, you must know its name. (If you don't know the name, you can use the DIR command; refer to the preceding section.) You type the file's name after the TYPE command and a space:

```
C> TYPE FILENAME.EXT
```

Press Enter to see the contents of the file, which is FILENAME.EXT in the preceding example. To see the contents of the LETTER.DOC file, for example, you would enter the following command:

```
C> TYPE LETTER.DOC
```

The file is then displayed on-screen.

- ✔ A really simple way to view — and edit — text files is to use the DOS Editor (skip merrily over to Chapter 16).

- ✔ If you get a `File not found` error message and you're certain that the file exists, you probably mistyped its name. Reenter the command and check your typing. Or you can use the DIR command to verify that the file exists.

- ✔ Text files usually end with TXT in their filename. The DOC ending is also popular, though DOC doesn't necessarily mean that it's a text file. Some common text filenames are READ.ME and README and sometimes README.TXT.

- ✔ If you still can't find the file, see the section "Finding a Lost File," in Chapter 19.

- ✔ You can't see all files, even though your application may display them perfectly. These "Greek" files typically contain special codes and functions for the computer, stuff that the program eats and then spits back at you as non-Greek information. Unfortunately, the TYPE command just isn't that smart.

Fancy-jargon section

Files you can see are referred to as *text* files or *ASCII* files. These files contain only regular alphabetical stuff, not computer code, and they're typically formatted in a manner that makes them easily displayed by the TYPE command. ASCII is the name of the coding scheme, and what it stands for is not important, although pronouncing it "ASK-ee" is. (Don't call it "ASK-two," or else you'll be pelted with small rocks.)

An easier yet more advanced way

If the file scrolls by too quickly, you can use the following version of the TYPE command:

```
C> TYPE LETTER.DOC | MORE
```

That's a TYPE command, the name of the file you want to type, a space, and the *bar* character, followed by another space and the word *MORE*. This command causes the file (LETTER.DOC, in the preceding example) to be displayed one screen at a time. Press the spacebar to see the next screen.

The secret to this command is the MORE filter, which is just a special program that reads text and then shows it back to you one screen at a time. The prompt - More - is displayed at the bottom of the screen, prompting you to press any key for more text. Another format is

```
C> MORE < LETTER.DOC
```

This command has the same effect as the longer version: The file LETTER.DOC is displayed one screen at a time. Is that command cryptic-looking, or what?

Changing Disks

To insert a 3½-inch floppy disk into a drive:

1. **Make sure that a disk is not already in the drive. If a disk is in the drive, eject the disk: Press the button by the drive's gaping maw — ptooey!**

2. **Insert the disk, label side up and toward you. (It goes in only one way.) Slide it in all the way. At some point, the drive "grabs" it and takes it in the rest of the way.**

- Access the floppy drive only after you've inserted a disk. If you do otherwise, you get a DOS error. See Chapter 23 for dealing with that kind of error.

- Never change a disk while you're using it. For example, wait until you've completely saved a file before removing the disk.

- If the drive door latch doesn't close, the disk isn't inserted properly. Try again.

- Keep your disk drive doors open when a disk isn't in the drive.

- Never force a disk into a drive. If it doesn't fit, you're either putting the disk in wrong, a disk is already in the drive, or what you're sticking the disk into isn't a disk drive. (Many times, disks get wedged into the space between two drives; don't be embarrassed — even the "pros" do it. In fact, a former editor-in-chief of mine confessed to me in an unguarded moment that he did it and had to practically disassemble his computer to get the disk out!)

- Okay, because sticking a disk between two drives is an issue, tape one or more of those tiny, sticky write-protect tabs that came with your disks over the space between your floppy drives — or just about any other slot on the front of your computer into which you might someday slip a disk.

- For more information on disks, see Chapter 13.

Changing Drives

A computer can pay attention to only one disk at a time. To switch the computer's attention from one drive to another, type that drive's letter followed by a colon. Press Enter to *log to* that drive. (Whichever drive the computer is using is referred to as the *logged drive;* in computerspeak, *using* equals *logged.*)

For example, to change from drive A to drive C, type

```
A> C:
```

To change from drive C to drive B, type

```
C> B:
```

A colon always follows a drive letter in DOS.

- Drive A is always the first floppy drive; drive C is always the first hard drive. A second floppy drive is drive B. Any additional drives in the system are lettered from D up through Z.

- ✔ Most modern PCs have huge hard drives, which they "partition" at the factory into hard drive C and hard drive D. Few people bother using their drive D, which is sad. Try typing **D:** at the DOS prompt to see whether your PC has a drive D.

- ✔ Most new PCs ship with a CD-ROM drive. The CD-ROM drive is often assigned letter D, but may have any letter from D through Z. CD-ROM stands for Compact Disc Read Only Memory. You can only read information from the CD-ROM, you cannot write to it (you know: create, delete, or change the files).

- ✔ On most systems, the DOS prompt indicates which drive you're using, or logged to. If it doesn't, see the section "Prompt Styles of the Rich and Famous," in Chapter 3.

- ✔ Don't change to a floppy drive unless a disk is in that drive. Refer to the preceding section.

- ✔ If you see the message `Drive not found,` that drive doesn't exist on the system. If you know this message to be untrue, see Chapter 23.

Technical Background and Other Drivel

Using a drive is the same as being logged to it. Whenever you're using your PC, you're logged to one drive or another. This information is usually reflected in the DOS prompt.

The *drive designator* is how you tell DOS to log to another drive. It's nothing more than the drive letter followed by a colon (not a semicolon). Otherwise, the drive letter by itself could be mistaken for a filename or the name of a program or DOS command, so you must type a colon whenever you're referring to a disk drive.

Even if you don't have a drive B, you can log to it by typing **B:** and pressing Enter. On single floppy drive systems, drive B is a *phantom* drive. DOS prompts you to *switch disks* when you change from drive A to drive B and back again. This switching is helpful when you are working with more than one floppy disk, but, generally speaking, it can be a real pain in the elbows. (Maybe someday Andrew Lloyd Webber will write an opera about the Phantom B Drive. Then again, maybe not.)

Changing Directories

Changing drives is no big deal. You can see drive A (or drive B, if you have it). And you know that drive C is inside the box somewhere, humming away. Changing directories is another matter, though. You do that by using the CD command, but it also involves a bit of techy-speak because the whole idea of directories (or subdirectories) isn't as entrenched in reality as the concept of your A and C drives. Therefore, all the changing directory information is handily stuffed into the following technical section.

Starting with Windows 95, the DOS subdirectory is called a *folder*. It's akin to your local municipality changing the sign on your street from Dead End to No Outlet: It's just a new name for something old. In fact, Microsoft still uses the term *subdirectory* in its documentation.

Really boring technical details — but read them anyway because you'll get lost if you don't

DOS is capable of dividing disks into individual work areas, called *directories*. Each disk has one main directory, the *root directory*. The root directory's symbol is the single backslash (\ ). All other directories on a disk are subdirectories of (or "under") the root directory.

Directories can have directories of their own, which can have even more directories. That is how a *pathname* is created. If your instructions tell you that your files can be found in the \SCHOOL\DATA directory, it means that the directory DATA is a subdirectory of SCHOOL, which is a subdirectory of the root directory. Note how the backslash is used to separate items:

\	The root
\SCHOOL	The SCHOOL directory under the root
\SCHOOL\DATA	The DATA directory under the SCHOOL directory under the root

This subject is painfully elaborated on later in this book, primarily all over Chapter 17.

CD command

To change to another directory on a disk, you use the CD command followed by the name of the directory:

```
C> CD \WORD\DATA
```

In this example, the CD command changes directories to the \WORD\DATA subdirectory. Note the space between CD and the directory's pathname.

To change to the root directory of any disk, use the command

```
C> CD \
```

 ✔ Directories and subdirectories are work areas on a disk.

 ✔ For more information on the root directory, see the section "The Root Directory," in Chapter 17; for information on pathnames, see the section "What Is a Pathname?" also in Chapter 17.

 ✔ A longer version of the CD command is CHDIR. Both do the same thing. I use CD because it's quicker to type. Well, that and I pronounce CHDIR as "cheddar" in my head and that makes me hungry.

 ✔ Directory names contain backslashes (\ ). A backslash is not the same character as the forward slash (/). See the section "Slash and Back-slash," in Chapter 10.

 ✔ The name of the directory you type after the CD command never ends with a backslash, though it may contain several backslashes. Note that not all directory names you type start with a backslash. (It depends on "where you are" on the disk, which is elaborated on in Chapter 17, in the sections "Current Directory" and "The Tree Structure.")

 ✔ If you see an Invalid directory type of error, you may not be entering the correct directory name. Refer to your sources for the correct path-name. Plan ahead: Ask them for the full pathname, and type that after the CD command.

Chapter 3

Life at the DOS Prompt

· ·

· ·

*P*erhaps one of the most disgusting ways to work with a computer is to type secret codes at a hieroglyphic prompt. Let's be realistic, though. What's the result of trying to make something too easy? It becomes boring. The DOS prompt may be cryptic, but it's definitely interesting. (Okay, and physical torture can be interesting, but that doesn't mean that we volunteer for it in droves.)

This chapter contains information about using the DOS prompt. Most of it consists of tips, though some of them give you valuable shortcuts and make using the prompt — obscure as it is — a bit easier.

Names and Versions

What this book calls *DOS* is really a computer program created by Microsoft (one that it would just as soon forget, too). Its version is called *MS-DOS,* short for Microsoft Disk Operating System.

Microsoft makes three other operating systems: Windows 95, Windows 98, and Windows NT. Oh, and don't forget PC DOS and other DOSes. All of them are based on the MS-DOS that Microsoft produces.

In addition to its name, DOS has version numbers. Six major releases of DOS have appeared, numbered 1 through 6. Each major release also has its own minor releases: There was DOS Version 1.0, 1.1, 2.0, 2.1, 3.0, 3.1, and so on. The minor release number is separated from the major release by a period or a dot. Also, the first minor release is 0, not 1.

To find out which name and version of DOS you're using, use the VER command:

```
C> VER
```

Press Enter and DOS displays its name and version number.

✔ Aside from being perhaps the simplest and most stupid DOS command, VER can be used to determine which version of DOS is installed on a computer. If you wind up using an alien computer, type **VER** to see which make and model of DOS is installed. That may explain why some DOS commands function weirdly or aren't available.

✔ If you type VER from a DOS window in Windows 3.11 you see:

```
MS-DOS Version 6.22
```

If you want to see the Windows version displayed type WINVER and press Enter:

```
Windows for Workgroups Version 3.11
```

✔ For Windows 95 and Windows 98, the version number displayed says Windows and not MS-DOS. For example:

```
Windows 95. [Version 4.00.950]
```

or

```
Windows 98 [Version 4.10.1998]
```

The Prompt, or What Do You Want?

The DOS prompt is how DOS tells you that it's ready for your input or for you to type something, enter information, or just idly sit back and swear at the computer. In this book, the following prompt is used as an example:

```
C>
```

The prompt on your system may look like this:

```
C:\>
```

✔ Sometimes the DOS prompt is called the *command prompt.* Same thing.

✔ The letter in the prompt tells you which disk drive you're using (or *logged to*). Refer to the discussion under "Changing Drives" in Chapter 2.

✔ The greater-than sign (>) is the all-purpose computer prompt. It means "What do you want?"

✔ Other variations of the droll DOS prompt exist. Some contain the name of the current directory, some may show the date and time, and some may look like Bart Simpson. (See the section "Current Directory," in Chapter 17, for information on the current directory; see the FOX television network to find Bart Simpson.)

✔ You can change your system prompt by using the PROMPT command. See the section "Prompt Styles of the Rich and Famous," later in this chapter.

Prompt Error Messages

Two common error messages are produced at the prompt: `file not found` and `bad command or file name`. `File not found` means that the file you've specified doesn't exist. Don't panic; you may have just typed it wrong. Check your typing. If that fails, see the section in Chapter 19 about finding a lost file.

`Bad command or file name` is similar to `file not found`, though in this case the message is really `program not found`. You may have mistyped the name of a program, added a space, or forgotten something. See the section "Where Is My Program?" in Chapter 21 for additional information on solving this problem.

✔ Individual programs produce their own unique error messages for `file not found`. Although the messages vary in syntax, they all mean the same thing.

✔ Other error messages are possible at the prompt, some of which really burn your buns. See Chapter 23.

Typing at the Prompt

You use the prompt by typing after it. All the text you enter at the keyboard appears on-screen next to the prompt. Of course, what you type are DOS commands, the names of programs, or general insults to the computer.

The information you enter at the DOS prompt is the *command line,* which is an assortment of words, cryptic and English, that direct the computer to do something. You send that information to DOS by pressing the Enter key. Only by pressing Enter is the information sent, which gives you an opportunity to back up and erase or to change your mind and press Ctrl+C or the Escape (Esc) key to cancel.

- As you type, the underline cursor on the screen moves forward. The cursor marks the spot on-screen where all text appears.

- If you make a mistake typing at the DOS prompt, press the Backspace key to back up and erase.

- If you want to discard the entire command line, press Esc. On some computers, the backslash (\ ) is displayed and the cursor moves down to the next line on the screen. You can start over from there. (Other computers may just erase the line and let you start over.)

- I don't need to mention that the DOS prompt is unfriendly. In fact, DOS is arrogant and understands only certain things. When it doesn't understand something, it spits back an error message (refer to the preceding section).

- On the bright side, you can't really do anything heinous at the DOS prompt. Most of the deadly things you can do involve typing specific commands and then answering Y (for yes). If you accidentally stumble into one of those situations, press N (for no). Otherwise, you can do little at the DOS prompt to damage your PC.

Beware of Spaces!

Beginners have three bad tendencies when they're using the DOS prompt: They don't type any spaces, they do type spaces, or they type periods.

Always keep this statement in mind: The DOS prompt is not a word processor. You don't need to type formal English; punctuation, capitalization, and spelling are often overlooked. So, never end a command with a period. In fact, periods are used only when you're naming files that have a second part, or *extension*.

Spaces are another sticky point. You must stick a space (and only one space) between two separate items, as shown in this example:

```
C> CD \FRIDGE\LEFTOVER
```

Here, the CD command is followed by a space. You must put a space after CD or any other DOS command.

In the following example, the program **WP** is run. It's followed by a space and the name of a file:

```
C> WP CHAP02.DOC
```

Just as you shouldn't type too few spaces, don't type too many spaces either. In the preceding example, the file named CHAP02.DOC has no space in it. If you're a touch typist, you may have a tendency to type a space after the period. Don't. Always type a command exactly as you see it listed in a book, magazine, or computer manual.

- ✔ Some books and magazines may use a funny typeface to indicate the stuff you type. This typeface may make it look like extra spaces are typed in a command, typically around the backslash (\ ) character. Watch out for this potential pitfall!

- ✔ A few DOS commands may end in a period, but only when that period is part of a filename, as shown in this example:

```
C> DIR *.
```

The preceding DIR command lists all files that don't have a second part, or *filename extension*. The *. is a legitimate part of the command. This instance is about the only one in which a DOS command ends with a period.

- ✔ If you forget to type a space at the proper place, you probably will get a bad command or file name error message.

If you have Windows 95 or Windows 98 and you want to use a long filename in a DOS command, enclose the filename (and its path) in quotes. For example:

```
CD "\My Documents\Financial Data"
```

Beware of User Manuals and English Punctuation!

Manuals and instruction books often tell you what to type at the DOS prompt, but there is no established convention for doing this.

This book uses the following method:

```
C> VER
```

The DOS prompt is shown followed by the text you enter. The text is shown in a different typeface from the rest of the text in the book. The prompt is always C> in this book, though it may appear in some other way on your screen.

Some manuals follow what you type with the word *Enter,* sometimes in a bubble or in some other happy typeface. That means to press the Enter key after you type the command; don't type the word *Enter* on the command line.

Some manuals list what you type on a line by itself, without the prompt:

```
VER
```

Some manuals include the command in the text — which is where this stuff can get tricky. For example, they may say

```
Enter the VER command.
```

VER is in uppercase, meaning that you type it at the DOS prompt. Sometimes, it may appear in lowercase, italics, or boldface. The worst is when they put the command in quotes:

```
Type the "DIR *.*" command.
```

In this example, you can gather that you type the DIR command, followed by a space, an asterisk, a period, and another asterisk. You do not type the double quotes surrounding the command. In this book, this command is specified as follows:

```
C> DIR *.*
```

So far, so good. When English punctuation rears its ugly head, however, you may see one of the following commands:

```
Type the command "DIR *.*".
Type the command "DIR *.*."
```

The first example is grammatically incorrect: The period is outside the double quote. Of course, the period ends the sentence — it's not part of the command you should type. The second example is what most computer book editors do to DOS commands. No, the period is not part of the command, although a period inside a quote is grammatically correct in that circumstance.

If you type the period as part of the DOS command, you see one of DOS's inflammatory error messages.

- ✔ You can enter DOS commands and program names in uppercase or lowercase. Most manuals and books, including this one, use uppercase.

- ✔ No DOS command ends in a period. Exceptions exist, but the point here is that if you see a command ending in a period in a manual or computer book, it's probably a part of English grammar and not something you need to type.

- ✔ DOS commands contain spaces. Spaces follow the name of the command, separating filenames and any other options typed after the commands.

- ✔ Using the DIR command displays filenames with spaces separating the name and the extension. When you type a filename at the DOS prompt, a dot separates the name and extension. Do not use spaces.

- ✔ No user manual is 100 percent correct. If you type the command exactly as it's listed and the computer still produces an error, try again with a space or without a period.
- ✔ General information on using your keyboard is covered in Chapter 10.

F3 Key

The F3 key provides a handy shortcut whenever you need to retype a DOS command. For example, to list files on the disk in drive A, you type

```
C> DIR A:
```

If the file you want isn't on that disk, remove it and replace it with another disk. Then, rather than retype the same command, press F3. You see the same command displayed:

```
C> DIR A:
```

Press Enter, and the command is executed a second time.

If this suggestion doesn't work, you may have a *keyboard macro* enhancement program operating. In that case, try pressing the up-arrow cursor key instead.

Canceling a DOS Command

The universal cancel key in DOS is Control+C, or Ctrl+C. Pressing this key combination halts most DOS commands. In some cases, it may even halt a DOS operation in progress.

To press Ctrl+C, hold down the Ctrl (Control) key and press C. Release the Ctrl key. You see ^C displayed on-screen and then another DOS prompt.

If Ctrl+C doesn't work, try Ctrl+Break. (The Break key is the same as the Pause key on most keyboards.) Ctrl+Break often works when Ctrl+C seems stubborn.

- ✔ Always try canceling a DOS command with the keyboard first. You never want to reset — or, worse, turn off — your computer to get yourself out of a jam.
- ✔ Application programs use their own cancel key, which is usually the Esc key. (They have exceptions, however. WordPerfect for DOS, for example, uses the F1 key.)

✔ The caret, or hat symbol (^), is used to denote *control*. When you see ^C, it means Control+C, or the Ctrl+C keystroke. Likewise, ^H means Control+H, ^G means Control+G, and so on. Some of these keys have significant meanings, which I don't need to get into here.

Prompt Styles of the Rich and Famous

The DOS prompt is a flexible thing. It can really look like anything you imagine, contain interesting and useful information, and so on. The secret is to use the PROMPT command.

Other books offer you a tutorial on the PROMPT command and how it works. Rather than bother with that, here are some popular prompts you can create. Just type the command as listed, and you have your own excellent DOS prompt.

Here's the standard, boring prompt:

```
C>
```

To create the standard prompt, which contains the current drive letter and a greater-than symbol, type

```
C:\> PROMPT
```

Here's the informative drive/directory prompt:

```
C:\>
```

The most common DOS prompt shows the current drive and directory and the greater-than sign. Type this command:

```
C:\> PROMPT $P$G
```

Here's the date-and-time prompt:

```
Fri 7-31-1998
12:34:25.63
C:\DOS>
```

This prompt contains the current date and time and then the drive and directory information found in the second example. Note that the date-and-time information is current only while the new prompt is displayed; it's not continually updated on your screen. Here's the command you should carefully type to produce that prompt:

```
C:\> PROMPT $D$_$T$_$P$G
```

To make your favorite prompt permanent, you have to edit your AUTOEXEC.BAT file and place the PROMPT command in it. This subject is covered in Chapter 16.

Additional, Worthless Information

The prompt can contain any text you like. Simply specify the text after the PROMPT command:

```
C:\> PROMPT Enter command:
```

or the ever popular

```
C:\> PROMPT What is thy bidding?
```

You cannot directly specify the following characters in a prompt command: less than (<), greater than (>), and the pipe (|). Instead, use the following: $L for less than (<); $G for greater than (>); and $B for the pipe (|).

Because the dollar sign ($) is used as a special prefix, you have to specify two of them ($$) if you want $ as part of your prompt. That's okay; when money's involved, greed is good.

Chapter 4

Easier DOS: The DOS Shell

. . . .

In This Chapter

▶ Starting and quitting the DOS Shell

▶ Changing the display in the DOS Shell

▶ Moving between different parts of the shell

▶ Copying files in the shell

▶ Deleting files in the shell

▶ Moving files in the shell

▶ Renaming files in the shell

▶ Finding a lost file by using the shell

▶ Changing from one drive to another

▶ Changing from one directory to another

▶ Running programs in the shell

. . . .

DOS comes with an easy-to-use (yeah, right) *shell program*. The word *shell* means that the program insulates you from cold, prickly DOS, keeping you in a warm, fuzzy graphics environment, supposedly making life easier on you. Inside the shell, you can do all the things you could do outside the shell, though everything's easier, thanks to the pretty graphics and fun, shell-like ways of doing things. Okay, so it may not be that easy, but it's free with DOS, so who's complaining?

Remember that all these functions are particular to the DOS Shell program, specifically the one that comes with DOS Versions 5.0 and 6.0. The DOS Shell isn't available with MS-DOS 6.2 onward (which includes Windows 95 and Windows 98). Microsoft no longer offers the program or makes it available.

Starting the DOS Shell

To start the DOS Shell, you type its name at the DOS prompt:

```
C> DOSSHELL
```

Press Enter, and in a few moments you see the DOS Shell program on your screen.

The DOS Shell was installed when your computer was first set up for DOS. If you see a Bad command or file name error message, your system was probably set up without the shell. Oh, well.

Do You Have a Mouse?

Let's be serious here: You can get the most from the DOS Shell program only if you have a mouse. You can do things without a mouse, but the shell was really designed with a mouse in mind.

- ✔ If you don't have a mouse, buy one. If you can't afford one, force someone else to buy a mouse for you.

- ✔ This same flawless logic also holds true for Windows: You need a mouse to run Windows. See Chapters 5 and 6 for the luscious details on Windows.

Quitting the DOS Shell

Okay, you've seen the DOS Shell. La-di-da. To quit the DOS Shell and return to plain old command-line DOS, press F3.

You can also press the Alt+F4 key combination to quit the shell.

If you have a mouse (and you should), you can click the File menu and then choose the Exit menu item.

If you don't have a mouse but would like to use the menus, press Alt+F to *drop down* the File menu, and then press **X** to quit the shell.

✔ The F3 key is compatible with the DOS Shell program offered with DOS Version 4.0 and with an older shell program called the Microsoft Manager. The Alt+F4 key combination is compatible with all versions of Microsoft Windows, used there to close a program or to quit the Windows environment.

✔ See Chapter 10 for more information on using a mouse and mouse terminology.

Changing the Display in the DOS Shell

You can look at the DOS Shell in a number of ways, all depending on the horsepower of your computer's graphics. (See Chapter 9 for more information on graphics and the PC's screen.)

Use the mouse to choose the Options menu by clicking it. Then click Display. If you don't have a mouse, press Alt+O and then type a **D**. What you see is the Screen Display Mode dialog box, as shown in Figure 4-1. Press the arrow keys to select one of three types of displays: text, graphics, or the number of lines of information on-screen. Click the OK button or press Enter to see the new screen, as shown in Figures 4-2 and 4-3.

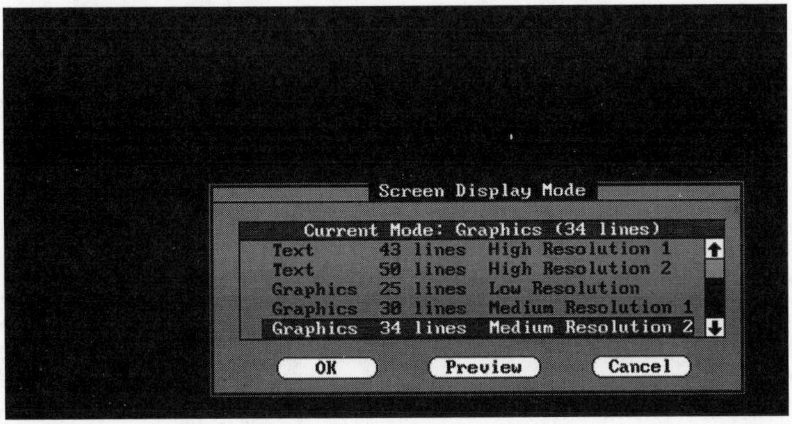

Figure 4-1: Clicking the Display item on the Options menu gives you the Screen Display Mode dialog box.

Screen Display Mode

Current Mode: Graphics (34 lines)
Text   43 lines   High Resolution 1
Text   50 lines   High Resolution 2
Graphics   25 lines   Low Resolution
Graphics   30 lines   Medium Resolution 1
Graphics   34 lines   Medium Resolution 2

OK   Preview   Cancel

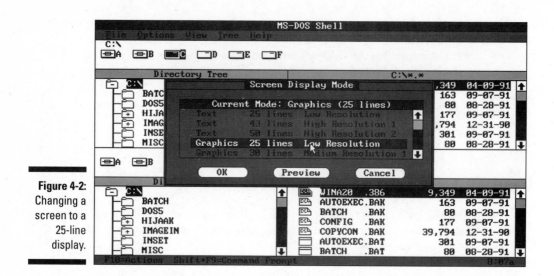

Figure 4-2:
Changing a
screen to a
25-line
display.

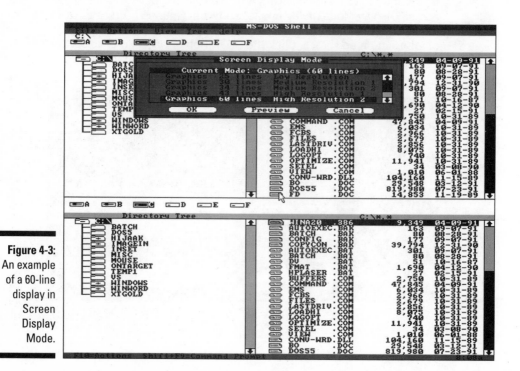

Figure 4-3:
An example
of a 60-line
display in
Screen
Display
Mode.

Another way to change the way the shell looks is to change its layout. You do this from the View menu. You activate the View menu by clicking it with the mouse pointer or by pressing Alt+V, as shown in Figure 4-4. Then, you can select from five views:

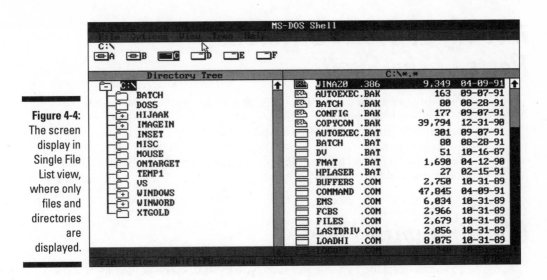

Figure 4-4:
The screen
display in
Single File
List view,
where only
files and
directories
are
displayed.

✔ **Single File List:** Shows only files and directories

✔ **Dual File Lists:** Shows two sets of files and directories (good for copying and comparing information, as shown in Figure 4-5)

Figure 4-5:
Changing
the layout of
the shell by
using the
View menu.

✔ **All Files:** Shows only files (good for locating lost files)

✔ **Program/File Lists:** Shows files, directories, and a list of programs to run

✔ **Program List:** Shows only programs to run

Moving between Different Parts of the Shell

You work in only one area of the shell at a time, which can be frustrating because your eyeballs may be trained on one part of the screen while the computer is "using" another part. Major pain.

To move between each of the different *panels* in the shell, click the mouse in the appropriate one or press the Tab key until that area's panel is highlighted.

Working with Files

To work with a file by using the shell, you must first select the file. You do this by using the mouse to click the file's name. That action highlights the file's name, letting you know that it's selected.

Copying files

To copy a file by using the mouse, first select it by clicking it. Next, drag the file to the proper subdirectory or disk drive, as shown on-screen. A confirmation dialog box appears; click in the Yes button's area.

To copy a file by using the keyboard, highlight the file by pressing the spacebar. Press the F8 key to copy the file. The Copy File dialog box appears; enter the subdirectory destination for the file.

- ✔ Remember that to copy files by using the mouse, you must first press the Ctrl (Control) key. If you forget to do it, the file is moved and the original file is deleted.

- ✔ Copying files in DOS is covered in Chapter 18.

- ✔ To copy a file in the DOS 5 shell, you must hold down the Ctrl key before you click the file. In DOS 6, you don't have to.

Deleting files

To delete a file, highlight it and then press the Delete key. A dialog box appears, asking whether you really want to delete the file. Select the Yes button if you do; otherwise, press Esc.

Deleting files by using DOS is covered in Chapter 18.

Moving files

To move a file, hold down the Alt key and then click the file. Using the mouse, drag the file to the destination directory or drive on-screen. A confirmation dialog box appears, asking whether you want to move the file. Click in the Yes area if you do; otherwise, press Esc to cancel.

If you lack a mouse, you can copy a file by first selecting it and then pressing the F7 key. Type a new destination for the file, and then press Enter.

✔ Moving a file by using the DOS command line is covered in Chapter 18.

✔ In DOS 5, you don't have to hold down the Alt key before clicking the file; just drag the file to move it.

Renaming a file

To rename a file, highlight it and then select the File menu's Rename option: Click the File menu by using the mouse and then click the Rename option. Or, if you only have a keyboard, press Alt+F and then press **N**.

A dialog box appears, giving you the file's original name plus a cute little box in which to type the new name.

✔ See the section "Name That File!," in Chapter 19, for more information on renaming a file; the section "Renaming a File," in Chapter 18, has the basic information on using the REN (rename) command.

✔ You can also use the shell to rename a subdirectory — which is something you cannot do at the DOS prompt. Simply highlight the directory name and then choose Rename from the File menu (as just described). Note that the same rules for renaming a file apply to a subdirectory.

Viewing a file's contents

To peek at a file's innards, highlight the file and then press Alt+F to drop down the File menu; press **V** to choose View file contents. Alternatively, you can highlight the file's name and press F9. Personally, I find that the F9 key works best.

Note that text files are displayed in a readable format. You can press the up- and down-arrow keys as well as PgUp and PgDn to scroll through the file for your viewing pleasure. (This method is much more enjoyable than tangling with the TYPE command. Ick.)

When you're done browsing, press Esc to return to the DOS Shell's main screen.

> ✔ Unreadable, or "Greek," files are displayed by using the horrid — and I hesitate to mention this subject — *hex dump* format. If this topic pleases you (or impresses your friends), cool. Otherwise, press Esc and hunt down more readable files.

> ✔ This feature is available only in the DOS Shell program that comes with DOS 6.

Finding a Lost File

Finding a lost file in the shell is a snap — much easier than any other way of finding a lost file. Here's what you do:

Click the File menu and then choose the Search item. If you don't have a mouse, press Alt+F and then press **H**.

Type the name of the file you want to find. Press Enter. After a moment, the search results are displayed. The file is listed by using its full pathname, which shows you where on the disk it's located. Press Esc to return to the shell.

> ✔ If the file isn't found, you see the message No files match file specifier. Odds are pretty good that the file isn't on that drive. Consider trying another drive; see the following section, "Changing from One Drive to Another," for details, and then try the file search again.

> ✔ See the section "Finding a Lost File," in Chapter 19, for methods of locating lost files without using the DOS Shell.

Changing from One Drive to Another

The shell shows you, near the top of the screen, a list of disk drives. Floppy drive A (and B, if you have it) is listed first, followed by drive C and any other hard drives attached to your PC.

To change, or *log,* from one drive to another, press the Ctrl key plus the letter of that drive. For example, to log to drive D, press Ctrl+D; to log to drive C, press Ctrl+C.

> ✔ You can also log to another drive by double-clicking it with the mouse.

> ✔ Refer to the section "Changing Drives," in Chapter 2, for basic information about logging to another disk drive.

Changing from One Directory to Another

To switch directories, you must make sure that the Directory Tree panel is active. Click in that panel by using the mouse or press the Tab key until that area's title is highlighted.

You select a directory by pressing the cursor keys or by clicking once on a directory's name by using the mouse. Any files in that directory are shown in the File panel to the right of the Directory Tree panel.

If the directory has a plus sign by it, it has subdirectories. Click on the directory by using the mouse or press the Plus (+) key to open the directory and list its subdirectories.

Refer to the section "Changing Directories," in Chapter 2, for some basic information about changing directories; Chapter 17 has lots of information on why and how directories are used.

Running Programs in the Shell

A program in the DOS Shell can be run in three ways. The first is to locate the COM or EXE program file in the list of files, highlight that file, and then press Enter to run the program.

The second way is to choose the Run menu option on the File menu. Click the word *File,* and then choose Run by using the mouse, or press Alt+F and then press **R** to choose the Run option. Then, type the name of the program to run in the box provided.

The third way is possible only if someone has configured the shell to show a list of programs at the bottom of the screen in the Main panel. Click in that area by using the mouse or press the Tab key until that area is highlighted. Then highlight the name of a program to run and press Enter.

✔ You may need someone else to set up the shell to contain a list of programs to run on your computer. This process is one of those things that's beyond the scope of what you need to know, so bug your computer manager or a friend into doing it for you. It really does make running things convenient.

✔ See Chapter 15 to read about some other programs that make life easier for people who hate DOS. Not all of them are free, like the DOS Shell, although many of them are easier to use.

Chapter 5

The Way Windows Was

*B*ecause DOS was so ugly and so many people complained about it, Microsoft graced PC users with a DOS Shell called Windows. Eventually, Windows grew in power and stature to become its own operating system. But before that, there was Windows 3.11 and its networking cousin, Windows for Workgroups.

Before Windows 95 came along, Windows offered a graphical look for your computer and your Windows software. If you're still using Windows 3.11 or Windows for Workgroups on your PC, then this chapter tells you what's what. You'll probably find Windows is a more fun and relaxed way of using a computer than the terse DOS command line (or at least the brochure says so).

Starting Windows 3.11

Windows should start automatically on your computer. If not, you can start Windows at the DOS prompt by typing **WIN**:

```
C> WIN
```

Be forewarned: If you use Windows, you'll need a mouse. See Chapter 10.

Starting Windows and running a program at the same time

Some programs can run only under Windows. Two of the most popular are Word for Windows and Microsoft's Excel spreadsheet. Normally, you would run these programs inside Windows, which involves hunting down pretty icons and double-clicking with the mouse. However, it's possible to start Windows and load these programs at the same time, saving needless wrist action.

For example, if you want to run Word for Windows at the DOS prompt, type:

```
C> WIN WINWORD
```

That's WIN, the command to start Windows, followed by a space and then WINWORD, the program that runs Word for Windows. No mess, no icons, no clicking.

To run Excel, type the following:

```
C> WIN EXCEL
```

Again, that's WIN for Windows, a space, and EXCEL to run the Excel spreadsheet.

- ✔ Of course, if you're already in Windows, you double-click the proper icon to run the program. These secrets are divulged elsewhere in this chapter.
- ✔ Why start Windows this way? If you're running only one program in Windows, then this removes the bother of messing with the Program Manager, the File Manager, and all those goofy games that come with Windows and get in the way from time to time.

Quitting Windows

To quit Windows, first hunt down the Program Manager window — the Windows main window. After you're there, select the File menu and then choose the Exit Windows menu item. A small box — a *dialog box* (though it only talks *at* you) — appears on the screen, proclaiming This will end your Windows session. Click the OK button to be hurled from the warm, loving Windows environment back to the hard, cold reality of the DOS prompt.

✔ Originally, there was no command to Quit Windows. Bill Gates was heard
saying, "Quit Windows? Who would want to do that?" But eventually he
relented, and they added the Exit Windows command.

The Beloved Program Manager

DOS has the DOS prompt and Windows has the *Program Manager*. Like the
DOS prompt, the Program Manager is the point from which you'll start all
your Windows applications and programs. Unlike the DOS prompt, the
Program Manager is a pretty window with lots of fun little icons and other
merriment (see Figure 5-1). The idea here is that fun and merriment make us
enjoy using a computer more. You and I know better, of course.

The Program Manager contains several of its own windows, called *group
windows*. Each group contains similar programs, which are represented by
one or more cute li'l icons.

Q: What's the difference between a DOS program and a Windows application?

A: About $300.

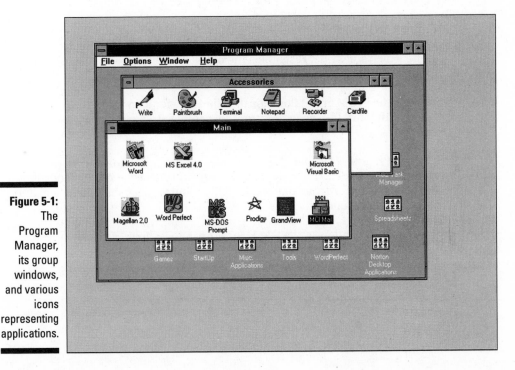

Figure 5-1:
The
Program
Manager,
its group
windows,
and various
icons
representing
applications.

To start a program in the Program Manager, you point the mouse at the proper icon and then swiftly double-click the mouse button: click-click. Both clicks have to happen nanoseconds apart, and you shouldn't move the mouse between them. That runs a program in the Program Manager.

✔ Additional information on minimizing icons and working with windows is covered in the section "Using a Window's Gizmos" later in this chapter.

✔ The icons are tiny and the pictures vague, but you can often tell what program the icon represents by reading the name below the icon.

✔ The Program Manager's group windows can be minimized to icon size, which conveniently shoves them out of the way, preventing "child-window overload." To reopen a minimized group icon, double-click it: Zowie! The window reappears.

You don't just *run* a program in Windows; you *launch* it. When one of your Windows manuals says to "launch an application," you know that phrase translates into "run this here program." You accomplish this by double-clicking the appropriate cutesy icon.

The Treasured File Manager

Unlike with the DOS prompt, you can't work with files in the Windows Program Manager. To work with files, you need to use the File Manager program, which somewhat resembles the old DOS Shell program discussed in Chapter 4.

To start the File Manager, look for the File Manager icon in the Program Manager. It looks like a squat, yellow file cabinet stolen from a Dr. Seuss cartoon.

Like the Program Manager, the File Manager contains childish windows, as shown in Figure 5-2. These are *file windows*. You can use more than one file window to see more than one group of files, and you can minimize them into icons at the bottom of the screen.

✔ Each file window in the File Manager window shows subdirectories on the left side, files on the right, and drive letter icons at the top.

✔ Refer to the section "Using a Window's Gizmos" later in this chapter for information on controlling a window, closing a window, minimizing, and other graphical gaiety.

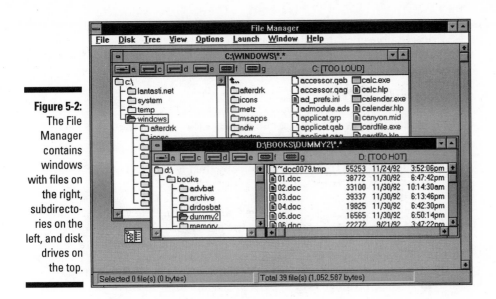

Figure 5-2:
The File
Manager
contains
windows
with files on
the right,
subdirecto-
ries on the
left, and disk
drives on
the top.

Changing drives in the File Manager

To look at files on another disk drive, click the letter of the drive you want (at the top of a file window). The subdirectories and files on that drive appear in the window's left and right panels, respectively.

✔ You can also press the Ctrl key plus a drive letter to see files on that drive. For example, Ctrl+D gives you a peek at drive D.

✔ If you double-click a drive letter icon, you'll open up a new file window displaying files on that drive. Ta-da, two file windows!

Changing directories

The files displayed on the right side of a file window are all in a particular sub-directory. The subdirectory is highlighted on the left side of the window. To see files in another directory, locate it in the scrolling list and click it once. The files in that directory will then be displayed on the right side of the window.

✔ Some directories have subdirectories — directories within directories. To see which they are, select the Tree menu and choose Indicate Expandable Branches. That causes little plus signs (+) to appear on the directories that have subdirectories — just like in the DOS Shell.

✔ Directories are marked by a folder icon. If they appear in the file side of the window, they're subdirectories. Double-click them to see what files they contain.

✔ If you double-click a directory with a plus sign, you'll see its subdirectories. Double-click that directory again to "close" it.

Copying a file

The best way to copy a file in the File Manager is to know where it is and where you want to copy it.

For example, suppose that you want to copy the file 256COLOR.BMP from your C:\WINDOWS directory to a disk in drive A.

Start by opening a file window for drive C and selecting the WINDOWS directory. In the file side of the window, find the file 256COLOR.BMP — or whichever file it is that you want to copy. Click that file once with the mouse to select it. The file becomes highlighted. Using the mouse, drag the file's icon to the drive A icon at the top of the window. Release the mouse button when the file is over the icon. Zap! The file is copied.

✔ If you want to copy the file to another directory, press the Ctrl key and drag the file to the subdirectory name on the left side of the window.

✔ Another way to copy is to open another file window. For example, you can double-click the drive C icon to open another window and then select a destination directory on the left side of the window. To copy files, drag them from one file window to the other.

✔ Sometimes a window may appear, asking whether you want to copy the file. Click OK.

✔ To copy a group of files, select them all with the mouse: As you click each new filename, press and hold down the Ctrl key. You can then work with the files en masse.

✔ The key command for copying a file is F8, just like in the DOS Shell (see Chapter 4).

Moving a file

Moving a file works just like copying a file, but without pressing the Ctrl key. Simply drag the file's icon from one folder to another and it's moved.

✔ The key command for moving a file is F7, just like in the DOS Shell (see Chapter 4).

Deleting a file

To rub a file out of existence in the File Manager, highlight the offending file's name in a file window. Then, squint your eyes and press the Delete key. Unlike DOS, where this action is covert and stealthy, the File Manager pops up a dialog box asking whether you're serious or not. Click OK to delete the file.

> ✔ Wholesale slaughter is possible if you select multiple files at a time: Press and hold the Ctrl key as you click each file doomed to extinction.

Renaming a file

To rename a file, highlight it, select the File menu, and choose the Rename item. Type the new name into the box and click OK.

There are two boxes on the screen for renaming a file. The top one contains the original name; the bottom one is where you type the new name. Remember to type in the bottom box! If you edit the top box, you aren't renaming anything.

Starting a program in the File Manager

You can run programs in the File Manager, which steals a little bit of the Program Manager's pride. Fortunately for the Program Manager, it has all the cutesy icons; the File Manager has terse program names.

To start a program, locate its filename in a file window. In Windows, the program files are all flagged with a rectangular icon, which is meant to instill the message "this is a program" in your brain (but fails miserably). After you find the icon, double-click it with the mouse and the program runs.

> ✔ Another way to run a program is to select the File menu and choose the Run item. A box appears, into which you can type the name of the program that you want to run — eerily similar to using the old DOS prompt. (The Program Manager has an identical Run command in its File menu.)

Running a Program in Windows

You have three ways to run a program in Windows. But why bother with the second and third ways when the first is so simple?

Locate a program's icon (little graphical picture) in the Program Manager's window. Double-click that icon. The program runs.

Sadly, this method works only for Windows programs and those applications someone has already installed for you in the Program Manager's window. You're best off if you can browbeat your guru into doing this for you. The following two methods aren't as nice.

The second method is to use the File Manager program, which shows you a list of files on disk. Look for the program names that end in the COM or EXE extensions to find the program you want to run and then double-click it. The program starts.

The third method is to type in the program's name, just as you would at the DOS prompt. You do this by selecting the File menu and then Run in either the Program Manager or the File Manager. Type in the full pathname of the program to run it. Hmm, just like DOS.

Note that only Windows-specific programs show up as graphical windows. Everything else looks the same way it does when you run the program under DOS. But don't be fooled: You're still in Windows. (Which also means don't just quit the program and shut off the computer when you're done; return to Windows by typing **EXIT** and quit gracefully from Windows at that point.)

Using a Window's Gizmos

Windows is a virtual FAO Schwarz of fun things to play with, stuff to drive you crazy, and interesting toys over which you'll waste colossal amounts of time. There are tiny buttons you "push" with the mouse, graphics that slide and stretch, things to poke, and stuff that drops down. In other words, there are gizmos on the screen, most of which control the way the windows look and how programs in Windows operate.

Changing a window's size

Your windows can be just about any size, from filling the entire screen to too small to be useful, and everything in between.

To make a window fill the entire screen — which is how it's the most useful — click the up-pointing triangle in the window's upper-right corner. (This changes the up-pointing triangle to a combination up- and down-pointing triangle thingy. Click that button again to restore the window to its original size.)

To turn a window into a doinky little icon at the bottom of the screen, click the lonely only down-pointing arrow button in the upper-right corner of a window. This action shoves the window out of the way but isn't the same as quitting. To restore the icon back into a window, double-click it.

When a window isn't full-screen or an icon, you can change its size by "grabbing" an edge with the mouse: Hover the mouse over one side of the window or a corner. Press and hold the mouse button and drag the window in or out to a new size. Release the mouse button to snap the window into place.

> ✔ Enlarging a window to full-screen size is called *maximizing*.

> ✔ Shrinking a window down into an icon is called *minimizing*.

> ✔ Positioning a window just so on the screen and then having Windows move it for no reason is called *frustrating*.

Scrolling about

Often, what you're looking at in a window is larger than the window. For example, if a tanned, svelte, and bikini-clad Claudia Schiffer walked by a very tiny window in your wall, you would be able to see only a small part of her bronzed form. If you could move the window up and down the wall, you could see more of her, but only one window's worth at a time. This is how *scrolling* works.

To facilitate scrolling a window around, one or two scroll bars are used. The scroll bar is a long, skinny thing with an arrow at either end and an elevator-like box in the middle. You use the arrows and elevator to move the window's image up or down or left or right, revealing other parts of the total picture.

Accessing a menu

Unlike in a DOS program (take WordPerfect — please!), in a Windows application all the commands and whatnot are included on a handy — and always visible — menu bar. It's usually at the top of a window.

Each word on the menu bar — File, Edit, and so on — is a menu title. It represents a pull-down menu, which contains commands related to the title. For example, the File menu contains Save, Open, New, Close, and other commands related to files.

To access these commands, click the menu title. The menu drops down. Then select a menu item, or command. If you don't like what you see, click the menu title again to make the menu go away, or select another menu.

You can access the menus by using your keyboard in two ways: Press the Alt key plus the underlined letter in a menu title. To select a menu item, type the item's underlined letter. Or you can press and release the Alt key, or just press F10 to access the menus. You can then use the arrow keys to point at the menu item you want.

Closing a window

Closing a program's window is the same thing as quitting the program; you make it disappear. The most common way to close a window is to double-click the long hyphen-thing square in the upper-left corner of the window.

Another popular way to close a window is to press Alt+F4. Why Alt+F4? The wind must have been blowing from Utah that day on the Microsoft campus, because Alt+F4 sure smells like a WordPerfect command to me.

Another way to close a window — striking because it's obvious — is to select the Exit menu item from the File menu. This also quits the program you're running.

If you close the Program Manager's window, you quit Windows.

Switching Programs

In Windows you can run several programs at once. Imagine the productivity boost! Dream of getting two things done at once! Then realize the chaos. Fortunately, you really don't run several programs at once as much as you can switch between two or more at a time without having to stop and restart, stop and restart, over and over.

Although Windows can run more than one program at a time, as a human — and I assume that most of us are — you can work only on the program whose window is up in front or "top o' the pile" or filling the entire screen. To switch to another program you have several options.

The Quick Way: The quickest way to switch programs is to grab the mouse and click in another program's window, if it's visible. Clicking in a window brings that window to the top of the pile.

Another Quick Way: Shove the current window out of the way, shrinking it down to an icon at the bottom of the screen. This doesn't quit the program — it just *minimizes* it, allowing you access to whatever other windows lie behind it. You accomplish the minimization process by clicking the down-pointing triangle button on the upper-right corner of the window.

Nonmousy Ways: If you run out of mouse methods for switching programs, you can try one of three keyboard methods. These are awful to remember, though I'm personally fond of the Alt+Tab key combination approach.

- **Alt+Tab:** Press the Alt and Tab keys at the same time — but hold down the Alt key and release the Tab key. This displays a little picture box in the center of the screen telling you which program is next. If you don't like that program, keep holding down the Alt key and tap the Tab key again. When you find the program you want, release the Alt key.

- **Alt+Esc:** Press the Alt and Esc keys at the same time. This switches you to the next program you have active (in the order in which you started the programs). You may have to press Alt+Esc a few times to find the program or window you want.

- **Ctrl+Esc:** Press the Ctrl and Esc keys at the same time. This summons the Task List window, which shows you a list of the programs currently running. Double-click a program in the list, and you are immediately switched to it. (You can also bring up the Task List by double-clicking the *desktop* or background, away from other windows.)

- To switch to another window, click it.

- You can use three key combinations to switch to another window or program: Alt+Tab, Alt+Esc, or Ctrl+Esc.

Minimizing a window by clicking the down-arrow button in the upper-right corner of the window does not quit that application. Instead, the program is shrunk down to icon size at the bottom of the screen. Double-click that icon if you want to access the program's window.

The General Commands

Windows-specific programs all share common commands. This allows you to easily learn new Windows applications, as well as to cut and paste information between two different applications. Ah, yes, more productivity boosting, thanks to Chairman Bill.

Copy

To copy something in Windows, select it with the mouse: Drag the mouse over text or click a picture. This action highlights the text or picture, which means it has been selected and is ready for copying.

After selecting, choose Copy from the Edit menu. The quick-key shortcut for this is Ctrl+C.

- After your text or picture is copied, it can then be pasted. You can paste into the same program or switch to another program for pasting.

- When you copy something, it's put into the Windows *Clipboard*. You can even look at the Clipboard's contents if you start the Clipboard Viewer application in the Program Manager. Unfortunately, the Clipboard holds only one thing at a time. Whenever you copy or cut, the new item replaces whatever was already in the Clipboard. (Such a Clipboard doesn't seem very handy, but Microsoft would like me to remind you here of all the time you're saving in Windows.)

✔ Primitive versions of Windows used the memorable Ctrl+Insert key combination as the quick-key shortcut for Copy.

Cut

Cutting something in Windows works just like copying: You select a picture or text and then select Cut from the Edit menu. Unlike with Copy, however, the picture or text you cut is copied to the Clipboard and then deleted from your application. The quick-key shortcut for this is Ctrl+X.

✔ After you cut text or a picture you can paste it from the Clipboard back into the current application, or you can switch to another application for pasting.

✔ Some old, oddball Windows applications may use the forgettable Shift+Del key combination as the quick-key shortcut for Cut. (Please don't try to make sense of this.)

Paste

The Paste command is used to take a picture or bit of text that's stored in the Clipboard and insert it into the current application. You can paste a picture into text or text into a picture. Ah, the miracle of Windows.

To paste, select the Edit menu and choose the Paste item. Or you can press Ctrl+V, the Paste quick-key shortcut.

✔ You can paste material cut or copied from any Windows application into another Windows application.

✔ The old, arcane key command for Paste was Shift+Insert — like that means anything.

Undo

The powers at Microsoft have graced us sloppy Windows users with the blessed Undo command. This command undoes whatever stupid thing we just did.

To undo, select the Edit menu. The first item on the list should be the Undo command — how convenient. The key command is Ctrl+Z.

- ✔ Undo undoes just about anything you can do: unchange edits, replace cut graphics, fix up a bad marriage, and so on.

- ✔ The old key command equivalent for Undo was Alt+Backspace. This makes no sense to me because the Alt+Shift (or Alt+Delete or Alt+Insert) keystroke isn't used by anything, and, heck, let's all go with the Windows programming gang over to Building 16 and have a latté and giggle about end users.

Getting Help

Windows has an incredible help system, and all Windows-specific programs share it. You can always activate Help by pressing the F1 key. From there you're shown the *help engine* that allows you to look up topics, search for topics, or see related items of interest all by properly using your mouse. Here are some hints:

- ✔ You can click green text to see related topics.

- ✔ You can click green underlined text (with a dotted underline) to see a pop-up window defining the term. (Press and hold the mouse button to see the pop-up information.)

- ✔ Browse forward or backward through the help topics to see an index or to look up a specific item.

The help engine is its own program. When you're done using help, remember to quit: Double-click the minus-sign thing in the upper-left corner of the window. Also refer to the section "Stopping a Windows Program (Safely)" which is located . . . why, it's next.

Stopping a Windows Program (Safely)

You end a Windows program by choosing Exit from the program's File menu. You can also exit by double-clicking the slot-like doohickey in the upper-left corner of the window, or by single-clicking said slot-like device and selecting Close from the menu that appears.

Non-Windows programs under Windows must be quit in the same way as you'd quit them under DOS: Press F7 for WordPerfect, /Quit for 1-2-3, and so on.

To exit Windows itself, double-click the minus-like icon thingamabob in the upper-left area of the Windows Program Manager window. Answer OK to the prompt. (When you're back at the DOS prompt, you can turn off the machine.)

> ✔ Just because you're no longer using a program in Windows doesn't necessarily mean that you've quit it. It's possible to switch between programs without quitting; refer to "Switching Programs" earlier in this chapter.

It's possible to run more than one copy of a program at a time in Windows. For example, you can have several Notepads running, each of which shows you a different text file for editing. Don't let this boggle you. As a word of advice: Quit any program you're not using. Doing so removes the confusion, and Windows runs a little faster when it has less to do.

General Advice

Use your mouse. If you don't have a mouse, you can still use Windows but not as elegantly. Ack, who am I kidding? You *need* a mouse to use Windows!

Have someone organize your Program Manager for you so you can click any program or file you want to run, and have him or her get rid of all those other programs you don't use that clutter up your screen.

Windows is a *black box* program in that a lot is going on in the background that you might forget about (see Chapter 15). Never reset while you're running Windows. And before you quit Windows itself, make sure you've properly quit from all the programs you're running under Windows.

Keep in mind that Windows can run several programs at once. Use the Task List (Ctrl+Esc) to see whether a program is already running before starting a second copy. (Yes, you can run several copies of a program under Windows, but you probably need to run only one.)

Be wary of seeing a DOS prompt when you're in Windows. The DOS program simply may be one of the Windows "programs"; seeing it doesn't mean that you've quit Windows, nor is it a sure sign that you can reset or turn off the computer. To be sure, type the EXIT command:

```
C> EXIT
```

If that doesn't return you to Windows, you're out of Windows, and it's safe to reset.

If a program crashes under Windows, big deal! Windows is constructed so that one dead program won't topple the whole computer. You simply close that program's window and keep on working — you can even start the program again after it has been properly disposed of. This is one of the neater aspects of Windows (when it works).

Chapter 6

DOS in Windows 95/98

*W*ith the dawn of Windows 95, DOS became an operating system Microsoft no longer supported. Which is good, I suppose, since DOS had so many shortcomings. Even so, lots of DOS software exists and a special DOS mode is available to anyone who has a Windows 95 or Windows 98 PC. This chapter covers the nuances of running DOS in that environment, and it does so with few lamentations.

✔ As far as DOS is concerned, there is little difference between Windows 95 and Windows 98. In fact, Windows 98 should really be called Windows 95 version 2.

✔ Because Windows 95 and Windows 98 are so similar, they're referred to collectively as *Windows* in this chapter. (Be careful not to confuse this with the older version of Windows, which is covered in the previous chapter.)

✔ If you want to know nearly everything you'll need to know about running DOS in Windows 95, go check out *DOS For Dummies*, Windows 95 Edition, (IDG Books Worldwide, Inc.) available everywhere. Most of it also applies to Windows 98 as well.

Summoning a DOS Prompt Window

Under the repressive thumb of Windows, DOS must run like any other program; you start up a "DOS prompt" window, which, uh, changes things somewhat. Even so, all the DOS commands you know and love — with a few exceptions — still work as you would expect. Oh, and you still get the same error message. But it's prettier because DOS is in a window.

To start the MS-DOS prompt window in Windows, follow these steps:

1. **Summon the Start menu.**

   Press the Ctrl+Esc key combination, which is always a surefire way to do it.

2. **From the Start menu, choose Programs.**

   You can press the **P** key here for a shortcut.

3. **Choose** MS-DOS Prompt **from the pop-up menu that appears.**

   You can use the arrow keys to highlight that item and then press Enter. Or, you can point and click with the mouse.

Lo and behold, a DOS window appears on-screen (see Figure 6-1). You can type a DOS command or type the name of a program to run — just like in the old days.

Figure 6-1: A DOS window in Windows.

To quit the DOS window, type the **EXIT** command. Or, you can close the window as you'd close any program window: Click the X button in the window's upper-right corner.

   ✔ After you have the DOS prompt window open, you can use DOS just like before. You can change the DOS window size as well as the size of the text you see in the window. Keep reading.

   ✔ You can actually run more than one DOS prompt window at a time, which is ideal, especially if you have more than one head.

✔ The command to close the DOS prompt window is EXIT. Type it at the DOS prompt and the window goes away.

✔ The EXIT command does not quit Windows; EXIT only closes the DOS prompt window.

Running your DOS programs

All DOS programs run the same under Windows 95 and Windows 98 hegemony as they did when DOS was king. Okay, they appear in a graphical window on-screen, but other than that, you get the same program.

You can run your DOS programs in two ways. The first is to run the MS-DOS prompt window, which is shown in Figure 6-1. Because it's a DOS prompt, all you need to do is type the name of your program and press the Enter key — as described in Chapter 2.

The second way to start a DOS program is the same way you start a Windows program: Look for the DOS program on the Start menu and run it from there. Or, you can locate the program by using Windows Explorer and double-clicking the program's icon to open it.

✔ Actually, you can use *dozens* of ways to start any program in Windows. It's as though Microsoft couldn't make up its mind about which way was best, so it suffocates us with options instead.

✔ The Program menu (from the main Start menu) may have a submenu titled DOS Programs or DOS Applications. Look there for any DOS programs you may have on your PC.

✔ Newer PCs (those that come with Windows 95 or Windows 98 installed) don't have any DOS programs available.

✔ All DOS programs run the same in Windows as they do in DOS. When you quit the DOS program, its window disappears from the screen. Or, if you're running the DOS program from a DOS prompt window, you return to the DOS prompt.

✔ See the section "Messing with a DOS Window," later in this chapter, for information on what you can do with a DOS program in a window.

Running Windows programs

It's also possible to run Windows programs from the DOS prompt. If you're eager to see Windows take a back seat again, nothing will delight you more than starting a Windows program by typing its name at the prompt. For example:

```
C> NOTEPAD
```

Typing this command and pressing Enter runs the Windows text editor, Notepad. (The Windows program starts up in its own window, leaving the DOS window "behind the scenes.")

TECHNICAL STUFF

✔ If you're used to writing batch file menus, you can use them to start your Windows programs: Just put the Windows programs on the menu as you would do with a DOS program.

✔ In some cases you have to specify a full pathname to run a Windows program. To run WordPad, for example, you type

```
"PROGRAM FILES\ACCESSORIES\WORDPAD"
```

Yes, that's a long filename and, yes, it must be enclosed in double quotes. But it runs WordPad for you.

Running more than one DOS program at a time

In Windows, you can *run* several programs at one time, even DOS programs. The key is just to start them up, each one in its own DOS cage, er, window. Each program runs independently of the other, making it look like you're getting a whole lotta work done at once!

TIP

Long filenames in DOS

One of the boasts of Windows 95 and Windows 98 is that they allow you to name a file just about anything by using just about any number of characters. This blessing passes over into DOS: You can use long filenames at the DOS prompt, if you like.

To make a long filename work, however, you have to enclose it in double quotes. For example:

```
C:\> COPY FILELIST.TXT "MY
     COMPUTER"
```

This command copies the file named FILELIST.TXT to the directory named "MY

COMPUTER." Any DOS command can work with long filenames in this manner; just remember the double quotes.

One other thing: Windows actually keeps two filenames for files with long names. The first name is a traditional, eight-character DOS filename. The second is the long name. You can see both names in the output of any DIR command; the long filename appears on the right, after the date and time.

To switch between each running DOS program, you can use any one of the fancy Windows program-switching methods. The most popular way is to locate the DOS program's button on the taskbar and click it to switch to that window. Also popular is the Alt+Tab key combination used to hop from one window to the next.

✔ To switch to another window, click it.

✔ Clicking a program's button on the taskbar switches you to that program.

✔ The best way to switch is to press the Alt+Tab keys. This method works especially well for DOS programs, where your hands are on the keyboard most of the time anyway.

Messing with a DOS Window

By framing DOS in a window, Microsoft is blessing you with a whole slew of new commands. They're not DOS commands; they're window commands. Maybe one or two of the commands directly affect the DOS program (and there's no point in going into them in this book), although some of the commands affect the window in which you see your DOS program. That's worth rumination for a few paragraphs.

Show me how it looked in the olden days

Want to run your DOS program full-screen? Press the Alt+Enter key combination. It switches any DOS program between full-screen and "windowed" mode.

✔ Press Alt+Enter once to switch to full-screen mode.

✔ Press Alt+Enter again to switch back to a window.

✔ Don't forget that you're in Windows when you run a DOS program full-screen! Type the EXIT command to be sure you're at a DOS prompt before you turn off your PC. And never turn off a computer when one of your DOS programs is running.

Changing a DOS window

A DOS program in a window can be changed like any program in a window can. You can do any of the following:

Move the window. To move a window, drag it about by its title bar: Point the mouse at the title bar at the top of the window. Press and drag the mouse, moving the window to a new location on-screen.

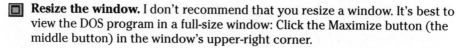 **Resize the window.** I don't recommend that you resize a window. It's best to view the DOS program in a full-size window: Click the Maximize button (the middle button) in the window's upper-right corner.

Shrink the window to an icon. Click the Minimize button to shrink the window to a button on the bottom of the screen. The Minimize button is the first of the three buttons in the window's upper right corner. Note that clicking this button does not stop the DOS program from running; it merely shoves its window aside.

The toolbar

To get the most from a DOS window, make sure that the toolbar is visible. Click the MS-DOS icon in the window's upper left corner. From the drop-down menu that appears, check to make sure that the Toolbar option has a check mark by it. If it does, press Esc. Otherwise, choose the Toolbar option to see the window's toolbar, as shown in Figure 6-2.

Figure 6-2:
The DOS
window's
toolbar.

Messing with the font size

 To change the font size, click the A button on the DOS toolbar. You see a dialog box displayed, which looks a lot like the one shown in Figure 6-3.

The important part is the Font size section in the upper right corner. That's where you choose a font size for your DOS window.

The lower right corner of the dialog box shows you how big the characters will look on-screen — a preview.

The lower left corner of the dialog box shows you how large the DOS prompt window is for a selected font. Because this size is in proportion to your monitor, you see how much of Windows DOS can hide.

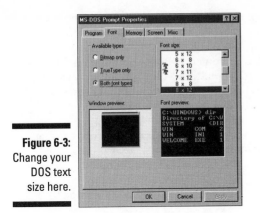

Figure 6-3:
Change your
DOS text
size here.

Choose various fonts until you find one with characters (lower right) of the perfect size and a window (lower left) of the perfect size. ***Remember:*** This is *work*. Feel free to do this kind of experimentation at the office.

After finding the perfect font, click OK. It's OK!

✔ Microsoft logic: Click "A" for *f*ont.

✔ You can also change the font by using the drop-down list on the left side of the DOS toolbar. The Font dialog box, however, is more useful — especially if you really don't know what you're doing (which is me, most of the time).

✔ One special type of font "size" to pick is Auto. No, it has nothing to do with cars. It allows the font size to change as you resize the DOS prompt window. If you're tired of seeing scrollbars, choose the Auto option.

Copying and pasting DOS stuff

Windows is all about copying, cutting, and pasting. That's one of its selling points. With DOS, Windows allows you to copy and paste as well. There's no cutting, though, probably because Microsoft fears what DOS users can do with a good pair of scissors.

 Copying. You can copy any chunk of text from any DOS prompt window. Click the Mark button on the DOS toolbar. Then, use the mouse to select a chunk of text on-screen. (You can select only text, not graphics, in a DOS window.) Press Enter and the text you selected is stored in the Windows Clipboard.

Pasting. You can paste the text you copy from one DOS window into any other DOS window. Just click the Paste button from the DOS toolbar. DOS "types" the text into your window — including any spaces you may have copied. You can paste into a DOS window (including the same DOS prompt window from which you copied), or you can paste into a Windows application.

Pasting from Windows to DOS. Any text you copy in Windows can be pasted into a DOS prompt window. The text is "typed" into the DOS prompt window just as though you typed it yourself at the keyboard. You cannot, however, paste graphics into a DOS prompt window.

- ✔ If you choose the Mark command and change your mind, press the Esc key to return your DOS window to normal operating mode.

- ✔ A DOS window has no Cut command.

- ✔ After selecting text, you can press the Enter key to copy it or click the Copy button on the DOS toolbar.

- ✔ In Windows, Ctrl+C is the Copy command. In DOS, it's the Cancel command.

- ✔ Oh, and Ctrl+V is used to Paste in Windows, although in DOS Ctrl+V means nothing (or it could be a specific command in your DOS application).

- ✔ You can also paste text by pressing Alt+Spacebar,E,P — which pops up the DOS prompt window's control menu, from which you choose the Edit⇨Paste command.

- ✔ When the paste button isn't highlighted, it means that there's nothing to paste. Yes, yes: Even if Windows will paste, DOS may not. Don't let this bug you.

- ✔ Anything copied or pasted in Windows is stored in the Windows Clipboard. The Clipboard can hold only one item at a time. If you copy (or cut) something else in Windows, it replaces the current contents of the Clipboard.

Important DOS-in-Windows Things to Remember

Since DOS is no longer in charge, you have to defer to the Windows way of doing certain things while you run DOS in Windows. You have to be wary of several things:

Thing 1. In Windows 95 and Windows 98, the DOS prompt is simply another "program." Especially if you see a DOS prompt "full screen" (the Alt+Enter thing), don't assume that you've quit Windows. To be sure, type the EXIT command:

```
C> EXIT
```

If that command doesn't return you to Windows (instead you see another DOS prompt displayed), you're not in Windows. It's then safe to reset or turn your PC off.

 Thing 2. Windows 95 and Windows 98 let you close a DOS window by clicking its X close button — just like any other Windows program. However, Windows does not let you close a DOS window while you're running a DOS program. When that happens, you see an error message displayed. Click OK. Quit your DOS program, and *then* close the DOS prompt window.

Thing 3. Do not run CHKDSK while you're in a DOS window. This could seriously mess up your files on disk. Use the Windows version of ScanDisk instead. Generally speaking, in fact, avoid using any disk utility in a DOS window. Other Windows counterparts behave better.

Thing 4. Deleting a file in DOS means that you have no way to recover it by using the Windows Recycle Bin. If you do major disk management, do it in Windows — unless your DOS disk-management software has an "undo" feature.

Generally speaking, starting with Windows 95, DOS has its hands tied. Most of the major things you would do with DOS — backup, disk optimization, disk repair — are done under Windows.

Thing 5. It's possible to quit Windows and return to a DOS prompt. When you see the Shut Down Windows dialog box, choose the Restart in MS-DOS Mode option. Click OK and you see a DOS prompt — and no Windows — just like in the old days. This method is an ideal way to run stubborn DOS games or use any DOS programs that don't behave well under Windows.

Thing 6. There is no Thing 6.

Part II
The Non-Nerd's Guide to PC Hardware

The 5th Wave   By Rich Tennant

"IT'S ABOUT A GROUP OF YOUNG, INEXPERIENCED GERMAN PROGRAMMERS ALL CRAMPED TOGETHER INSIDE THIS HOT, TINY COMPUTER ROOM FIGHTING THE VIRUS OF THEIR LIVES DURING THE EARLY YEARS OF NETWORK COMMUNICATIONS."

In this part . . .

Wow! Hardware. It's tools, Owen! Man toys. Things you can . . . uh . . . hey! Wait a second! This here is *computer* hardware! No drills! No saws! Just silly things like floppy drives, microprocessors, and . . . a mouse? Weird.

There's much that goes into the hardware side of your computer. Most of it you can blissfully ignore. In fact, you need to know only what all the big pieces are called, and you'll be just fine. Any detail beyond that is for the computer scientists or the folks who fix your computer to muss with. Yes, you can be a happy and productive computer owner and never know what an EEPROM is.

This part of the book covers computer hardware, specifically those items you use every day, plus a few other goodies that DOS controls. And what exactly is "hardware," anyway? Well, simply put: If you can drop it on your foot and it makes you go "ouch," it's hardware.

Chapter 7

Your Basic Hardware: What It Is and Why

In This Chapter

▶ Defining and explaining the various parts of a computer system

▶ Understanding how a microprocessor fits into the big picture

▶ Learning what a math coprocessor is and what it can do for you

▶ Discovering where your disk drives are located and what they're called

▶ Using a port to connect interesting external devices to your PC

▶ Using printer ports and serial ports

▶ Using your PC to keep track of the date and time

*T*he truth is, you just can't go around calling everything a whatsis. It would be grand, but there comes a point when you need a doodad — or a jobbie or a thingamabob. Then, eventually, you've developed your own, personalized form of technospeak — a language only you can understand. After all, rumor has it that lawyers started out that way — and look where it got them!

This chapter defines a few common things associated with your computer. It describes them by using a variety of terms, including geegaw, doojigger, and madoodle. The idea is to explain your basic PC hardware minus the complex geometric math.

The Nerd's-Eye View

Time for the big picture. Note the items listed in Table 7-1 and their locations. Furthermore, make sure that you can identify each one on your PC.

Table 7-1	Basic Computer Hardware Components
Item to Find	**Typical Nerd Description**
Monitor	Video display, or CRT (cathode ray tube)
Keyboard	Manually dexterous input mechanism, or "101 Enhanced"
Computer box	System unit, console, or combative FFC Class B approved anti-EMF regulated shield with titanium white finish
Floppy drive A	Primary disk-based I/O storage device with removable media, or floppy drive A
Floppy drive B	Optional second disk-based I/O storage device with removable media, or floppy drive B (if present)
Hard drive(s) C	Primary fixed disk, nonremovable, high-speed, maximum-capacity, hermetically sealed SCSI 960 Mach 3 whopper
CD-ROM drive	Massive read-only storage device; primary means by which software is distributed
Tape drive	Optional streaming serial access backup device
Removable drive	Zip drive, magneto-optical drive, or other massive storage device
Printer	Laser, color, whatever

Inside the computer box are various other items: stuff you can't see because, well, it's inside the box. Table 7-2 lists the items you would be able to locate there if, like Superman, you had X-ray vision.

Table 7-2	Internal Computer Components
Item Inside	**Typical Nerd Description**
Memory	RAM, or memory chips or banks, or SIMMs, DRAM, SRAM, EDO RAM, RAMALAMADINGDONG
Main circuitry board	The motherboard, system board, planar board
The computer's brain	The microprocessor, or the central processing unit (CPU), or by its number/name
Expansion cards	PCI, ISA, PCMCI, direct bus expansion daughterboards
Power supply	210 watt, U/L listed, AC/DC power converter
Other stuff	Goobers

✔ Very few PCs come today with two floppy drives. That configuration was a holdover from the early days when PCs lacked hard drives. If you do have a second floppy drive, it's drive B. To avoid confusion, it helps to label each drive by using a sticker or one of those letter-puncher devices. Don't just label them A and B either; label them drive A and drive B or, better still, A: and B: (with colons, which is how DOS refers to them).

✔ For more information on computer memory, see Chapter 8.

✔ The back of your PC contains lots of connections for various devices and other goodies you can hook up to a PC. For example, both the printer and your monitor hook up to your PC's rump. For information on other things you can plug in back there, see the section "What Are Ports?" later in this chapter.

The Microprocessor

The computer's main microchip is called a *microprocessor*. The type found in most PCs is the Pentium, which is the microprocessor's first name. Its last name can be "Pro" or "II" (two) or MMX or Celeron, each of which denotes a different type of Pentium based on speed, capability, and price.

Telling whether you have one microprocessor or another inside your computer box is a job best left to the gods. The only time this information should be a concern of yours is when some piece of software requires one microprocessor and you have another. You'll know this, of course, because the program won't run.

✔ The microprocessor is not "your computer's brain." That's a common metaphor, but it's just not true. A computer with a brain is something scary — like a politician with a brain. No, your computer's microprocessor is more like a calculator. It doesn't have brains, which I should know because my accountant uses a calculator all the time.

✔ The "brains" in a computer are actually the software.

✔ Before the Pentium, computer microprocessors were named after famous numbers. There was the 8088/8086, the 80286, the 80386, and the 80486. Generally, the bigger the number, the faster and more powerful the computer (well, at the time).

✔ The Pentium could have been called the 80586, or 586, for short. The Pentium II is an 80686, more or less.

✔ You can buy software programs that tell you the kind of microprocessor you have in your computer as well as what kind of video display you have and other information that's not apparent to most people. Most software that performs "diagnostics" coughs up such advice. Refer to the shelves of your local software store.

Pentium Jokes

- ✔ Pentium. Little. Yellow. Different.

- ✔ The doctor said that all that bending is hard on your Pentium.

- ✔ "And here's another slide of Athens. That's Helen in front of the Pentium."

- ✔ Thanks to local industry, our freshwater supply is polluted with Pentium (though the fish have gotten much smarter).

- ✔ "Where, pray tell, is Deuterium?" "Why, he's gone with Pentium to the Oracle at Delphi."

- ✔ You've tried dusting them; you've tried spraying them. Why not try Pentium?

- ✔ Did you hear about that new dirty magazine in Latin? *Pentium Housium.*

- ✔ Whole-Wheat Corn Goobers cereal now comes with 11 vitamins and minerals, including iron, zinc, Paladium, and Pentium.

Disk Drives

Disk drives are storage devices. Several kinds are available.

Floppy drives. This type of disk drive uses removable floppy disks for storage. Although some software comes on floppy disks, because of their limited capacity, most floppy disks are used to transport files (between one computer and another, for example).

Hard drives. This type of disk drive stores massive amounts of information. It's the primary thing you use for storing DOS, your programs, and all the junk you create on your PC. Unlike with other types of disk drives, however, you cannot remove your hard drive. (Well, not without a screwdriver and some solid determination.)

CD-ROM drives. A CD-ROM drive is a removable form of storage. Like the hard drive, it stores massive amounts of information. Unlike with the hard drive, you can remove a CD-ROM disk. Also, you cannot write information to CD-ROM drives; they're "read only," meaning that information is stored on them and cannot be altered.

Removable drives. A whole gaggle of removable drives is available. Essentially, they store lots of information in a compact form, such as zip disks or magneto-optical disks. As with a floppy disk, you can remove these types of disks from one computer and use them in another. They're often slower than a hard drive, though, and have a limited storage capacity.

To see what's stored on a hard drive, use the DIR command. (Refer to the section "DIR Command," in Chapter 2).

Under DOS, your cherished disk operating system, disk drives are referred to by letters. The first floppy drive on all PCs is called *drive A,* or the A drive. The second floppy drive, whether or not you have one, is *drive B.* The first hard drive on any computer system is almost always *drive C,* with additional drives given letters of the alphabet from D through Z.

If you have a PC with one floppy disk, one hard drive, and a CD-ROM (the standard configuration), here's how everything breaks down:

Floppy disk	Drive A
Hard disk	Drive C
CD-ROM	Drive D

The floppy disk and hard disk are always drives A and C, respectively. The CD-ROM may or may not be drive D. For example, you may have a *huge* hard drive that's just so goldarn big that it's actually drives C *and* D. Here's how your drives would be named:

Floppy disk	Drive A
Hard disk	Drive C
Hard disk	Drive D
CD-ROM	Drive E

The moral? Don't always expect your disk drive letters to match up with every other computer on the planet. This advice is important because computer manuals don't assume that, for example, your CD-ROM is drive D. It may or may not be. So pay attention!

✔ After you know which drive has which letter, write it down! Tape that information to the front of your PC. (Don't tape over the breathing slits in the front of the computer.)

✔ Hard drives are internal mechanisms. On most PCs, you cannot see the hard drive. If you can see it, it looks like a floppy drive but with tiny air holes rather than a disk slit.

✔ On each disk drive is a *drive light.* The light is on only when the computer is accessing the disk, either reading or writing information. It's important that you do not remove a floppy disk while that light is on.

✔ Refer to the section "Changing Disks" in Chapter 2 for instructions on removing and ejecting disks from floppy drives.

✔ Older PCs sported a different size floppy drive: 5¼-inch. This disk was of a different type than the 3½-inch size disks of today. If you have an older drive, consider having it replaced with the newer, 3½-inch size.

What Are Ports?

The term *port* refers to a "hole" in the back of the computer or a festive dessert wine. You can plug in any one of a variety of external devices with which the computer can communicate through a port.

Presently, two popular kinds of ports are in a PC: the *printer* port and the *serial* port.

> ✔ Other external devices, such as the keyboard and monitor, are connected via their own special ports. Sometimes, external disk drives are added, again, via some form of unique port.

> ✔ A special type of port is available on some PCs. Technically, this port is the *analog-to-digital,* or *A-to-D,* port. A variety of scientific and real-world monitoring devices and such can be plugged in to that port. However, most people refer to this port by the device that's hooked up to it 99 times out of 100: the *joystick* port.

> ✔ You get no visual clue to determine which port is which. (Well, what did you expect?) Even the experts have to struggle through trial-and-error sometimes; ports on a PC do look similar. If you ever find out for sure, label them.

The printer port

Mysteriously enough, the printer port is where you plug in your printer. The printer cable has one connector that plugs into the printer and a second that plugs into the computer. Both connectors are different, so it's impossible to plug in a printer backward.

> ✔ For more information on printers, see Chapter 11.

> ✔ Printer ports are also called *parallel* ports or (to old-time nerds) *Centronics* ports. People who refer to ports in this manner should be slapped.

> ✔ Other devices can be connected to a printer port, though typically the only one you have is the printer. Examples of other devices are voice synthesizers, network connections, external hard drives, extra keyboards, and choo-choo train sets.

The serial port

The serial port is much more flexible than the printer port; it supports a variety of interesting items, which is why it's generically called a serial port rather than a this-or-that port.

TECHNICAL STUFF

Port deciphering hints you may skip

Ports connect to external devices by means of cables. These cables have connectors on both ends that are shaped like the letter *D*. From this arrangement, we get the term *D-shell* connectors.

Your typical monitor port has a 15-line D-shell connector, whereas your typical serial port has a 9-line D-shell connector. This stuff isn't worth mentioning, except for the fact that both D-shell connectors are the same size and can be easily confused.

The parallel port uses a 25-line D-shell connector. On some older systems, the serial port uses the same 25-line D-shell connector. (Curiously, all external modems still use the 25-line D-shell connector.) This situation was done purely for spite, and it caused many PC owners countless hours of agony discovering which port was which.

You often plug the following items into a serial port: a modem, a serial printer, a scanner or other input device, or just about anything that requires two-way communications. Most computers come with two serial ports.

✔ A serial port can also be called a *modem* port.

✔ Serial ports are also called *RS-232* ports. No, that's not a Radio Shack part number. Instead, it refers to Recommended Standard 232, which I assume is the 232nd standard The Committee came up with that year. Busy guys.

✔ You can plug a computer mouse into a serial port. In that case, the mouse is called a *serial mouse*. The mouse can also be plugged in to its own port, called — shockingly enough — a *mouse port*. (Refer to your local pet store for more information on mice or turn to Chapter 10.)

Oddball ports

Several new types of ports may also crop up on various and sundry PCs. Here's a samplin':

USB. The *Universal Serial Bus* is a new port designed to replace the serial port, keyboard port, and mouse port with one, single, everything-plugs-in-here port. These ports are standard on most PCs sold in the late 1990s, though at the time this book was written, few USB devices are available for plugging in to USB ports.

Firewire ports. The *firewire port* is another attempt to have a versatile port on a PC to which you can attach a wide variety of useful devices. For example, one firewire port could have attached to it an external hard drive, a scanner, a modem, another hard drive, a CD-ROM drive, another hard drive, power tools, the garage door opener, another hard drive, the machine that goes "boop" in a hospital emergency room, a garden weasel, and even more hard drives. You get the idea.

SCSI ports. A *SCSI* ("scuzzy") *port* enables you to connect as many as six external or internal devices to a computer. These devices include hard drives, CD-ROMs, scanners, and other devices. It's not as versatile as firewire is supposed to be, but many more devices are available that use SCSI than use firewire.

Definitely skip over this port stuff

Serial ports are complex in that you must *configure* them. Printer ports are set up to work in a specific manner and require no configuration. With a serial port, however, you must configure both the port on your computer and the device with which you're communicating.

You have to configure four items on a serial port: the speed at which the port operates; the data word format, or the size of the bytes you're sending; the number of stop bits; and the parity. This process is a real hassle only when you need to connect a serial printer (see the section "Serial Connection," in Chapter 11). To get everything working right, you must occasionally make a full-moon sacrifice to the UNIX god or sing "Zip-A-Dee-Doo-Dah" while holding your nose and hopping on one foot.

Definitely skip over this starboard stuff

On a ship, the left side as you face forward is called *port*. The right side is called *starboard*. These terms apply even when you face the rear (aft) of the ship: Then the ship's left side, now on your right, is still called "port"; ditto for "starboard."

The Date and Time

Most computers come with an internal clock. The clock is battery operated, which enables it to keep track of the time, day or night, whether or not the PC is plugged in.

To check or change the current time, use the TIME command. Type the word **TIME** at the command prompt, and DOS responds with what it thinks is the current time. Here's an example:

```
C> TIME
Current time is 11:13:55.13p
Enter new time:
```

Type the new time by using the hour:minutes format; there's no need to enter seconds or hundredths of a second. (If you work for the government, there's no need to enter the minutes value either.) If the given time is close to correct, just press Enter to keep it. Don't worry: You don't reset the clock to 12:00 a.m. if you don't enter a new time.

You use the DATE command to view or change the current date. It works like the TIME command:

```
C> DATE
Current date is Tue 10-19-1999
Enter new date (mm-dd-yy):
```

Type the new date by using the format indicated.

DOS uses the date and time you enter when it creates or updates a file. The date and time are then shown in the directory listing along with each file. If you want to see just the current date or time, press Enter when you're asked to enter the new date or time. Pressing Enter doesn't alter the date or time. (Refer to the section "DIR Command" in Chapter 2 for more information on the directory listing.)

✔ If the computer's clock battery goes dead, you have to replace it. Before you become incensed, see the section "The Computer Has Lost Track of the Time," in Chapter 20.

✔ If you have an earlier 8088/8086 system, it may have a different kind of clock/timer installed. You may have to run a special utility program to permanently change or set the date and time. The DATE and TIME commands don't affect your computer's internal clock.

✔ The format for the date and time varies depending on how your computer is set up. DOS uses a date-and-time format based on your country or region. This book assumes the typical (and, I'll agree, backward) U.S.A. method of listing the date.

✔ Who cares whether a computer knows what day it is? Well, because your files are time — and date — stamped, you can figure things out, like which is a later version of two similar files or of two files with the same name on different disks.

The Year 2000 Looms

If you follow the panicked media, you may have heard that every computer in the world will stop working at midnight on January 1, 2000. That's because computers store the current year as "99" rather than as "1999." When the clock rolls over (rumor has it), the computer will think that it's really the year 0 and start using Roman numerals or something equally disastrous.

Relax.

If you have current versions of all your software, the Year 2000 "bug" shouldn't affect you. Unfortunately, this means having *Windows* software because, starting with Windows 98, Microsoft has fixed things so that the year 2000 won't cause anyone's PC to crash.

The only time you may have trouble is with older (read: DOS) programs that don't understand the date change. I know that this book is written for you specifically, but if your software doesn't understand the new year 2000, it's *seriously* time to buy some new stuff.

Chapter 8

RAM (Or Memory, the Way We Were)

*I*n the PC Land of Oz, the Scarecrow would be singing, "If I only had some RAM. . . ." *Memory,* or *random-access memory* (RAM), is a storage place in a computer, just like disk space. Unlike disk storage, memory is the only place inside the computer where the real work gets done. Obviously, the more memory you have, the more work you can do. Not only that, but having more memory also means that the computer is capable of grander tasks, such as working with graphics, animation, sound, and music — and your PC remembers everyone it meets without ever having to look twice at his or her name tag.

This chapter is about memory inside your computer — *RAM,* as it's called in the nerdier circles. Every computer needs memory, but, sadly, life just isn't that simple. Different kinds of memory exist — different flavors, different fashions for the different seasons. This chapter goes into all that.

Don't Forget Memory

All computers need memory. That's where the work gets done. The microprocessor is capable of storing information inside itself, but only so much. The excess is stored in memory. For example, when you create a document by using your word processor, each character you type is placed into a specific location in memory. After a character is there, the microprocessor doesn't need to access it again unless you're editing, searching or replacing, or doing something active to the text.

After something is created in memory — a document, spreadsheet, or graphic — it's *saved* to disk. Your disk drives provide long-term storage for information. Then, when you need to access the information again, you *load* it back into memory from disk. After the information is there, the microprocessor can again work on it.

The only nasty thing about memory is that it's volatile. When you turn off the power, the contents of memory go poof! It's okay if you've saved to disk, but if you haven't, everything is lost. Even a reset zaps the contents of memory. Always save (if you can) before you reset or turn off your PC.

Common PC Memory Questions

"How much memory do I need?" The amount of memory you need depends on two things. The first, and most important, is the memory requirement of your software. Some programs, such as spreadsheets and graphics applications, require lots of memory.

The second and more limiting factor is cost. Memory costs money. Although it's not as expensive as it was back in the old stone-tablet days of computing, it still costs a bunch. For example, 16MB of RAM costs less than $30. When the second edition of this book came out, 16MB cost about $800. (That's almost $4,200 in dog dollars!)

Most computers sold today come with 32MB or 64MB of memory. You have options for up to 256MB. However, your DOS programs use only the first 640K of that memory, which is called *conventional,* or *DOS, memory.* This memory is the most important.

Any extra memory you have in your computer is a bonus. Extra memory comes in the form of *extended* memory. Some DOS programs (mostly games) can use it; most don't even need it.

✔ Windows (all versions) needs extended memory.

✔ Why doesn't DOS need a great deal of memory? Because DOS is text-based. Text doesn't consume the oodles of memory required by graphical programs like Windows.

✔ For more information on memory terms, see the following section; for information on expanded or extended memory, see their sections later in this chapter.

"Can I add more memory to my PC?" Yes. You add memory typically because your applications need more. The programs just don't run (or run sluggishly) without more memory.

✔ If a program keeps flashing that red MEM at you, pull out a large-caliber sidearm and shoot the computer. Or see the section "Upgrading Memory," later in this chapter.

"Can I lose computer memory?" No. Your computer has only a finite amount of memory, but it cannot be "lost" to anything. Programs use memory when you run them. For example, when you run WordPerfect, it eats up a specific amount of memory. When you quit WordPerfect, however, all that memory is made available to the next program. While a program runs, it "grabs" memory for its own uses. When the program is done, it lets the memory go.

✔ See the section "Conventional Memory," later in this chapter, for information on running the MEM command to see how much memory your computer has.

"What about copying programs?" Copying programs uses memory, but don't confuse disk "memory" with computer memory, or RAM. You can copy a huge program from one disk to another without worrying about running out of memory. DOS handles the details.

Computer memory can never be "destroyed." Even after a huge program runs or you copy a very large file, your system still has the same amount of RAM in it.

Disk "memory" is just storage space on disk. It's possible to store on your hard drive a program that's huge in size — hundreds of megabytes — more than could possibly fit in memory. How does that work? Some say that it's voodoo. Others say that it's because DOS loads only a small portion of the file into memory (RAM) at one time. Who knows what the truth *really* is?

Memory Terms to Ignore

Many interesting terms orbit the memory planet. The most basic of these terms refers to the quantity of memory (see Table 8-1).

Table 8-1		Memory Quantities	
Term	*Abbreviation*	*About*	*Actual*
Byte		1 byte	1 byte
Kilobyte	K or KB	1,000 bytes	1,024 bytes
Megabyte	M or MB	1,000,000 bytes	1,048,576 bytes
Gigabyte	G or GB	1,000,000,000 bytes	1,073,741,824 bytes

Memory is measured by the *byte*. Think of a byte as a single character, a letter in the middle of a word. For example, the word *spatula* is seven bytes long.

A whole page of text is about 1,000 bytes. To make this figure a handy one to know, computer nerds refer to 1,000 bytes as a *kilobyte,* or one *K* or *KB*. (Actually, 1K is equal to 1,024 bytes, probably because 1,024 is two to the tenth power. Computers love the number two.)

The term *megabyte* refers to 1,000K, or one million bytes. The abbreviation *MB* (or *M*) is used to indicate *megabyte,* so 8MB means eight megabytes of memory. (Actually, one megabyte is 1,024K, which equals somewhat more than one million bytes of information; the actual amount is mind-boggling.)

Further than the megabyte is the *gigabyte*. As you can guess, it's one billion bytes, or about 1,000 megabytes. The *terabyte* is one trillion bytes, or enough RAM to bring down the power on your block when you boot the PC.

- ✔ Just in case you didn't know, RAM stands for *random-access memory*. It doesn't mean anything useful.
- ✔ A specific location in memory is called an *address*.
- ✔ Bytes are composed of eight bits. The word *bit* is a contraction of *binary digit*. *Binary* is base two, or a counting system in which only ones and zeroes are used. Computers count in binary, and we group their bits into clusters of eight for convenient consumption as bytes.
- ✔ The term *giga* is actually Greek; it means *giant*.
- ✔ You have no reason to worry about how much *ROM* (read-only memory) you have in your computer.

Conventional Memory

Normally, any computer would just have "memory." Under DOS, however, different terms apply to different types of memory. The memory where DOS runs programs is called *conventional memory.* (It may also be called *DOS memory* or *low DOS memory.*)

When a program says that it needs 512K or 384K of memory to run, what it refers to is conventional memory.

Your PC can have as much as 640K of conventional memory installed. The maximum amount means that you can run almost any program.

Any extra memory — memory beyond the basic 640K of conventional memory — is *extended* memory. Another type of memory used specifically by DOS programs is called *expanded* memory. Which is which and why you should care are covered later in this chapter.

To see how much memory you have in your computer, you can use the MEM command. After typing MEM at the DOS prompt, you see a summary of all the memory in your computer, similar to that shown in Figure 8-1.

```
Memory Type          Total   =   Used  +   Free
-----------          ------      ------     ------
Conventional          640K         44K       596K
Upper                  91K         91K        0K
Reserved                0K          0K        0K
Extended (XMS)     21,285K        165K    21,120K
-----------          ------      ------     ------
Total memory       22,016K        300K    21,716K

Total under 1 MB      731K        134K       596K

Largest executable program size       596K (610,720 bytes)
Largest free upper memory block         0K        (0 bytes)
MS-DOS is resident in the high memory area.
```

Figure 8-1: The MEM command spews forth memory statistics.

The key value to look for appears toward the end of the long and complex output. Look for the line that says `Largest executable program size`. It tells you how much conventional memory you have available (out of 640K). In Figure 8-1, the value is 596K (which is 610,720 bytes to the IRS).

If extended (XMS) memory or expanded (EMS) memory is available, you see summaries for those values as well. Your system may have one, both, or neither.

✔ If your PC has less than 640K of RAM, you can add memory to boost your total. See the section "Upgrading Memory," later in this chapter.

✔ You see only commas in the big numbers with MS-DOS 6.2 and later (refer to Figure 8-1). Older versions of DOS display the numbers all chunkily-wunkily.

The 640K Barrier

Conventional memory is limited to 640K. That's all the memory DOS has for running programs. Even if you have megabytes of RAM installed in your computer, you have only 640K in which to run programs. Thus, it's called the *640K barrier.*

This stuff is kind of dumb, of course; powerful PCs don't need artificial limitations set on them. I mean, they can tear down the Berlin Wall and eliminate communism, but the smartest engineers in all the land can't pass the 640K conventional memory barrier. Well, actually, they did figure out how to pole-vault over the 640K barrier. It's complicated and involves the installation of extra memory.

The solutions for skirting around the 640K barrier involve adding more memory to your system. The solutions are provided in the form of either *extended* or *expanded* memory, both of which are covered in the following sections.

Most programs can work fine in 640K, though for many newer programs it's a tight fit.

✔ The reason for the barrier in the first place is how the original IBM PC was designed. Way back in 1982, 640K seemed like plenty. As the PC has evolved and as programs become more sophisticated, however, the 640K limit affects everybody.

Upper Memory

A region of memory exists just above the 640K barrier. This region is called *reserved memory,* although, starting with DOS Version 5.0, it has become known as *upper memory.*

Upper memory is used only by memory-management programs that store various and sundry things there. All this happens by magic, so there's no need explaining it in any detail here. Just sit back and be amazed.

Expanded Memory

Early DOS users found the 640K DOS barrier a real pain in the neck, so a temporary solution was devised. It enabled extra memory to be added to a PC, memory that DOS programs could use. That memory was given the name *expanded memory,* or *EMS,* for Expanded Memory System.

Only a few programs used expanded memory, primarily DOS spreadsheets. Other than that, expanded memory is kind of a white elephant. All versions of Windows can "simulate" it for those DOS programs that need it. Otherwise, this type of memory will forever be a footnote in the annals of computer memory history.

Extended Memory

Extended memory is any memory beyond 640K. Oh, for the sake of making sense, just say that extended memory is any memory beyond the first megabyte of RAM in your PC. If you have an 8MB computer, for example, you have 7MB of extended memory. If you have just bought a 32MB PC, you have 31MB of extended memory.

Extended memory is meat on the table for power-mad programs, like Windows and other operating systems, such as Windows NT, OS/2 and UNIX, that demand the most from your computer. Although MS-DOS uses extended memory for some special purposes, for the most part, it is other greedy software that requires this type of memory.

Managing Memory

Memory management is something unique to DOS. Other operating systems do it automatically; with DOS, you need extra help. Oh, you could do everything just fine without a memory manager. But you would probably run out of memory quickly in that situation. No, it's best to use a solid PC memory-management product, something like QEMM, for example. That way, you get the most from your memory, and your programs love you for it.

> ✔ Memory management on a PC is possible only if you have an 80386, 486, or Pentium-type microprocessor. (See Chapter 22 to see which type you have.)

✔ With Windows, memory management is handled automagically. Even if you use DOS, Windows takes care of all the details and configures memory for you. You don't have to mess with anything. Heed the following advice only if you're using a non-Windows computer.

MemMaker solution

Having lots of memory in your PC shouldn't be an antagonizing thing. Never should you have to mess with terms like extended or expanded or upper memory. To prove it, MS-DOS 6 has a nifty utility that configures, manages, and controls all the memory in your PC. It's called MemMaker, and it's painless and quick to use. Everyone should follow along with these instructions to optimize their PC's memory with MemMaker:

1. **Make sure that you're at the command prompt. Quit Windows or your menu program or whatever. Remove any floppy disk you may have sitting in drive A.**

2. **Run MemMaker. Type the following line at the command prompt:**

   ```
   C> MEMMAKER /BATCH2
   ```

   That's `MEMMAKER`, a space, a slash, and then `BATCH2`.

3. **MemMaker is a full-screen program that optimizes your PC's memory. Because you typed the /BATCH2 option when you started MemMaker, it runs all by itself, and you can just sit there and watch (or go to the fridge and get a nice snack). If you do sit and watch, don't be alarmed when MemMaker resets your PC a few times.**

4. **You see a final screen full of statistics. The third column of numbers (under the Change column) tells you how much more memory you have now than when you started, but — oh! — there it goes, gone from view. Oh, well.**

5. **You're done.**

✔ These steps set up your PC to use expanded memory (EMS). This kind of memory is okay for just about any system.

✔ MemMaker makes changes to your CONFIG.SYS and AUTOEXEC.BAT files. Do not mess with these changes! (Indeed, it's usually a bad idea to go ripping through either file without knowing what it is you're doing.)

✔ If you're using another memory manager, MemMaker asks to disable it before it optimizes your PC's memory. You see a message that reads something like `The Bromidic memory manager is running on your computer`. If someone else set up your computer, choose the Exit option and ask that person to ruminate over your old memory manager versus MemMaker. If you're fed up with the old memory manager, choose the Delete option and plow right ahead.

✔ If MemMaker says anything about deleting a "corrupted" MEMMAKER.STS file, press Enter and just keep on going.

✔ The IBM version of DOS, PC DOS, comes with a memory-optimization program called *RamBoost*. It works similarly to the memory management available with MS-DOS, though you don't have to fix anything; RamBoost works every time you start your PC.

✔ If you don't start MemMaker with the /BATCH2 switch, you have to read all the screens and press Enter about four or five times. Pressing Enter selects the "go-ahead" option in all cases, which is what I recommend. However, by starting MemMaker with the /BATCH2 option, it just goes ahead anyway, saving you all that time and wear and tear on your Enter key.

"How often should I optimize memory?"

Memory managers work each time you start your PC. Using various types of magic, DOS obeys the memory manager's instructions and puts memory in order. However, another way to use the memory manager is to *optimize* your memory. This action is done once when you first install the memory manager and can be done again — but only on an as-needed basis. For example, running the DOS 6 MemMaker to optimize your memory a second time doesn't save you more memory.

To get the most from your memory manager, you should optimize your memory only under one of the following circumstances:

✔ When you first install the memory manager

✔ After you add more memory to your PC (or you remove memory — which is unlikely)

✔ After you add a new device driver or TSR (memory-resident program) to your PC

✔ After you run a disk-compression program

✔ After you edit either your CONFIG.SYS or AUTOEXEC.BAT files

✔ When you buy a new computer or one that hasn't had its memory optimized yet (and in that case you would be running your memory manager for the first time anyway)

Editing CONFIG.SYS and AUTOEXEC.BAT is covered in Chapter 16.

Upgrading Memory

Adding memory to your computer is Lego-block simple. The only problem is that the typical Lego block set (the cool Space Station or Rescue Helicopter set, for example) costs $17. Your computer, on the other hand, may cost 200 times that much. Upgrading memory involves five complex and boring steps you should not take lightly:

1. Figure out how much memory you need to add. For example, if your system has only 512K, you need another 128K to give yourself the full 640K of conventional memory. If you need expanded memory, you have to buy an expanded memory card for your system — plus memory to put on the card. If you have a Pentium system, all you need is extra memory.

2. Figure out how much memory you can install. This step is a technical one. It involves knowing how memory is added to your computer and in what increments. You should simply tell the shop or your favorite technical guru how much you think you need, and they'll tell you how much you can have.

3. Buy something. In this case, you buy the memory chips themselves or you buy the expansion card into which the memory chips are installed.

4. Pay someone else to plug in the chips and do the upgrade. Oh, you can do it yourself, but I'd pay someone else to do it.

5. Gloat. After you have the memory, brag to your friends about it. Heck, it used to be impressive to say that you had the full 640K of RAM. Then came the "I have 4 megabytes of memory in my 386" round of impressiveness. Today? Anything less than 64MB, and your kids roll their eyes at you.

   ✔ The primary reason for upgrading memory is to enable programs to run more efficiently on your system. In light of that, upgrade only when your software requires it or doesn't otherwise run.

   ✔ If you want to try it yourself, go ahead. Plenty of easy books on the subject of upgrading memory are available, as well as how-to articles in some of the popular magazines. I recommend having someone else do it, however.

   ✔ Be sure to run your memory manager again after upgrading your memory. Refer to the preceding section for scant details.

   ✔ More information on these memory terms is covered throughout the first part of this chapter.

Chapter 9

The Video Display (That's the Computer Screen)

*P*erhaps the most important part of any computer is the screen, or what a nerd would call the *video display monitor* or even a *CRT* (cathode ray tube). In the old days, the wrong kind of display could fry your eyeballs. I remember riding down the elevator with bug-eyed people desperately searching for Visine. Today's computer screens are easier to look at and can produce much more stunning displays. Visine sales are down considerably.

This chapter is about the video display, computer screen, monitor, or the thing you look at when you use a computer. There's really not much to do with the display as far as DOS is concerned, although you will encounter some terms that will bug you to no end. In fact, more acronyms are associated with the computer screen than anything else (except for the government).

Your PC Graphics System

The image you see when you use your computer is the responsibility of two devices. The first is the monitor itself — the computer screen. The second part, hidden deep within the PC's console, is the *graphics adapter*. It's the circuitry that controls the monitor.

"So why should I care?"

Because the monitor and graphics adapter must work together to bring you the kind of quality graphics and text that you, as a demanding PC user, expect. Well, that and it makes this chapter twice as long.

What Makes a Graphics Adapter?

Graphics adapters are judged by their colors and resolutions. They have other goodies as well, although colors and resolution are the biggies.

Colors simply refers to the number of colors that can be displayed on-screen at one time. For example, the VGA display can show as many as 16 million colors on-screen at one time. Maybe more. I'll have to check.

Resolution refers to the number of dots, or *pixels,* on-screen. The more pixels, the higher the resolution and the finer the image. The measurement here is horizontal by vertical resolution. A typical PC graphics screen is 800 pixels wide by 600 pixels tall.

You have a trade-off between resolution and color: A computer display can only have more of one or the other, not both. A high-resolution display gives you few colors. A large number of colors gives you low resolution. This situation works, however, because the numerous colors fool the eye into thinking that you have more resolution. (A typical TV has a low resolution but a nearly infinite number of colors.)

For the text screen, resolution is measured by the number of horizontal (columns) and vertical (rows) characters. A typical color display shows 80 characters across by 25 characters down.

The text colors for all the color adapters remain the same: You can have as many as 16 foreground text colors and 8 background colors.

Funky Text

The standard *resolution* for text on your computer's display is 25 rows of 80 columns of text. That gives you about half a page of written text or, if you're looking at a graphics image, from the top of someone's head to just above his navel.

All color displays are capable of switching between 80 columns and 40 columns. The text gets twice as wide ("fat text," I call it). To make the text 40 columns wide, you can use this command:

```
C> MODE 40
```

That's 40, as in 40 columns wide. To switch the display back to 80 columns, you use this command:

```
C> MODE 80
```

Again, it's 80, for 80 columns wide. That's about it for the width of your screen under DOS. For the number of rows, you have several choices, depending on the kind of display you have. The best way to determine the number of rows is to try them out.

```
C> MODE CON LINES=43
```

That's the MODE command, a space, CON, a space, and, finally, the word LINES, an equal sign, and 43 — the number of lines you want to display. Press Enter. Type the DIR command a few times to prove to yourself that you now have 43 lines of text on-screen.

The following command is the same MODE command as in the preceding example, except that the number of lines is increased to 50:

```
C> MODE CON LINES=50
```

This example produces a readable display, although the characters are really scrunchy.

Changing the text screen with the MODE command does not change the font when you're using DOS in a window. Refer to Chapter 6 for information on changing the size of text using Windows 95 or Windows 98.

To return the display to normal, type

```
C> MODE CON LINES=25
```

✔ DOS supports screen modes for only 25, 43, and 50 lines.

✔ If the screen modes still don't work, you probably have an older PC that is incapable of the various text screen modes.

✔ Some programs can take advantage of the smaller, more compact text. WordPerfect supports several of the text modes, as does Lotus 1-2-3. You have to refer to your application's manual for the details (but only if this stuff really intrigues you).

A bothersome explanation of what's going on

The MODE command is used to change the modes of a variety of computer devices. In fact, the MODE command is so confusing that it's listed more times than any other command in some books on DOS (11 times in the old DOS 3.3 manual!).

The MODE 80 command is used to set the color monitor to a width of 80 columns. The number of rows on-screen remains at 25.

The MODE 40 command is used to set a color monitor to a width of 40 columns, which appear twice as fat as on the standard display. The number of rows stays at 25.

✔ Most graphics adapters come with special programs that offer additional, way-out modes. The adapter in my PC enables a display of 132 columns by 43 rows! Even WordPerfect supports it, although the text is very small and hard to read.

Other Popular Questions You Don't Have to Read

What are the other questions I'm asked? Here's a list along with my answers.

"Should I buy the newest graphics adapter?" Nope. It takes years for the software to catch up with a new adapter. Chances are, at this stage in the game, any new adapters have goodies to offer only to demanding graphics users. You probably aren't one of them.

"Which graphics adapter is best?" Name brands don't really matter, especially if you're buying a PC from a national dealer. They install whatever works best for them. However, if you're using high-end graphics applications, you may consider going with the brand your software manufacturer recommends.

"Can I pick up a used display screen?" Bad idea.

"What about 3D Video?" Although I'm unclear about what exactly "3D Video" is, I know that certain DOS games run better on computers that have 3-D graphics cards. The games run on other graphics cards as well, but, honestly, I cannot tell the difference.

Chapter 10

Keyboard and Mouse (Or Where Is the "Any" Key?)

•••

In This Chapter

▶ Finding special keys on the keyboard

▶ Pressing the "any" key

▶ Using the Caps Lock, Num Lock, and Scroll Lock keys

▶ Determining the difference between the slash and backslash keys

▶ Knowing when to press Enter and when to press Return

▶ Pressing the Alt+S key combination

▶ Pausing a long text display by using the keyboard

▶ Cursing at the WordStar cursor-key diamond

▶ Making the keyboard more (or less) responsive

▶ Dealing with a keyboard that beeps at you

▶ Understanding how a mouse fits into the big picture

▶ Using a mouse

▶ Understanding what all the mouse terms mean

•••

I may be weird, but I think that a good keyboard can make a good computer. Nothing beats the full responsiveness of a real keyboard, when the keys punch down evenly and are light to the touch. Some keyboards have a built-in click; others may have some pressure point or feel-only click. These features give you the impression that the computer's designers wanted you to feel like you're in control while you use the machine. Who cares whether you're typing out mysterious DOS commands when the keyboard feels so good?

This chapter is about the computer keyboard and all the fun things you can do with it. Your keyboard is the direct line of communication between you and the computer. You can use the keyboard in subtle ways and type with special keys. Knowing how to use them is like making funny or rude noises with your mouth: Although they may be socially unacceptable, they offer, in the right situations, a unique form of payoff.

Oh, and this chapter also describes the most common of computer rodents: the mouse.

Keyboard Layout

The typical keyboard supplied with most of today's computers is referred to as the enhanced 101-key keyboard. Yes, it has 101 keys on it. You can count them on your own, and you can examine each key individually. In Figure 10-1, you should note four main areas:

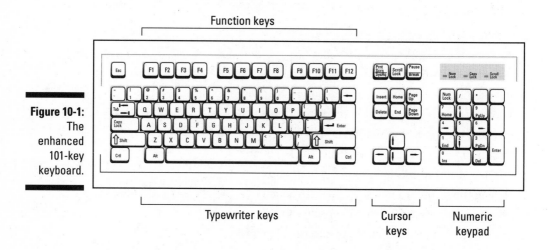

Figure 10-1: The enhanced 101-key keyboard.

The function keys, labeled F1 through F12: Perform various functions depending on the application. (No two applications use the same function keys for the same function — which you should be expecting by now.)

The typewriter keys: Laid out like the standard typewriter keyboard. All the alphanumeric keys are there, plus a handful of special computer keys and symbols.

The cursor-control keys: Called *cursor keys,* or *arrow keys;* used to move the cursor on-screen. Four directional keys form an inverted T pattern, with six specialized keys above them. These keys are used most often in editing text.

The numeric keypad: Contains the numbers 0 through 9, plus the period, an Enter key, and various mathematical symbols. The keypad can be used for fast numeric entry, and it serves a second function as a backup cursor keypad. (See the discussion in the section "The Keys of State," later in this chapter, for more information.)

✔ Some older keyboards lack the F11 and F12 keys as well as the separate cursor-control keys. They may also have their function keys in two columns to the left of the typewriter keys.

✔ Important keys to look for are the Esc (Escape) and backslash (\) keys. These keys are used quite often, and over the history of the PC keyboard, they've been quite migratory. The only reason for pointing out this information is that the Esc key used to be next to the Backspace key. Confusing the two was painful; Esc erased the entire line, whereas Backspace erased only one character.

✔ Computers use the following symbols for mathematical operations: + is for addition; – is for subtraction; * is for multiplication; and / is for division. The only important special symbol here is the asterisk — not the little *x* — for multiplication. This symbol is universal in all areas of computerdom.

✔ Some newer PCs come with three *bonus* keys (making the total 104, although they still call it a 101 keyboard). These keys are used in Windows 95 and Windows 98. Two of them even have the Windows logo on them. The third has an icon of a menu with a mouse pointer. The key with the menu icon serves no useful function in DOS. The keys with the Windows logo cause the Start menu to pop up (even if you're at a DOS prompt in full-screen mode).

✔ You may encounter one of the new ergonomic keyboards that seem to be cropping up. Many computer manufacturers are offering these ergonomic keyboards to increase your comfort when you're spending hours toiling at the computer.

So Where Is the "Any" Key?

Nothing is more frustrating than hunting down that elusive *any* key. After all, the screen says, Press any key to continue. So where is it?

Any key refers to literally any key on your keyboard. Let me be specific: When it says to press the "any" key, press the spacebar. If you can't find the spacebar or you think that it's the place where you order drinks on the starship *Enterprise,* try pressing the Enter key. Enter key = any key.

You can press almost any key on the keyboard for the "any" key. The problem is that some keys don't respond and are ill-suited to be "any" keys. These keys include the Shift keys, Caps Lock, Pause, the 5 key on the numeric keypad, and other "dead" keys. You can pound away on them all you like, and the program will never continue.

Why do they say "Press any key" rather than "Press spacebar to continue?" I guess that it's because they want to make things easy for you by giving you the whole keyboard to choose from. If that's really the case, why not just break down and say, "Slap your keyboard a few times with your open palms to continue"?

The Keys of State

Three keys affect the way the keyboard behaves. I call them the keys of state: Caps Lock, Num Lock, and Scroll Lock.

Caps Lock works like the Shift Lock key on a typewriter. Press Caps Lock once to turn it on. After you do that, all the alphabet keys on the keyboard (26 of them, at last count) produce uppercase letters. Press Caps Lock again to turn it off. Note that, unlike a typewriter, Caps Lock shifts only the letter keys; all the other keys on the keyboard remain the same.

Num Lock controls the numeric keypad. Press Num Lock once to turn it on. When Num Lock is on, the numeric keypad produces numbers (like you suppose that it would). Press Num Lock again to turn it off. When Num Lock is off, the numeric keypad doubles as a cursor keypad. The arrow keys, Home, PgUp, and others take precedence. (This arrangement is the way most DOS users prefer to use the numeric pad, as a cursor keypad.)

The Scroll Lock key is vaguely defined and doesn't do anything under DOS. In some spreadsheet programs, Scroll Lock has the effect of "locking" the cursor keys. Rather than press an arrow key to move the cell selector to another cell in the spreadsheet, with Scroll Lock on, the whole spreadsheet moves in the direction of the arrow key. Although other applications may use the Scroll Lock key differently, under DOS, it serves no direct function. (Press it a few times on someone else's computer to irritate a friend.)

The positions of the Caps Lock, Num Lock, and Scroll Lock keys vary. Figure 10-2 shows the locations on an enhanced 101-key keyboard. Other keys that are not keys of state, such as the Shift keys, are where you would expect them to be on any typewriter: Two control keys are on the outside edges of the typewriter area, in lower corners, and the two Alt keys are inside, on either end of the spacebar. Although laptop keyboards and older PC keyboards have these keys in different locations, they're still labeled Shift, Ctrl, and Alt.

Interesting yet skippable information on reverse state keys

When Caps Lock is on, you can use the Shift key to reverse the case of a letter. When Caps Lock is off, press the Shift key plus a letter to get a capital letter. With Caps Lock on, however, pressing the Shift key plus a letter produces a lowercase letter.

The same weirdness affects the numeric keypad and the Num Lock key. With Num Lock on, pressing a key on the numeric keypad produces a number key, although pressing the Shift key and a number key produces the corre-

sponding arrow key. For example, pressing Shift+4 on the keypad with Num Lock on gives you the left-arrow key. When Num Lock is off, pressing Shift plus a key gives you the corresponding number key.

Yeah, this stuff is confusing. If you play around with the keyboard and the Caps Lock, Num Lock, and Shift keys, you can see what's going on. But why fill your head with such trivial matters?

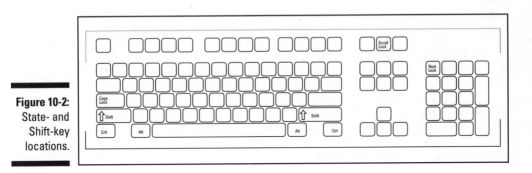

Figure 10-2:
State- and
Shift-key
locations.

✔ If your keyboard has a Caps Lock, Num Lock, or Scroll Lock light, it is on when the corresponding state key is on.

✔ If your Caps Lock key is backward (sometimes it gets that way), the only way to fix the situation is to reset. For example, if the Caps Lock light is on but you aren't seeing uppercase letters, reset to remedy the situation. (Exit your applications first!)

Slash and Backslash

Two slash keys are used under DOS. The first is the forward slash (/), the most common of the two. This slash leans forward, like it's falling to the right. On most computers, it's used to denote division, such as 52/13 (52 divided by 13). In English, it's used to divide various words or, most often, as an incorrect replacement for a hyphen.

The backslash is a backward-slanting slash (\) that leans to the left. This character is used in DOS to represent the root directory. It also appears in pathnames to separate the various directory names. (For more information on the root directory and directory names, see Chapter 17.)

Enter or Return?

All PC computer keyboards have two keys labeled Enter. Both keys work identically, with the second Enter key placed by the numeric keypad to facilitate the rapid entry of numbers.

The Enter key is used to end a line of text. After entering the text, press Enter, and the information becomes *locked in*. After you press Enter at the DOS prompt, the command you typed is sent off to DOS for scrutiny. In a word processor, however, you press the Enter key to end a paragraph. (The words *wrap* automatically at the end of a line, meaning that you don't have to press Enter to end each line.)

So, what is the Return key? Many early computers sported a Return key. It's essentially the same thing as the Enter key. In fact, some computers had both an Enter and a Return key.

The difference between Enter and Return is only semantic. Enter has its roots in the electronic calculator industry. You pressed Enter to enter numbers or a formula. Return, on the other hand, comes from the electronic typewriter. Pressing the Return key on a typewriter caused the carriage to return to the left margin. It also advanced the paper one line in the machine.

The Tab key is also used in some applications (mainly databases) to end the entry of information in a *field*. As on a typewriter, pressing Tab moves the cursor over eight spaces or to the next *tab stop,* though pressing Tab on some computers causes the computer to produce a can of a refreshing diet beverage.

You may freely skip over this trivia

When you press the Enter key, the computer generates two different characters. The first is the *carriage-return* character. This character has the effect of moving the cursor to the leftmost column on the screen, just as a carriage return on a manual typewriter does. (Remember whacking the carriage-return bar?)

The second character produced is the *line feed*. This character moves the cursor down to the next line on the screen. Again, in the ancient days of typewriting, the line feed advanced the paper in the machine. In fact, the carriage return/line feed was usually performed by whacking the same lever.

In computerspeak, you often encounter the terms *carriage return/line feed* or the abbreviation CRLF. (Am I the only person who pronounces that "crullif"?) They simply mean that you press the Enter key, or they refer to the two secret characters that end a line of text.

Alt+S Means What?

Alt+S could mean anything, actually. (It's up to each application to assign meanings to certain keys.) The important thing is to know what to do when you see Alt+S or even Alt-S.

The Alt key works like the Shift key on the keyboard. In fact, three kinds of shift keys are on the keyboard: Shift, Alt, and Ctrl. This information baffles most people because the typewriter has only one shift key, the Shift key.

The positions of the Alt, Ctrl, and Shift keys on the enhanced 101-key keyboard are shown in Figure 10-2.

You use the Alt, Ctrl, and Shift keys similarly: Press and hold Alt, Ctrl, or Shift, and then type another key on the keyboard (usually a letter of the alphabet, though function keys are commonly paired with the shift keys).

You produce an uppercase *S* by pressing Shift+S, though no one needs to say "press Shift+S" because most typewriter-using people know that it works that way. With three shift keys on a computer, however, you have to specify things. Pressing Alt+S means pressing and holding the Alt key and then pressing **S**. No character appears on-screen; instead, the program may do something, such as save a file to disk.

The Ctrl key works the same way. When you read "Press Ctrl+C," press and hold the Ctrl (Control) key, type a **C**, and then release both keys.

✔ Even though you may see Ctrl+S or Alt+S with a capital *S,* it doesn't mean that you must type Ctrl+Shift+S or Alt+Shift+S. Those are actually separate keystrokes where you press three keys at one time. In fact, you can use the Ctrl and Alt keys with or without the Shift key, so most users skip it.

✔ The functions of all the Alt and Ctrl keys differ from application to application.

✔ Keep in mind that you can use Alt, Ctrl, and Shift with the function keys. In fact, WordPerfect users will recognize 40 function-key combinations using these shift keys plus ten function keys.

✔ The Ctrl+key combinations have an abbreviation: The caret, or hat character (^), is used to denote Control. When you see ^C, it means the keystroke Ctrl+C or the Control+C character.

Ctrl+S and the Pause Key

In DOS, you can use several Ctrl-key combinations to give you more power over your PC. The two most common are Ctrl+S and Ctrl+C.

Ctrl+C is the universal DOS cancel key combination. It stops any DOS command and cancels just about anything you're typing — a good thing to know. (For more information, refer to the section "Canceling a DOS Command," in Chapter 3.)

The Ctrl+S key combination is used to freeze information, suspending it as it's displayed on-screen. You can read rapidly scrolling text by pressing Ctrl+S in a panic-driven frenzy and then . . . the screen stops, dead in its tracks. Press Ctrl+S again (or any key), and the display scrolls again. All this stuff happens until all the information is displayed or until you press Ctrl+S again to stop.

To test Ctrl+S, you have to display a long document. Typically, you do it with the TYPE command, as shown in this example:

```
C> TYPE LONGJOHN
```

As the file LONGJOHN is displayed, it scrolls wildly up the screen. Pressing the Ctrl+S key combination stops it, and you can read a little. When you're ready to see more text, press Ctrl+S, Enter, or the spacebar. To freeze the screen again, press Ctrl+S.

The Pause key on some keyboards has the same effect as Ctrl+S, and it's only one key to press. Unlike with Ctrl+S, however, you must press any key other than Pause to get things rolling again. I prefer pressing Enter as my "any" key.

✔ The Pause key may also be labeled Hold.

✔ You can always cancel any long display by pressing Ctrl+C.

✔ For more information on the TYPE command, refer to the section "Looking at Files," in Chapter 2.

✔ The Ctrl+P key combination switch is another handy DOS control-key function. (See the section "Printing DOS," in Chapter 11.)

The WordStar Cursor- and Cursed-at Key Diamond

WordStar was the first popular and most widely used word processor for the personal computer. Not just DOS computers but also the Apple II, a slew of CP/M "boxes," and the old TRS-80 (the "trash-80") could run WordStar. Back then, it was the Cadillac of word processors. Sheesh, it even had *block* commands and featured *word wrap*. How could anyone compete? It showed you where the page ended — right there on-screen!

Because most keyboards at the time lacked cursor keypads, the folks who made WordStar came up with an interesting alternative for moving the cursor around. They came up with the WordStar *cursor-key diamond*. This set of control-key combinations on the keyboard represents pressing certain arrow keys, whether or not your computer already has enough arrow keys.

I'm bringing all this stuff up because many popular programs still offer the WordStar cursor-key diamond and control-key commands. Generally, the application also supports the standard cursor-key commands. If not, Table 10-1 lists them all. Figure 10-3 shows the WordStar cursor-key diamond as mapped out on your keyboard.

Figure 10-3:
The
WordStar
cursor-key
diamond
diagram.

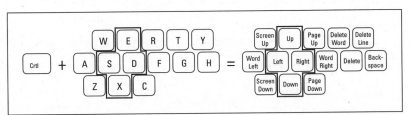

✔ You don't have to memorize Table 10-1, though after awhile the use of these key commands may seem logical to you. (I pray that it never happens.)

✔ Different applications use different key commands to do similar things. The only way to be certain is to refer to the manual, although the basic cursor keys plus the control keys listed in Table 10-1 are usually common to all DOS programs.

✔ In the DOS Editor, you use the WordStar cursor key commands to edit a file, as explained in Chapter 16.

Table 10-1	The WordStar Cursor-Key Diamond and Control-Key Commands	
WordStar Command	*Command Key*	*Command Function*
Ctrl+E	Up arrow	Moves the cursor up one line
Ctrl+X	Down arrow	Moves the cursor down one line
Ctrl+S	Left arrow	Moves the cursor left (back) one character
Ctrl+D	Right arrow	Moves the cursor right (forward) one character
Ctrl+R	PgUp	Moves up to the preceding page (screen)
Ctrl+C	PgDn	Moves down to the next page (screen)
Ctrl+A	Ctrl+Left	Moves left one word
Ctrl+F	Ctrl+Right	Moves right one word
Ctrl+W	Ctrl+Up	Scrolls the screen up one line
Ctrl+Z	Ctrl+Down	Scrolls the screen down one line
Ctrl+G	Delete	Deletes current character
Ctrl+T	Ctrl+Backspace	Deletes current word (or Ctrl+Delete)
Ctrl+H	Backspace	Deletes preceding character

Controlling the Keyboard

You can use the MODE command to control two aspects of the keyboard: how long you have to wait after pressing a key for more characters to appear and how fast those characters are repeated.

The PC keyboard sports a feature that IBM dubbed the *typematic:* If you press and hold any key, the character is repeated. Press and hold the I key, for example, and soon you have a dozen or so *I*s all across the screen. That's the typematic at work.

The initial pause before the key repeats is referred to as *delay*. It can be set to any time interval from ¼-second to a full second. The speed at which the key repeats (after it starts repeating) is the *rate*. Keys can repeat at any rate from 2 to 30 characters per second. Both the *rate* and the *delay* are set by using the MODE command in this format:

```
C> MODE CON RATE=20 DELAY=2
```

The MODE command in this line sets the computer to the standard typematic repeat and delay: MODE is followed by a space and then CON (which somehow means the keyboard). The word RATE is followed by an equal sign and 20, for a 20-character-per-second repeat rate. The word DELAY is followed by an equal sign and 2, which means that it starts to repeat ¾- (or ½-) second after the key is held down.

Now suppose that you're a heavy-handed typist. To avoid having keys repeat on you all the time, you could enter

```
C> MODE CON RATE=20 DELAY=4
```

This command sets the delay to ¾ of a second, or one second, even. That should eliminate the repeating keys you see all the time. (You must list both the *rate* and *delay* words after the command.)

If you want your keyboard to be slippery slick, enter this command:

```
C> MODE CON RATE=32 DELAY=1
```

Press Enter, and you get an idea of how annoying an overly responsive keyboard can be. Enter the first command listed here to restore your computer — or just whack the Reset switch (Ctrl+Alt+Delete) if it severely annoys you.

The MODE command in this capacity works with only certain keyboards. If you have an older PC, you may not be able to change the delay and repeat rates.

My Keyboard Beeps at Me!

On a typical PC, you can type ahead as many as 16 characters. A word processor is usually capable of eating those characters as fast as you type them. Sometimes, however — when you're accessing a disk or the computer is out doing something, for example — you can still type. Apparently, the keyboard remembers as many as the last 16 keys you typed, and then . . . it starts beeping at you, once for each key beyond the 16 you've already typed. Those extra keys, typed as you hear the beeps, aren't displayed. Essentially, your keyboard is "full."

You can do nothing about this situation. Some special programs, utilities, or keyboard enhancers may give you more than 16 characters to type ahead. Generally speaking, however, when the keyboard starts beeping, just stop typing and wait a few moments. Then wait a few minutes more — I had a program that took two full minutes to come back to life!

If the keyboard continues to beep, you've locked it up! The only way to escape this peril is to reset (press Ctrl+Alt+Delete) or press the Reset button or turn the PC off and on again.

Remember *not* to reset if you're using DOS in Windows. Instead, just close the DOS window if it's behaving stubbornly. Restart another DOS Prompt window, and you'll be okay.

Having a Mouse

The computer mouse is a handy pointing device used primarily in graphics programs. It comes in two parts: the mouselike, handheld device, usually as big as a fat deck of cards that can fit in the palm of your hand; and the software that tells DOS and all your programs that you have a mouse.

The mouse faces toward you with its tail going back to the computer's rump. There, it plugs in to either a serial port or a special mouse port. The mouse usually has one or more buttons on top, which you press with your index finger.

The mouse software is installed in either your system configuration file, CONFIG.SYS, or your AUTOEXEC.BAT file. You should have someone else install it, preferably at or near the time when he or she attaches the mouse to your computer. If you want to dabble with editing your CONFIG.SYS or AUTOEXEC.BAT files yourself, see Chapter 16.

The mouse works by being rolled around on the desktop. To use a mouse, you need a relatively wide area of space on your desktop. Look around your desktop. Do you see an open, flat area about 8 inches by 12 inches in size? I didn't think so. To use a mouse, you have to give it some room. On my desk, I get by with about a 4-x-4-inch square for the mouse.

✔ If you're using DOS in Windows, you don't need to set up mouse software, as just described. Windows automatically configures your PC to use a mouse in DOS. You don't have to do anything else.

✔ Not all DOS programs use the mouse. So even though you see the mouse in the DOS window, don't assume your program has suddenly become mouse smart.

✔ You may want to invest in a mouse pad, a handy device on which to roll the mouse. It gives the mouse's little ball-foot more traction than your typical Formica pressboard computer desk.

✔ For more information on the serial port, refer to the section "The Serial Port," in Chapter 7.

Using a Mouse

The mouse just doesn't become immediately useful; you must have software that takes advantage of it. Fortunately, a standard method exists for using the mouse that makes it a rather painless part of PC computing.

The mouse controls a *pointer* or *mouse cursor* on-screen. It may be the same as the text cursor, the one you see all the time at the DOS prompt, or it may be its own unique cursor, pointer, or square block. Sometimes, the mouse cursor is just anyone who barges into the room and starts yelling at the furless little guy.

When you move the mouse around, rolling it on your desktop, the pointer on-screen moves in a similar manner. Roll the mouse left, and the pointer moves left; roll it in circles, and the pointer mimics that action; drop the mouse off the table, and your DOS prompt changes to read Ouch! (Just kidding.)

The mouse should have one or more buttons on it. You press them with your index finger while keeping the mouse under the palm of your hand on the desktop. You use the button (or buttons) to manipulate various items on the computer screen. It goes like this: You move the mouse, which moves the cursor on the screen over to something interesting. You click the mouse button, and something even more interesting happens.

What happens, of course, depends on the software you use. If the mouse has more than one button, each button may perform different functions. It's all up to the application; as with many other things in DOS, you get no standards, no rules, no guidelines — it's personal computing run amok!

Mouse Terminology

Various mouse terms are associated with using a mouse. These terms are quite simple, and, thanks to millions of dollars of research by Apple Computer, they make sense! Only by using your mouse do these terms become obvious to you. It really pays to have a mouse and an application that supports the mouse in order to appreciate these terms. In case you don't, I've defined the terms in this section anyway.

Button

The *button* is the device on top of the mouse. Pressing the button is referred to as *clicking,* though clicking has another definition (covered in a later paragraph).

Pointer or cursor

The thing the mouse moves around on the screen is called the *mouse pointer.* I call it the pointer. Some applications call it the *cursor,* which is easily confused with the true cursor God created, the DOS text cursor.

Click

A *click* is a press of the mouse button. Often, you read "click the mouse on the NO button." This message means that a graphic something-or-other is on the screen with the word *NO* on it. Using the mouse, you hover the pointer over the word *NO.* Then, with your index finger, click the mouse button. This action is referred to as *clicking the mouse* on something, usually something on-screen. (You can roll the mouse around on your forehead and click it there if you like — just make sure that no one's looking.)

Double-click

A *double-click* is like a click-click, two rapid clicks in a row. You double-click in many applications to quickly select some item. (Although the time between clicks varies, it doesn't have to be *that* quick. Also, don't move the mouse around between the clicks.)

Drag

To *drag* something with the mouse, you press and hold down the mouse button and then move the mouse around. On the screen, this action has the effect of grabbing something (pressing the button) and then moving it about on-screen (dragging it). When you release the mouse button, you "let go" of whatever it was you were dragging.

Select

Selecting is the process of highlighting something, making it the target for whatever future plans you have. For example, you select a box by clicking that box. You select text by dragging the cursor over the text you want; that action *highlights* the text, which is similar to marking a block of text.

Chapter 11

The Printer (Making the Right Impression)

*Y*our PC needs a printer to get that all-important hard copy — a permanent record of your work, output, efforts, what-have-you. Without a printer, you would have to lug the PC around everywhere and show people your stuff on the monitor. That's tacky.

Lots of printers are out there. The problem is that few standards exist; unlike PC monitors, which are all basically "Super VGA" but made by many manufacturers, each printer manufacturer does things differently. This situation isn't a problem as long as you stick to the major brands. When you don't, however, it's time to rev up that chain saw. . . .

This chapter is about using a printer with your computer. By themselves, printers are harmless enough. But, umbilically connect one to the evil PC — nay, the child of Satan himself! — and you're bound for trouble. In this chapter, you find out how to get out of trouble and put your firm thumb of control over your printer.

Getting Connected

Every PC should have at least one printer attached. It's connected via a separate cable: One end of the cable connects to the PC; the other, to the printer. It's fairly obvious which end goes where, though on some PCs it's easy to confuse the printer port for a serial port.

You can have as many as three printers connected to your computer. The number of printers you can connect depends on how many printer ports your PC has. The typical PC has one printer port, called _LPT1_. You can buy more, if you like.

After the printer is properly connected, you can test it by printing something. Examples of printing under DOS appear later in this chapter. I recommend that you dive in to some application and then test printing in there.

 ✔ It's also possible to have a serial printer installed on your computer. This printer connects to the PC via a serial port — not a parallel port. (See the following section for more information.)

 ✔ If you're plugging in cables in the back of your PC — they can be any cables, from the printer cable to a keyboard cable — make sure that your PC is off. Having a PC on while you plug something in can lead to some rather unpleasant results.

 ✔ If the printer doesn't work, you may have it connected to the wrong port. Try plugging the cable into another, similar connector on the rear of your PC.

 ✔ For more information on ports, refer to the section "What Are Ports?" in Chapter 7.

DOS's Forgettable Printer Names

DOS refers to everything it controls by a _device name_. The name for the printer is _PRN_, a nice, handy, three-letter word (without vowels) that means "printer." So far, so good.

DOS can control as many as three printers for each PC. The device name PRN actually refers to only the first printer, the _main_ printer. The real, secret names for the three possible printers are _LPT1, LPT2,_ and _LPT3_. LPT stands for _line printer_. It's probably one of those massive, 1940s-type computer devices.

I bring this subject up because, well, I'm a nerd. Beyond that, you may occasionally see these names used and confused. For example, you may be asked, Is your laser printer connected to LPT1? As far as I can translate this question, it means "Is your printer hooked up to the first printer port?" Beware of these types of deceptive terms that weave their way into computer manuals and books.

Serial Connection

Of the 1,700 or so printer makes and models available for the PC, a handful operate from a serial port — not the almost-sane printer port, which you would expect. These printers are usually older models or printers designed for use on non-IBM-type computers.

Nothing is bad about owning a serial printer. This type of printer works just fine, and connecting one to your computer is as easy as plugging in the special serial printer cable. That's the easy part. The hard part comes in setting up the computer and telling DOS about it.

The first part is to set up the printer to a specific speed, or *baud,* and a *data word format.* You do this by holding the manual in one hand and setting some minute switches on the printer with the other. Although I really have no idea how your particular printer does it, what you want to do is set it to either

```
9600, 8, N, 1 (the fast setting)
```

or

```
2400, 8, N, 1 (a slower setting)
```

Refer to the manual for the proper settings or something that looks similar to these examples.

On the DOS side, before you can use the serial printer, you must give DOS two commands. The first is used to set up the serial port in the exact same manner as you've set up the printer:

```
C> MODE COM1:9600,N,8,1
```

In the preceding line, the MODE command is followed by a space. Then comes COM1 and a colon, which represents your first serial port. That's followed by the speed (9600, in this example) and then N, 8, and 1 to match the 8, N, and 1 you set your printer to. If you specified a different speed (2400, for example), substitute it for 9600 here.

The second step is to tell DOS that its printer device, called PRN, is now on the serial port rather than the printer port. You do that with this command:

```
C> MODE LPT1=COM1
```

Ugh. Real Greek, no less. Basically, this line shows the MODE command, a space, the hieroglyph LPT1 (meaning DOS's primary printer), and then COM1 (which indicates the first serial port to which your printer is attached).

After entering those two commands, you can use your printer under DOS — even in applications — as you would a parallel printer.

These commands are confusing. Trust me on this: No one I know has memorized them. Even I had to look them up to write them down here. You're forgiven if you repeatedly have to refer to this section to start your computer each day.

  ✔ If these commands are something you will type every day when you start your computer, why not make them a part of your AUTOEXEC.BAT automatic start-up file? (See Chapter 16 for the details.)

  ✔ Note that the serial printer cable is a special kind of cable, usually labeled as a "serial printer cable." You cannot use the same serial cable as you would to connect a modem, for example; it doesn't work.

  ✔ For more information on parallel and serial ports, refer to the section "What Are Ports?" in Chapter 7; for information on setting up a serial port, refer to the section, "The Serial Port," in Chapter 7.

Going Online

Before a printer can print, three things must happen: The printer must be connected to the computer; you must have paper in the printer; and the printer must be *online* or *selected*.

Somewhere on your printer is a button. That button may be labeled *Online* or *Select*. Pressing it puts the printer in "ready" mode, making it ready to print. If the printer is offline or deselected, it's still on but not ready to print. Usually, you take a printer offline to advance paper, change a font, or unjam it. You can print again only by putting the printer back online or selecting it.

  ✔ Most Online, Select, and Ready buttons have a corresponding light. When the light is on, the printer is ready to print.

  ✔ If the printer lacks an Online, Select, or Ready button, the printer is probably ready for printing all the time.

Form Feeding

The act of ejecting a sheet of paper from a printer is referred to as a *form feed*. Most printers have a button for this purpose. It's called, remarkably enough, Form Feed, though sometimes the label Eject is used. To eject a page of paper from a printer, you first take the printer offline by pressing the Online or Select button and then press the Form-Feed or Eject button. Zwoop! Out flies a sheet of paper.

This button seems rather silly — until you need a full sheet of paper to shoot from the printer. Even more important, a laser printer doesn't spit out a sheet of paper until it has printed the whole thing. If you want to see what you've printed and you haven't printed a full page, you must take the printer offline and press the Form-Feed or Eject button. Press Select or Online to turn off the little light.

  ✔ For more information about the Online or Select buttons, refer to the preceding section.

  ✔ Most nonlaser printers also have a *line-feed* button. This button simply advances the paper one line of text each time you press it. As with form feed, you must have the printer offline or deselected to use the line-feed button.

Forcing a Page Out

A special character called the *form feed* is the Ctrl+L character, often shown as ^L. When this character is sent to the printer — any printer — it's an immediate instruction to the printer to eject a page. Although typing Ctrl+L produces the form-feed character, knowing how to send it to the printer isn't obvious.

To send the Ctrl+L keystroke to the printer, type this DOS command:

```
C> ECHO ^L > PRN
```

That's the ECHO command, a space, and then the form-feed character produced by pressing Ctrl+L. (That's not the caret and L characters.) This stuff is followed by a space, the greater-than symbol (>), another space, and then the letters PRN (for printer). Press Enter, and the printer spits up a page.

The Page Didn't Come Out of My Laser Printer!

Laser printers are fast and their output snazzy, but they don't print until one of two situations occurs:

1. The laser printer prints if you've printed a whole page full of text, not before. With a laser printer, nothing is really put down on paper until you fill up a sheet.

2. You can always force a laser printer to print what has been sent to it so far by giving it a form feed. You press a special button on the printer or use a secret DOS command. Both these methods are covered in the preceding section.

In a Jam?

Paper flows through your printer like film through a projector; each sheet is magically ejected from a laser printer like the wind blowing leaves on an autumn day. Poppycock! Paper likes to weave its way through the inner guts of your printer like a 4-year-old poking his fingers into your VCR. When this happens, your printer can become jammed.

For inkjet printers, you can unjam most paper by opening the cover and yanking the paper out.

If you have a dot matrix printer, unjam it by rewinding the knob. Turn off the printer first! This action disengages the advancing mechanism's death grip on the paper platen, which makes it easier to back out the jammed paper. If the paper is really in there tight, you may have to remove the platen. When that happens, you have to take the printer apart to get at the problem; call someone else for help unless you want to take it apart yourself.

For laser printers, a light flashes on the printer when the paper gets jammed. If the printer has a message readout, you may see the message `Paper jam` displayed in any of a variety of languages and subtongues. Make your first attempt at unjamming by removing the paper tray. If you see the end of the paper sticking out, grab it and firmly pull toward you. The paper should slip right out. If you can't see the paper, pop open the printer's lid and look for the jammed sheet. Carefully pull it out either forward or backward. You don't have to turn the printer off first, but watch out for hot parts.

Printing problems explained, which you can ignore

Each line sent to the printer ends in two special codes: the *carriage return* and *line feed*. The carriage return tells the printer to start printing on column one again — on the left side of the page. The line feed, following the carriage return, tells the printer to print down on the next line on the page. Simple enough.

The problem is that not every computer sends the printer a carriage return/line feed combination. Some computers send only a carriage return. When that happens, no line feed takes place and all your text is printed on one ugly, ink-stained line.

To solve the problem of printing on one line, the printer can be told (via a switch) to supply its own line feed automatically after each carriage return received. That way, if your computer is dumb enough to send only the carriage return to end a line, the printer supplies the line feed and everything prints as you've intended.

The problem of double spacing happens when that same add-a-line-feed switch is on and the computer is already sending a carriage return/line feed combo. In that case, the printer adds, at the end of the line, its own line feed, giving a double-spaced effect. Turning off the tiny switch fixes that problem.

Sometimes, printers jam because the paper you're using is too thick. If that's the case, removing the paper and trying it again probably won't help; use thinner paper. Otherwise, paper jams for a number of reasons, so just try again and it will work.

Printing on One Line or Massive Double Spacing

Two common printer flubs are the "Everything is printing on one line!" expression of panic and the "Why the heck is everything double-spaced all the time?" annoying interrogation. Both problems are related, though solving them doesn't involve lying on a couch and talking about your mother.

Somewhere on your printer is a series of tiny switches. The computer weenies call them *DIP switches*. Flipping one of those tiny switches solves your problem, whether everything is printing on one line or you're seeing all your text double-spaced. (They're both the same problem, which is covered in the information that follows, which you can ignore.)

The switch is identified in your printer manual. It has the name "Add line-feed" or "Automatic linefeed" or "LF after CR" or something along those lines. To fix your problem, flip the switch. Because it's a tiny switch, you may have to mutilate a paper clip to reach in and flip it. (Just turn off the printer first.)

✔ If flipping this switch is something you don't feel like doing, have someone else do it.

✔ If you cannot locate the switch on the back of your printer, it may be inside, under the printing mechanism. If so, turn the printer off when you're in there fumbling around.

✔ If the preceding suggestion doesn't fix the problem right away, turn the printer off, wait, and then turn it back on again.

Printing the Screen

A special button on your keyboard — a feature — causes all the text you see on-screen to be printed. It's called the Print Screen key, though that particular key may be labeled Print Scrn or Prt Scn or something even more cryptic.

The technical term for printing the screen is a *screen dump*. Normally, I wouldn't mention that term here, but I personally find it hilarious: "Excuse me, dear, I've got to take a screen dump." Riotous stuff!

To practice, make sure that your printer is online and ready to print. Then press the Print Screen key. Zip-zip-zip. A few minutes later, you see a copy of your screen on the printer. (If you have a laser printer, you have to eject the page; refer to the discussion in the "Form Feeding" section, earlier in this chapter.)

✔ For more information about the keyboard, refer to Chapter 10.

✔ If the printer isn't on and you hit the Print Screen key, one of two things may happen. The first (and, hopefully, what happens all the time when you accidentally press Print Screen) is that nothing happens. Whew! The second thing that may happen is that the computer waits for the printer so that it can print your screen. And it waits. And waits. Turn the printer on and watch it print; you have no way to cancel out of this process with Ctrl+C.

✔ In Windows (all versions), the Print Screen key takes a "snapshot" of the screen, saving it as a graphical image in the Clipboard. From there, you can paste it into a Windows graphical program for, well, whatever. Windows does not let DOS do a screen dump.

Print Screen Woes

The Print Screen key isn't the miracle that most people suppose it is. For example, if your screen shows lines and boxes along with text, you may not see those characters displayed. In fact, you may see lots of *m*s or colons or other odd characters or even italic text.

The reason for the Print Screen garbage is that your printer isn't capable of printing the IBM *graphics set*. If your printer can somehow wiggle itself into an IBM-compatible mode, you see the characters just fine. Otherwise, you have to live with all the *m*s and whatnot.

Another Print Screen woe is that the *screen dump* only copies text. If you're using a graphics program and are looking at a picture of the latest screen god or goddess seductively biting his or her lower lip — and, by God, you want a hard copy of that to tape up by your pillow — pressing the Print Screen key won't help you. Unfortunately, Print Screen copies only text, and any attempt to *dump* a graphics image (no matter how badly you crave it) results in garbled output — and emotional disappointment.

✔ Some programs are available that replace DOS's lame Print Screen key with a smarter program, one that prints graphics. See your local software-o-rama for the particulars.

✔ If you press Print Screen and your printer is turned off (or disconnected), the computer sits there and waits for the printer to do something — forever, if need be. Turn the printer on — or reboot.

Printing DOS

The normal way you use DOS is to type a command and expect (hopefully) that DOS displays on-screen something that pleases you. In fact, all your interaction with DOS is shown on-screen, which, I admit, comes in handy. Even more handy is to sometimes have a *hard copy* of all DOS's output — a transcript of your DOS session, but without having to send the $2 to "Transcripts" at some P.O. box in Jersey. To create the hard copy, you use the *DOS print switch,* which is actually a keyboard command.

If your printer is on and ready to print, you can press Ctrl+P to activate the DOS printing function. After pressing Ctrl+P, DOS sends all output to both the screen and the printer. Everything is displayed and printed, even embarrassing errors. More importantly, you see vital information, such as file listings, displays, and other trivia.

To turn off the DOS printing function, press Ctrl+P again.

- ✔ If you just want to print a single file, refer to the section "Printing a Text File," in Chapter 18.

- ✔ If you just want to print a directory listing (the output of the DIR command), see the following section.

- ✔ Laser printers don't print anything until a full page is generated. To see what you've printed before then, refer to the discussion in the section "Form Feeding," earlier in this chapter.

- ✔ The only way to be sure that you've turned off the DOS printing function is to press Enter a few times. If the DOS prompt doesn't appear on your printer, the printing is turned off. If it does, try Ctrl+P again.

- ✔ Ctrl+P is what computer wizards call a toggle. A *toggle* is a single command that turns something both on and off, going either way each time you use the command.

Printing a Directory

The handiest thing to print is a list of files on disk. Under DOS, you use the DIR command to see a list of files. But that command only spits out the file information to the screen. To send the information to a printer, first make sure that the printer is on and ready to print and then type

```
C> DIR > PRN
```

That's the DIR command, followed by a space, the greater-than symbol (>), another space, and then PRN (which means "printer" in the Land of No Vowels).

- ✔ If you're using Windows (any versions), you cannot use Explorer or My Computer to get a hard copy of your directory. The only way to do it is as just described (from the DOS prompt).

- ✔ If you want to use any of the DIR command's options, sandwich them between DIR and the greater-than symbol (>). Note that the /P (pause) option would be rather silly at this point.

- ✔ If you print a directory to a laser printer, you may have to eject the paper from the printer to see the output; refer to the discussion in the "Form Feeding" section, earlier in this chapter.

- ✔ You don't see the directory on-screen when you use this command. If you want to see it there, use the DOS printing function, as discussed in the preceding section.

Why Does It Look Funny?

Printing anything from DOS has its consequences: If your printer cannot display the IBM graphics characters, they appear as other, odd characters on your hard copy. Seriously, the best place to print anything is from an application. Even then, though, you may not get what you want from your printer.

The answer lies in a piece of software called a *printer driver*. Like a slave driver, the printer driver utterly controls the printer, telling it to do exactly what the application wants. Why can't the application do this itself? Because no standard DOS printer exists. Hundreds of printers are in use, any one of which you may have attached to your PC. To tell your application which printer you have, you must set up the printer by directing the application to talk to it via a printer driver.

Installing a printer driver is usually done when you first set up an application (as described in Chapter 14). You select your printer's name and model number from a list, and then your application and your printer can work in sweet harmony. That isn't always the case, though.

Sometimes, someone (maybe you) selects the wrong printer driver. Or, worse, the application may not support your printer. As an example, WordPerfect has printer drivers for more than 1,000 different printers. My mailing-label program (which I don't name because I'm sorry that I bought it) supports only five printers — and I don't have any of them. Needless to say, the output from that program looks terrible (but, what the hey — only the post office has to read the labels).

Because each application enables you to set up your printer differently, it is impossible to mention all the possibilities here. If you cannot find the proper driver or locate your printer by name, you can always opt for the *Dumb printer* option. It's where the program controls your printer in text-only mode. It may not be the miracle of computers you dreamed of, but it works.

Windows made the idea of a printer driver obsolete — which is one of its (few) benefits. If you're running DOS programs under Windows, however, you *still* need a proper printer driver for your software. Sorry.

Those Funny Characters at the Top of the First Page

Occasionally, you may see some odd characters at the top of every page or just the first page you print. For example, you may see a ^ or &0 or E@, or any of a number of ugly-looking characters you didn't want there and that don't show up on-screen. It requires a major "Hmmm."

Hmmm.

Those characters are secret printer-control codes. Normally, the characters are swallowed by the printer as it prepares itself to print. The problem is that the software on the computer is sending your printer the wrong codes. Because your printer doesn't understand the codes, it just prints them as is. Hence, you see ugly characters.

The solution is to select the proper printer driver for your software. You want a printer driver that knows your printer and how to send it the proper codes. This stuff is best done by the person who (supposedly) installed the software on your computer. It can be changed in most cases. But you had better make someone else do it for you.

Chapter 12

More on Modems

. . . .

In This Chapter

▶ Discovering what a modem does

▶ Understanding the horrors of communications software

▶ Calling another computer

▶ Getting online

▶ Getting offline

▶ Dealing with the most common communications problems

▶ Defining communications terminology

. . . .

*F*air warning: The subject of telecommunications is not simple, and nothing I can do in writing will make it simple. Why? Because the modem and communications vendors have come up with 50 jillion different ways to do things and some of the most arcane jargon this side of quantum physics to describe it. Which *port* is your modem plugged in to? What is its *speed?* What *duplex* mode, *start and stop bits, transmission protocol,* and other gobbledygook make using a modem a nightmare?

The best possible way to use your modem is to get somebody else to set you up from soup to nuts, including preparing a *dialing directory* and walking you through the basics for the kinds of things you need to get done. In this chapter, I review just the basics, in case it helps.

Now, the bad news: When it comes to modems and online communications, Windows beats the pants off DOS. Sure, you can still do a great deal with DOS, so if it's your only operating system, you're okay. If you really want to get into modems, however, the best software runs under Windows.

What Does a Modem Do?

A *modem* is a device that translates the digital information from your computer into audio signals that can be sent over common phone lines (see Figure 12-1). In a way, the computer sends painful bits and bytes to the modem, which then converts them into sounds and "sings" them over the phone line (and I'm not talking operatic here). Using the modem, you can send information to another computer by calling its modem on the phone.

Figure 12-1:
A typical PC external modem.

You control a modem, and therefore talk with another computer, by using *communications software,* also called *telecom software.* It controls the modem, dials up other computers, sends information, and does just about everything in a complex and confusing manner. (Seriously, communications software is perhaps the most consistently cryptic of any application.)

✔ The most common device to plug in to a serial port is a modem. In fact, the serial port is often referred to as a *modem port.* Refer to Chapter 7 for the lowdown on ports.

✔ *Modem* is a contraction of the words *m*odulator-*dem*odulator. Rather than call it a *lator-lator,* though, they chose *mo-dem.* Also, the computer world has more modem jokes than anything else, typically "How many modem do you want?"

✔ Modems are judged by their speed — how fast they can talk to each other. Although your computer can chat with a modem at blistering speeds, the modem is limited (by design and price) by how fast it can talk. The speed value is measured by *bits per second,* or *bps.* See the section "Communications Terminology Explicated," at the end of this chapter.

Hooking up your modem

Two kinds of modems exist: internal and external. An internal modem sits inside your computer, snugly wedged into an expansion slot. An external modem sits outside the computer and must be connected to a serial port via a modem cable.

Internal modems have several advantages. The most obvious is that they're hidden from view, tucked inside the PC, which means that they don't eat up desk space or a power socket on the wall. It may also mean that the modem came with software, which removes another computer decision process.

To plug in your internal modem, locate someone whose fear level about such things is lower than yours and bribe that person heavily. Although you can install it yourself, I recommend the safe approach of having someone else do it.

External modems have several advantages. The most obvious is that you can see them and their pretty little lights, which tell you whether the modem is still breathing or has passed on to a higher plane of existence. You can also turn off an external modem if the need arises, and you can easily adjust its speaker volume.

Anyone can install an external modem: Take it out of the box and peel back the Styrofoam and wrapping. Set it on your desktop. Plug the power cord into the wall. Plug the phone cord into the wall (and optionally plug the phone that was plugged into the wall into the modem). Plug one end of a modem cable into the modem. Plug the other end into your PC.

Plug, plug, plug your modem, gently into the wall; merrily, merrily, merrily, merrily, comm is such a ball!

Personally, I prefer external modems. The reason is portability. A modem I bought in 1985 was used on a TRS-80 computer, Apple II, Macintosh, NeXT workstation, and PC. An internal modem would have been useful only on a PC it can plug into.

All that's left is wrestling with communications software.

Communications Software

A communications program is software that controls the connection between your computer and some other remote computer system, such as an online service (like America Online) or a local BBS (like the other services but cheaper — and free — and run by some kid in your neighborhood) or even the Internet.

Communications software does a great deal, which is probably why it's so darn cryptic. Basically, it has to coordinate several elements:

- ✔ Your computer's serial port
- ✔ The modem itself
- ✔ Setting things up to call another computer
- ✔ Talking with the other modem that answers the phone
- ✔ Doing interesting things while you're talking to the other computer
- ✔ Odd terminology

The nice part is that after you've set the various options, using the communications software and your modem is a cinch (which is why I recommend having someone else configure your *dialing directory*).

- Some online services, such as America Online, require special software rather than a general-purpose communications program.

- Yes, AOL has a DOS version of its software. I haven't checked it out recently, so I can't vouch for how good the version is or how well it is supported.

- What you're doing with communications software is calling another computer. That computer's modem answers the phone and talks to your modem, and then the two computers start sending information back and forth to each other. While you're connected, you're essentially running a program on that other computer. This stuff is the weird part of communications that makes some people sit in their chairs for hours without moving.

The Internet and DOS

Sure, DOS can do the Internet. In fact, the Internet itself originated on UNIX computers, and almost every program there is very DOS-like. (DOS is actually a primitive copy of the advanced UNIX operating system.) So, originally, all Internet stuff was text-based. DOS could handle it just fine.

Today, with the World Wide Web, the Internet is quickly becoming graphical. Sure, e-mail is text-based (mostly). And sending files back and forth with FTP can be text-based. The reason that the Internet is anything today, though, is because of the Web.

DOS software exists for using the Internet. DOS-based Web browsers are even available, some of which display Web pages in their full graphical glory. Even so, it would be unwise of me to recommend anything here; the software is mostly shareware and because of DOS's unfortunate demise at the hands of Microsoft, DOS Internet software probably won't be around for long.

If you're in the market to browse the Internet, get Windows. You don't have to pull the Windows 95 upgrade either; just get Windows 3.11, which Microsoft still supports. Plenty of decent Internet software exists for Windows 3.11, which you can use merrily under DOS.

If you're a DOS diehard and still want to surf the Web . . . Good news! There are graphical Internet browsers available. Some are even free. A good one is called Arachne available at `http://www.naf.cz/arachne/`. Arachne runs best with an 80386 PC or higher with 512K or more memory. You might also check out a DOS-based browser called SPIN (Saturnus Personal Internet Navigator) which can be found at `http://www.spin.saturnus.nl/engels/`.

Calling Another Computer

Before you call another computer, your communications software must tell your modem certain things about the computer system you're about to dial up. You must do this for each other computer you call, because each computer that answers the phone is different (and that's probably because of some arcane law passed during the Bush administration).

Assuming that your modem is hooked up right and your communications software works (more or less), you need to know the following basic (yeah, right) information about the other system — the one you're about to phone:

- The speed (for example, 28,800 bps)
- The number of data bits (7 or 8)
- The parity (odd, even, or none)
- The number of stop bits (usually 1)

Both your modem and the other modem must agree on these items if any communication is to take place. Modems are stubborn. If any one of these items doesn't match up, the other modem may answer, but it won't understand what your modem is saying — it's like when a lawyer calls you unexpectedly. This is the reason that you must make your modem match the other modem.

The following is the most typical setting:

> 28,800 bps for the speed, 8, N, 1

This example translates into a modem that talks at 28,800 bps and uses 8 data bits, no parity, and 1 stop bit. That's called a *data word format* of 8, N, 1. The other popular data word format for PCs is 7, E, 1:

> 28,800 bps for the speed, 7, E, 1

Chances are, most systems you dial up use 8, N, 1. If not, 7, E, 1 should be your selection.

- You must set these settings before you call the other computer. You cannot change them after the call has been made.

- How you control these settings depends on your communications software. Thanks to the rule that no two PC programs should be alike, each telecom package does things differently.

- Common values for a modem's speed are 300, 1200, 2400, 9600, 14,400, 28,800, 36,300 and 57,600 bps. Faster values also appear. The idea is to match your modem's speed with the speed of the other modem. If a variety of speeds is listed, use the fastest speed your modem has that's compatible with the answering modem.

✔ Other, truly weird settings for the data word format exist. With a PC, you can get by nearly all the time with 8, N, 1.

✔ There are other weird aspects of a modem you may or may not want to know about; see *PCs For Dummies* (IDG Books Worldwide, Inc.) for more information.

Dialing the modem

Modems work just like phones: They dial a number. Another modem should answer, in which case both modems start singing to each other and the connection is made (as long as you've properly set up the gobbledygook in the preceding section).

Ah, but before you call, you have to know the other computer's number. After you find that out, you use your communications software to dial that number.

For example, press Alt+D to bring up a dialing command. Then, enter the phone number — **1-555-234-5678**, for example. Press Enter (or whatever your communications program dictates), and the modem dials that number.

After one or more rings, the modem you're calling should answer the phone and send its distinctive warble. The pitch of the warble varies as the two modems compare notes, and then it falls abruptly silent; then (if all goes well), you see the word CONNECT on your screen. Wait a second or two, and then follow the on-screen instructions of the service you're calling.

✔ If you don't see anything right away, press Enter. This action may wake up the other computer.

✔ If you don't get a response or you get a long stream of garbage characters across the screen, hang up. Use the Hang-up or Disconnect command in your communications package. You can try calling again, which sometimes works. (Hey, modems are moody.) Or consider changing the data word format from 8, N, 1 to 7, E, 1 or vice versa. Or just toss up your arms and call your guru.

✔ One of four things can happen when you call up another computer: The other computer answers — which is great and what you want; or it's busy, which happens frequently; or there's no answer, in which case you can call back right away or later; or a human answers. If a human answers, do that person a favor and don't call back using your modem. The places that publish modem (or BBS) numbers frequently make mistakes. Don't bug poor Mrs. Henderson by redialing her phone every 30 seconds from midnight to 2 a.m.; she probably hates computers more than you do.

✔ Assuming that you aren't calling Mrs. Henderson's house, many communications programs have automatic redial features. That way, you can redial a busy computer over and over until it answers. (However, this is a poor excuse to sit and stare at a computer for an hour, so I recommend calling back once every ten minutes because most people spend about that long online anyway.)

✔ Calling with a modem is just like using the phone. The phone company (for now) does not charge any more for modems making phone calls than for people. Long-distance and toll charges still apply.

✔ When you're using your modem, no one else can call you. I know, this sounds dumb, but few people realize that they're using the phone because it's not immediately in their ear. Incidentally, if you pick up the phone while the modem is working, you hear a horrid high-pitched squeal — the modem in action. If you talk, you see random characters on your screen, or you may break the connection. (Other people in the house do this more often than you.) For this reason, I recommend getting a second phone line for your modem.

Logging in

When the modem you're calling answers, it says "Hey, wake up!" to its computer. That computer then runs special software. What you're doing online is using that software remotely, from your own computer. You can send messages to others who use the system, read your mail, join a conference, play online games, send files to the system, or have the system send you files. Oh, it can all be so much fun. Everything starts with logging in, though:

```
LOGIN:
```

You have to tell the other computer who you are. You do this by typing your full name or nickname at a login prompt. Sometimes, the prompt says LOGIN; at other times, it may just ask for your full name or first and then last names. If you've never called the system, read the instructions on-screen to see how you can become a member and get your own account.

After you enter your login ID, you're prompted for a *password*. This secret word is used to ensure that you are who you logged in as. After your password is entered and verified, you continue to use the online system.

✔ Many systems have interesting ways to log in. Some just come up right away; others require you to press Enter first. For example, CompuServe has you press Ctrl+C to get a prompt asking for your ID and password. Whatever the case, be sure to read any instructions on-screen, which should tell you what you can do next.

Calling another human by using your modem

Suppose that you and that crazy Earl both go down and buy modems at the same time. You hook them up, and then Earl calls and suggests that you phone each other up so that you can "chat" electronically. This is a fun thing to do when you first get your modem (but old-timers seriously roll their eyes over the thought).

To make it happen, you both should agree on your modems' speed and data word format. Let me help: Set your communications programs and modems to 2400 bps, 8, N, 1. Sure, your modem may be able to go faster, but you can barely type at 300 bps, so 2400 bps is more than fast enough.

The next thing you have to decide is who gets to call whom. One of you must be the calling computer, and the other must direct your

communications package to answer the phone. Then, the caller must dial up the answerer. This process is much more complex than it sounds, though. If you're just sitting there and you see RING on-screen, type ATA and press Enter, and your modem answers the phone. (Don't ask me how that works.)

After you're connected, start typing at each other! You don't see what you type unless you activate the local echo command. Or check to see whether your communications package has a special chat mode and use it. Keep in mind that if you have anything important to say, you can always pick up the phone and talk verbally. This method is definitely much quicker than watching Earl always back up and correct his typing mistakes.

 ✔ If you're just calling another person who's expecting you, just type something and see whether you get a typed response from that person.

 ✔ If, when you type, you see double letters or no letters, you have to switch your *duplex*. It's also called *local echo* in most communications programs (and it's usually the Alt+E key combination that controls it).

Doin' the Online Thing

Online means that something is connected. Your printer is online when it's actively paying attention to your computer and printing whatever the computer tells it to print. With a modem, you're online when you're actively conversing with another computer.

Most of what you do online is dictated by the other computer. You can read messages, peruse your mail, chat, and so on. Because all this stuff is handled by the remote computer, you just sit there and type. Sometimes, however, you have to tell your computer to do something. I can think of three big issues:

Capturing a file. Directing your communications program to start recording what you're receiving from the other computer. You can send the information to a file on disk or to your printer.

Uploading. Sending a file to the other computer. First, you tell the computer that you're sending it a file. You explain what type of file you're sending, give it a name, and answer whatever other questions you're asked. Then, you send the computer that file. This process involves selecting a mode for sending, such as XMODEM or ZMODEM.

Suppose that you're sending REPORT.XLS to the office's computer. You dial up the office computer, log in, and then weave your way to the place where you upload the file. You tell the office computer that you're sending it REPORT.XLS. It asks which protocol you use and provides a list:

```
1. ASCII
2. XMODEM
3. YMODEM
4. ZMODEM
```

Your communications software supports all these protocols, so you pick ZMODEM. The office system says Start uploading your file. On your end, you tell your communications software to send a file by using ZMODEM, and then you enter the filename.

You're alerted when the file is sent, at which time you continue using the office computer as you did earlier.

Downloading. The opposite of uploading. When you download, you tell the other computer to send you a file. It works the same way that uploading works; because more people download than upload, however, here are the steps in brief outline form:

1. **Locate the file you want to download. The other computer has a command that displays a list of files. Examine the list carefully or use a Search or some such command to locate the file (or files) you want.**

2. **Tell the other computer that you want to download. Choose the Download option. The exact name varies, depending on which computer you're calling.**

   The next two steps may be reversed on some systems.

3. **The other computer asks you for the name of the file you want it to send you. Type the filename. Sometimes it asks for a number, so you type the number instead.**

4. **The other computer asks how you want the file sent. This is the *protocol* question. Select a protocol (XMODEM, YMODEM, ZMODEM, or Kermit) based on what your communications software can handle. XMODEM is the most common; ZMODEM is the best.**

You've told the other computer what to send and how to send it. Now you have to tell your communications software to receive a file.

5. **Type your communications program's Download or Receive File command. In most cases, it's the PgDn key.**

6. **Select the protocol. It must match what you told the other computer: XMODEM, YMODEM, and so on.**

7. **Type the filename.**

8. **Go for it!**

The other computer sends the file, and your computer should receive it 100 percent okay. That's why "protocols" exist — to ensure that the file you get is the file the other computer sent.

Your communications software lets you know after the file is fully received. Mine beeps at me, which I find annoying, but it's handy because I can hear it in the other room and don't have to sit and watch a 15-minute download.

✔ As you can guess, you have a massive opportunity for screwing up here. Downloading is one of the most complex aspects of using already complex communications software. My advice is to try it first by using the preceding eight steps. Then, if you're still in the dark, refer to your horrid communications manual. At least that way you have a bit of experience when you look in there, and maybe that experience can help you decipher what they're trying to say.

✔ In the Windows 3.11 Terminal communications program, the *Binary* protocol is the same thing as ZMODEM elsewhere.

Online Attitude

Online telecommunications is a new and exciting way to communicate. Just as with learning a foreign language, however, you should be aware of some rules about online communications before you take the plunge. Don't get me wrong; this stuff can be fun. I do it all the time and have made quite a few enemies of my friends.

✔ Happy people go modeming.

✔ You can't "see" anyone you "meet" online, so don't assume anything about them. Modem people are old and young and come from diverse backgrounds, though studies show that they're typically male, upper income, and Republican. Still, don't hold that against them.

✔ Please don't type in ALL CAPS. Type your letters and comments in mixed case — like you do in writing a letter. To most online people, all caps reads LIKE YOU'RE SHOUTING AT THEM!

✔ Don't "beg" for people to send you e-mail. Participate in discussions or just be obnoxious, and you'll always have a full mailbox.

✔ The art of written communication is lost on the TV generation. When people use the phone to communicate, they hear inflection and gather extra meaning. Unfortunately, online messages lack these nuances. And, since we all don't have the written vocabularies that we should, jokes, side remarks, and kidding can easily be taken seriously (way too seriously). Remember to keep it light. Adding "ha-ha" occasionally lets people know that you're having fun instead of being an online jerk. Speaking of which. . . .

✔ Many online jerks are out there (ha-ha). The best policy to take with them is to ignore them. No matter how much they steam you, no matter how ludicrous their ideas or remarks — golly, even if they're Libertarians — don't get into a "flame thrower" war with them.

✔ In an online debate, ignore anyone who quotes "the dictionary" as a source. I hate to break it to you, but no National Institute of English defines what words mean. Dictionaries are written by people as ignorant as you and I. Heck, I could write and publish a dictionary if I wanted to and make up entirely new definitions for words. Nope, the dictionary is not a source to be quoted.

✔ An online debate isn't over until someone compares someone else to Adolph Hitler. Calling the person a Nazi or the generic "fascist" also counts.

✔ Never criticize someone over spelling. English is a beautiful and rich language, utterly lacking in logic or spelling rules. Phonics — ha! *It* starts with a *p,* for Pete's sake! There's no sense in drilling people on their spelling (unless it's truly awful, in which case you're probably dealing with a 12-year-old).

Saying Bye-Bye

When you're done using the remote computer, you should tell it good-bye — which is only polite. Use whichever command it has to hang up the phone. Always let the other computer hang up first. This practice enables it to clear your call properly, stop charging you online access fees, and so on.

✔ Sometimes, the good-bye command is on a menu. It may be H for Hang-up, G for Good-bye, O for Off, or E for Exit. If you have a command prompt, you may have to type the command. For example, on CompuServe, you must type **BYE** and press Enter. On MCI Mail, you type **EXIT** and press Enter. Other variations include LOGOFF, LOGOUT, and QUIT. When in doubt, type **HELP**.

✔ Only if the other computer appears dead or just totally confused should you hang up on your end: Tell your communications software to hang up the phone.

The Most Common Sources of Problems

After you get going, telecommunications can be easy. Yeah, and I've heard that some weirdoes can rip out their toenails without any sensation of pain. You may encounter some problems from time to time. Chances are that they're probably one of the following:

✔ **Not having the right cable between your computer and your modem.** It must be a standard RS-232 serial cable or *modem cable*. You cannot use a serial printer cable or a *null modem cable*.

✔ **Not having the modem connected to the correct port on your computer.** Most PCs have two serial ports, COM1 and COM2. Most communications programs assume that you use COM1. If not, tell your software that you're different and are using COM2.

✔ **Using a modem that is not fully Hayes compatible.** Your communications software assumes your modem to be Hayes compatible. If it's not, you have to select a proper modem driver or just sit in a pile of ash and weep bitterly because some bozo sold you an incompatible modem.

Unzipping the ZIP File Mystery

Occasionally, you may download a strange type of file with the extension ZIP. You may be all proud and happy that you actually got everything to work and then be crushed because that cool painting program you downloaded is named PAINT.ZIP and — Lord only knows why — it doesn't run. Boo-hoo. Sniff, sniff.

Any file ending in ZIP is called an *archive*. It's actually a collection of several files, all of which have been compressed and compacted into one handy ZIP file. This technique is the way most downloads are stored on BBSs and other online systems. Rather than have you toil with downloading dozens of files one after the other, the files are all stored in a single ZIP file. Because the files are compressed, they take up less space on disk and take even less time to download. The only problem is getting the files out of the ZIP file — *unzipping* them, so to speak.

To unzip a ZIP file, you need a special program, a *utility* called PKUNZIP. It's part of a group of programs available from PKWare, the company that makes

PKUNZIP and its companion program, PKZIP. These programs are the number-one PC file-archiving programs available for DOS and the source of all those ZIP files you may encounter while modeming.

Using PKUNZIP is easy. Just type **PKUNZIP**, a space, and then the name of the ZIP file you want to decompress (or "explode"):

```
C> PKUNZIP PAINT.ZIP
```

In this example, PKUNZIP is followed by PAINT.ZIP, the name of a file you downloaded. After pressing Enter, you see PKUNZIP go to work, extracting all the files sitting tight in the ZIP file archive and saving each one to disk. In a few moments, the operation is complete and you can play with your downloaded program (or programs).

✔ The easiest way to get PKZIP is to download the file from a BBS or national online service. The program is named PKZIP*xxx*.EXE. The *xxx* part of the filename is replaced by numbers, indicating the PKZIP version number. After downloading, type **PKZIP*xxx*** (the name of the file you downloaded), and it "explodes" into the various PKZIP and PKUNZIP utilities. Use the COPY or MOVE command to put those files in your PC's UTILITY subdirectory or store them in a special place where you always have access to them, as described in Chapter 18.

✔ The honest way to get PKZIP is to order it from PKWare directly. It advertises in national computer magazines and changes its address and phone number too often for me to justify putting it down here.

✔ Even if you don't order PKZIP from PKWare, you're expected to pay for it. This type of software is not "free" just because you downloaded it. Pony up. Check the file named ORDER.DOC for ordering information.

✔ PKZIP comes with a manual "on disk." Check the file named MANUAL.DOC for more information.

✔ ZIP files don't have to contain dozens of files. Sometimes, they contain only one file, though because the file is in an archive, it takes up less space on disk and is quicker to download than if it had not been compressed.

✔ No, ZIP files have nothing to do with disk compression and programs such as Stacker. Although the idea is the same, only one file is compressed, not a whole disk.

✔ Other archiving programs similar to PKZIP are available, though not as popular. Each has its own unzipping utility and its own filename extension: ZOO, LZH, ARC, PAK, and so on. Because this subject opens a whole can of worms — a compressed can, at that — I give you permission to bug the online system's operator or online guru for help with those types of archives.

Communications Terminology Explicated

I'm not trying to mentally agitate you with terminology, but computer communications is full of it (so to speak). This section defines specific terms related to online communications. I've tried to describe them in as sane a manner as possible.

Baud. A modem's speed is often referred to as *baud,* though that term is technically incorrect. The speed is really measured in bits per second, or bps, which is defined in this section. I have no reason to bring this matter up other than I'm granting you license to correct anyone who refers to bps as "baud rate."

BBS. An acronym for an electronic *b*ulletin-*b*oard *s*ystem. It's a local, typically hobbyist-run online computer system. BBSs have more of a neighborhood or community flavor than the big, impersonal national systems.

bps (speeds). An acronym for *b*its *p*er *s*econd, the speed at which a modem can communicate. A speed of 2400 bps translates roughly into 240 characters per second, which is almost 2,400 words per minute that can be sent between two computers.

Carrier. The tone that two modems sing to each other. You hear it used most often when someone says that they've "dropped the carrier." Although an impressive mental image of the U.S.S. *Nimitz* splashing down into the Caribbean appears, think of it instead as hanging up the phone.

Chat. To type at someone else while you're online. Chatting can be a great deal of fun. It can also be boring to sit and watch some of the slowest typists in the world — and then experience the agony as they backspace over the whole line of text to correct a spelling mistake.

Communications settings. Refers to the modem's speed and data word format, which must be tailored to each BBS you call.

Data word format. Involves three elements: the word length (8 or 7), the parity (odd, even, or none), and the number of stop bits (1 or 0). The most common data word format in PC communications is 8, N, 1. The second most common is 7, E, 1. These settings must match those of the computer you're dialing.

Download. To copy a file or program from the computer you're calling to your own computer.

Duplex. Refers to how characters appear on-screen. *Full duplex* means that you send characters to the other computer, and everything you see on the screen comes from the other computer; also known as *no echo. Half duplex* means that the characters you type appear on-screen directly; also known as *local echo.* You can freely ignore this term. Only when you can't see what you're typing should you put your computer in local echo mode.

E-mail. Also known as electronic mail — personal, private messages you can send to other people who dial into the same computer you do. Getting lots of mail is perhaps the most rewarding part about online communications. (Please don't beg for others to send mail to you; just participate and you get mail.) By the way, the people at the post office are thinking of starting an e-mail delivery system. The problem is that they can't figure out how to slow it down.

Host. Another term for the computer you're calling, the one answering the phone.

Log in. To identify yourself to the host computer. You log in by entering your name or a special nickname or ID number.

Online. To be connected and chatting with another computer.

Speed. *See* bps.

Upload. To send a file from your computer to the host computer.

XMODEM, YMODEM, ZMODEM, and so on. File transfer protocols; programs and files are typically sent from one computer to another by using XMODEM, YMODEM, ZMODEM, or a number of other methods for sending files without errors.

Chapter 13

All You (Don't) Want to Know about Disks

● ●

In This Chapter

▶ Understanding why disks are really *hardware*

▶ Buying disks

▶ Preparing a disk for use by DOS (formatting)

▶ Formatting different sizes of disks

▶ Learning what not to do with disks — the no-no's

▶ Determining which type of disk is which

▶ Changing a volume label

▶ Write-protecting a disk

▶ Reformatting an already formatted disk

▶ Duplicating disks

● ●

*B*oth computers and humans have two kinds of long-term storage. The internal storage in a human is provided by a wet, slimy thing called a *brain*. It's fast on the uptake and can store volumes of information but is sluggish on the retrieval. Inside a computer, the hard drive provides fast but limited storage and retrieves quickly.

Humans supplement their brain-storage device with storage media, such as scraps of paper with things written down on them. Computers use floppy disks, on which information can be written and removed from the computer, taken elsewhere, or just stored. Both systems have their pluses and minuses.

This chapter is about using *floppy disks,* the removable long-term storage devices used by computers. You use floppy disks to make safety copies of your important files, move files between computers, back up information from the hard disk, and play a limited-distance version of Frisbee. Floppies can be frustrating or fun, but above all, they must be formatted (see the section "Formatting a Disk," later in this chapter).

Why Are Disks Hardware?

A common misconception among computer users is that a floppy disk is actually software. This is not so. Floppy disks are hardware. Keep in mind that hardware is something you can touch or drop on your foot. (Although a floppy disk doesn't hurt as much as a monitor that has been dropped on your foot, it is still hardware.) See Figure 13-1 for a peek at what these floppy disks look like.

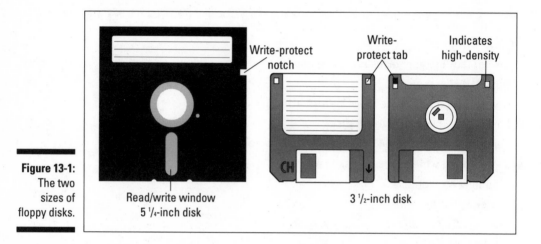

Figure 13-1:
The two
sizes of
floppy disks.

Write-protect notch

Write-protect tab

Indicates high-density

Read/write window
5 ¼-inch disk

3 ½-inch disk

The confusion comes about because floppy disks store software. The software is on the disk, magnetically encoded. Just as you wouldn't call a compact disc "music," don't confuse the floppy disk with the software that's recorded on it.

Buying Disks

You should always buy disks that match the size and capacity of your floppy drives. Under most circumstances, they're the high-density 3½-inch disks. You may find low-density disks available: Avoid them. Buy only the high-density stuff.

Older PCs may also sport a 5¼-inch-size floppy disk drive. Buy high-density disks for that type of drive as well.

- A high-density 3½-inch floppy disk can store 1.4MB of information.

- The high-density 3½-inch floppy disk is also called an "80 Track, 135 TPI" disk. These terms are used primarily by the geeky among us.

- A high-density 5¼-inch disk can hold 1.2MB of information.

- If you have only a low-capacity drive, which means that you have a very old PC, buy the low-capacity, DS/DD disks. You cannot use the high-capacity disks, and you shouldn't even buy them.

- Nothing is wrong with buying discount disks in bulk. I do it all the time.

- Do not buy so-called *quad-density* disks. These disks are for an older PC disk format that no longer exists.

- Do not format high-capacity disks to a low-capacity. See the section "Formatting a Low-Capacity Disk in a High-Capacity Drive," later in this chapter, for more information.

- Don't buy low-capacity disks and "notch" them so that they format to a higher capacity. This technique was a fad about ten years ago; I'm hoping that none of the notching machines exists anymore.

- Also: Don't mess with extended-density (ED) floppy disks. They were in a funky IBM format. As far as I know, I'm the only person in a 500-mile radius who has an ED disk drive (on a very old PC).

Formatting a Disk

Before you can use a disk, it must be formatted. For most of the disks you buy, this process isn't a big deal because all the major brands sell their disks preformatted. It says so right on the box: formatted disks. If so, you don't have to prepare the disk before you use it.

If your floppy disks are not formatted or you're unsure, you have to format them because you can use floppy disks on a variety of computers — not always DOS computers. For DOS to use the disk and store information on it, you must format that disk the way DOS likes. You format it with the FORMAT command.

To format a disk, first place it label side up and toward you and insert it into drive A. (Close the drive's door latch after inserting a 5¼-inch disk.) Type this line:

```
C> FORMAT A:
```

After pressing Enter, you're asked to insert the disk. That's already done, so press Enter again and the disk begins formatting.

After formatting is complete, you're asked to enter a *volume label* for the disk. Press Enter (unless you want to type a label name; it's optional). If you want to format another disk, press **Y** when it asks you and then remove the first disk and replace it with another. Then press any key to continue formatting.

You can also format disks in drive B (if your computer has a drive B). Here's the command you use:

```
C> FORMAT B:
```

Follow the same steps as listed for drive A.

- ✔ Never format any drive other than A or B; you should always use the two FORMAT commands listed in this section when you're formatting disks.
- ✔ The disk you format must be the same size and capacity of the drive you're using: high-capacity disks for high-capacity drives; low-capacity disks for low-capacity drives.
- ✔ If you see the message Track 0 bad or Disk unusable, see Chapter 23.
- ✔ You can format a low-capacity disk in a high-capacity drive; see the following section.

Formatting a Low-Capacity Disk in a High-Capacity Drive

It's possible to format a disk of lower capacity in a high-capacity drive. You would format this way to make your computer compatible with computers that have only the lower-capacity drives or if you're using cheaper, low-density disks. If that's never your situation, you have no need to format this way.

To format a low-capacity disk in a high-capacity drive, you must first get the low-capacity disk. Never format a high-capacity disk to a lower format. (It renders the disk useless.)

Insert the low-capacity disk into your high-capacity drive, label up and toward you. For a 5¼-inch drive, latch the drive's door shut after you've inserted the disk.

If you're formatting a low-capacity (360K) disk in a high-capacity 5¼-inch drive, type this FORMAT command:

```
C> FORMAT A: /F:360
```

That's FORMAT, followed by a space, A and a colon (meaning drive A), a space, /F and a colon, and then the number 360. Press Enter and follow the instructions on-screen. Keep in mind that if you answer Y when you're asked Format another?, you still format the low-capacity disks.

If you're formatting a low-capacity (720K) disk in a high-capacity 3½-inch drive, type this FORMAT command:

```
C> FORMAT A: /F:720
```

This FORMAT command is the same one listed in the preceding example, except that you type the number 720 rather than 360. Follow the same instructions listed under the first FORMAT command. Remember that any additional disks you format by answering Y are formatted at 720K.

✔ If you want to format the low-capacity disk in drive B, substitute B: for A: in either of the preceding commands.

✔ If the FORMAT command refuses to format the disk for any reason, you can force it to format by adding the /U option. Here are the modified commands:

```
C> FORMAT A: /F:360 /U
C> FORMAT A: /F:720 /U
C> FORMAT A: /F:1440 /U
```

Again, *do not* use these commands to force-format a high-capacity disk to a lower capacity. Always use low-capacity disks when you're formatting at low capacity.

Which Disk Is This?

Ever pick up a disk and wonder silently, "Where the heck did this disk come from?" If you do that frequently, I have one maxim for you:

Label Your Disks!

Every box of disks — even the cheapies — comes with several sticky labels. Here's how you use them:

1. **Write information on the sticky label by using a pen.**

   Describe the disk's contents or give it a general name: *Files for home* or *Backup stuff* or *Emergency disk* or . . . you get the idea.

2. **Peel the label off and gently apply it to the disk.**

There. That's easy. With all your disks labeled, you never have to worry about wondering what's on them. And you can find commonly used disks more quickly.

✔ If you don't label a disk, you can use the DIR command to find out what's on it. Refer to the section in Chapter 2 about the DIR command.

✔ As a suggestion, label disks immediately after you format them. That way, all formatted disks have labels. If you find a disk without a label, that tells you that it's probably unformatted. (Check it with the DIR command first, however, to be certain.)

✔ You may also want to write the capacity of the disk (1.2MB or 360K, for example) on the label. This info helps out in situations in which you have many computers with different kinds of drives in them.

✔ You can write on the labels after they're on the disk. Use a felt-tip pen and don't press too hard. If you use a ballpoint pen or pencil, you may dimple the disk inside and ruin any data there.

✔ You can peel and remove a label from a disk if you want to change it.

✔ Don't write on the disk's sleeve rather than the label. Disks can change sleeves.

✔ Programs are available that enable you to create custom labels for your disks, even putting filenames and the disk's contents on a nifty little sticky label.

✔ Don't confuse the sticky label with the *volume label*. The volume label is an electronic name you attach to a disk when it's formatted. See the section "Changing the Volume Label," later in this chapter.

✔ Don't use Post-Its as disk labels. They fall off when you're not looking and can sometimes get stuck inside your disk drives. I'm not speaking from experience here. Nope. No way would I have ever done that. Unh-unh.

What Kind of Disk Is This?

Even if a disk is labeled, sometimes it's hard to tell whether it's a low-capacity or high-capacity model. The following tips should clue you in to which disk is which:

If the disk is a 360K 5¼-inch floppy:

First of all, the disk is probably about 15 years old, so look for signs of caked-on dust.

It may have a label that contains one of the following: DS/DD; double sided/double density; 40 TPI, or 40 Tracks Per Inch; or even "Disk for the brand-new IBM PC-XT."

As a visual clue, if you remove the disk and look at its center hole, you see a reinforcing _hub ring_. The 1.2MB disks typically lack this feature.

If the disk is a 1.2MB 5¼-inch floppy:

One of the following clues may be written on the label: the letters _HD_ or the term _high-density;_ double sided/high-density; Double Track; or 96 TPI, or 96 Tracks Per Inch.

The visual clue is the absence of a reinforcing hub ring typically found on most 360K floppies.

If the disk is a 720K 3½-inch floppy:

It may have one of the following clues written on its label: DS/DD; double sided/double-density; DD; Double Track; or 135 TPI, or 135 tracks per inch.

The primary visual clue is that the disk is missing a hole in the lower right corner. (This hole is opposite from the write-protect hole.)

If the disk is a 1.4MB 3½-inch floppy:

The 1.4MB disk may have one of the following clues on its label: DS/HD; double sided/high-density; or the interesting graphic (double line) letters _HD_. (The HD is usually your best clue; all the manufacturers use it.)

The key visual clue is the extra, see-through hole in the lower right corner of the disk. The lower-capacity disks lack this hole.

Using the CHKDSK Command to Check a Disk's Size

If a disk is formatted, you can use the CHKDSK ("check disk") command to determine its size. The CHKDSK command is known as _check disk,_ which is kind of what CHKDSK looks like without all the superfluous vowels. Basically, this command reports information about your disk, most of it technical.

Do not run the CHKDSK program in Windows! Run CHKDSK only when you're using DOS by itself, you have quit Windows 3.11 or restarted your computer in MS-DOS mode for Windows 95 and Windows 98.

To see how much information you can store on a floppy disk, and therefore see its size or capacity, type **CHKDSK** at the DOS prompt, followed by **A:**, indicating the drive holding your floppy disk. Press Enter, and prepare to be overwhelmed:

```
C> CHKDSK A:
```

After pressing Enter, you see something like this:

```
Volume DOS HAPPY    created 01-20-98 8:16p
Volume Serial Number is 0D1B-0FF8
    1,457,664 bytes total disk space
      832,000 bytes in 38 user files
      625,664 bytes available on disk
          512 bytes in each allocation unit
        2,847 total allocation units on disk
        1,222 available allocation units on disk
      655,360 total bytes memory
      617,552 bytes free
```

Four chunks of information are here, most of it trivia. The most important is the first number value, which tells you the size of your disk. In this example, the number says that the disk has 1,457,664 bytes of *total disk space,* so this disk is a 1.4MB, formatted floppy disk. Other values are divulged in this table:

Floppy Disk Size	Long, Involved Number Displayed
360K	365,056
1.2MB	1,228,800
720K	730,112
1.4MB	1,457,664

- To check the capacity of a disk in drive B, substitute B: for A: in the preceding CHKDSK command.

- The value bytes available on disk tells you how much space is left on the disk for storing files.

- The commas appear in the CHKDSK output only with MS-DOS Version 6.2 and later. Earlier versions of DOS don't have the handy commas. Also, the MS-DOS 6.2 CHKDSK command is riddled with information about running the ScanDisk program instead. See Chapter 17 for information about ScanDisk.

- The danger in running CHKDSK in Windows 3.11 is that you may be tempted to "fix" a file that CHKDSK flags as broken. The truth is, under Windows 3.11, CHKDSK doesn't really know what's broken and what's not. Its fix may actually crash the computer, delete important files, or otherwise mess up your day.

> ✔ See Chapter 17 for information about how to deal with any errors
> CHKDSK may report.

Changing the Volume Label

When you format a disk, the FORMAT command asks you to enter a *volume label*. This electronic name is encoded on the disk — not the sticky label you should apply later. Giving your disk a volume label can be a good idea, especially if your sticky label falls off the disk. In that case, you can find out the name of your disk electronically by using the DIR command. The volume label appears at the top of the DIR command's output, and you can use the handy VOL command to find a disk's volume label. Type

```
C> VOL A:
```

or

```
C> VOL B:
```

The VOL command reports back the disk's volume label, or it may tell you that the `disk has no label`.

After you've formatted a disk, you can change the volume label by using the LABEL command. Type **LABEL**, and then follow the instructions on-screen:

```
C> LABEL
```

After pressing Enter, you see the current label for the drive as well as the cryptic `volume serial number`. DOS asks you to enter a new label up to 11 characters long. The label can contain letters and numbers. If you want a new label, type it. If you don't want to change the label, don't *type* anything, but *do* press Enter.

If you enter a new label, DOS changes it on the disk. You can use the VOL command again to verify the new label.

If you just pressed Enter and your disk already had a label, DOS asks whether you want to delete the old label. If so, press **Y**. Otherwise, press **N** and you keep the original label.

To change the label on a disk in any drive, follow the LABEL command with that drive letter and a colon. Here's an example:

```
C> LABEL A:
```

In this example, the label is examined or changed for drive A. Substitute `B:` for `A:` in this example to replace the label on drive B.

REMEMBER

✔ You can follow the VOL command with any drive letter and colon. You use this command to see the volume label for any other disk in your system.

✔ Insert a floppy disk in drive A or B before using the LABEL or VOL command on those drives.

Write-Protecting Disks

You can protect floppy disks in such a way as to prevent yourself or anyone else from modifying or deleting anything on the disk.

To write-protect a 5¼-inch disk, go grab one of those tiny, Velamint-size tabs that came with the disk in the box. Peel the tab and place it over the notch in the disk, which should be on the lower left side as you insert the disk into the drive (refer to Figure 13-1). With that notch covered, the disk is write-protected.

To write-protect a 3½-inch disk, locate the little sliding tile on the lower left side of the disk as you slide it into the drive. If the tile covers the hole, the disk can be written to. If you slide the tile off the hole (so that you can see through it), the disk is write-protected (refer to Figure 13-1).

When a disk is write-protected, you cannot alter, modify, change, or delete anything on that disk. And you cannot accidentally reformat it. You can read from the disk and copy files from it, but changing the disk — forget it!

To un-write-protect a 5¼-inch disk, peel off the little tab. Although this action renders the disk sticky, it's a livable problem. You can un-write-protect 3½-inch disks by sliding the tile over the hole.

Reformatting Disks

Disks must be formatted before DOS can use them, and after they're formatted, you can reformat them. You can format them under two circumstances: when you want to totally erase the disk and all its data or accidentally.

Obviously, you shouldn't erase a disk you don't want to erase. All the data on the disk goes bye-bye. The only way to avoid this situation is to be careful: Check the disk with the DIR command first. Make sure that it's a disk you want to reformat.

Personally, I erase disks all the time. I have stacks of old disks I can reformat and use. The data on them is old or duplicated elsewhere, so reusing the disk is no problem. Here's the FORMAT command you want to use:

```
C> FORMAT A: /Q
```

That's the FORMAT command, a space, and then A and a colon, which directs the FORMAT command to format a disk in drive A. That's followed by another space and a slash-Q. That line tells DOS to *Quickformat* the disk. It's very fast.

If DOS refuses to Quickformat the disk, try this FORMAT command:

```
C> FORMAT A: /U
```

This command is the same as the last one but with a slash-U rather than a slash-Q. This command tells DOS to *unconditionally* format the disk. It takes longer than a Quickformat, but it generally works.

- ✔ If you want to reformat a disk in drive B, substitute B: for A: in these examples.

- ✔ Note that you cannot Quickformat a disk to a different size. In fact, you shouldn't be reformatting disks to a different size anyway. If you must, use the /U option, as just shown.

- ✔ Quickformat only newer disks. If a disk has been sitting around awhile, use the FORMAT command without the /Q. Although that method takes longer, the FORMAT command does a better job to ensure that the disk is still usable.

- ✔ After formatting a disk, you see a list of statistics. If one of the statistics mentioned is xxxx bytes in bad sectors, you have a bum disk on your hands. My advice: Toss the sucker. If you still have the receipt and the store said that the disks were "fully guaranteed," you can try to get your money back. Good luck!

- ✔ You can recover accidentally reformatted disks by using MS-DOS 6.2. See the section "I Just Reformatted My Disk!" in Chapter 21.

Duplicating Disks (The DISKCOPY Command)

To make a duplicate of a file on disk, you use the COPY command. (Refer to the section "Duplicating a File," in Chapter 18.) To make a duplicate of a floppy disk, you use the DISKCOPY command. DISKCOPY takes one floppy and makes an exact duplicate of it, even formatting a new disk if it was previously unformatted.

Here are two things you cannot do with the DISKCOPY command:

- ✔ Use DISKCOPY to create two disks of different sizes or capacities.
- ✔ Use DISKCOPY with a hard disk or a *RAM drive*. (If you don't know what a RAM drive is, go to the refrigerator and reward yourself with a cool, carbonated beverage.)

When you copy disks, DOS refers to the original disk as the *SOURCE*. The disk to which you're copying is the *TARGET*.

To make a copy of a disk, first write-protect the original, the source. (Refer to the section "Write-Protecting Disks," earlier in this chapter.) Put your write-protected original in drive A. Close the drive's door latch for a 5¼-inch disk.

Type this command at the DOS prompt:

```
C> DISKCOPY A: A:
```

That's DISKCOPY, a space, and then A: twice (which means that drive A is mentioned twice and separated by a space). Press Enter and DOS examines the disk, spews out some technical mumbo jumbo, and then

```
Reading from source diskette . . .
```

The drive churns away for a few moments. Then, you're asked to insert the target:

```
Insert TARGET diskette in drive A:
Press any key to continue
```

Remove the source disk and insert your duplicate disk. Close the door latch if you have a 5¼-inch disk. Press Enter.

```
Writing to target diskette . . .
```

Take a few seconds to put the original (the "source") back in a safe place. When the operation is complete, you can use the duplicate rather than the original.

- ✔ When the operation is complete, DOS asks whether you want to use DISKCOPY again. Press **Y** if you do or **N** if you don't.
- ✔ In MS-DOS 6.2, after the copy is complete, you're asked whether you want to make another duplicate of the same disk — another TARGET. Press **Y** if you do or **N** if you don't. Then you're asked whether you want to copy another disk (another SOURCE). Press **Y** if you do or **N** if you don't.
- ✔ You can use DISKCOPY in your drive B by substituting B: for A: in the preceding command.
- ✔ You can use the following DISKCOPY command if and *only* if your drives A and B are of the same size and capacity:

```
C> DISKCOPY A: B:
```

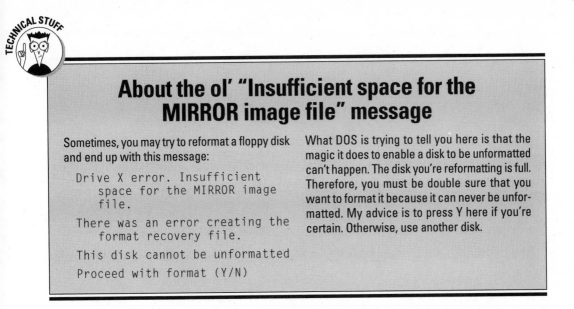

About the ol' "Insufficient space for the MIRROR image file" message

Sometimes, you may try to reformat a floppy disk and end up with this message:

```
Drive X error. Insufficient
    space for the MIRROR image
    file.
There was an error creating the
    format recovery file.
This disk cannot be unformatted
Proceed with format (Y/N)
```

What DOS is trying to tell you here is that the magic it does to enable a disk to be unformatted can't happen. The disk you're reformatting is full. Therefore, you must be double sure that you want to format it because it can never be unformatted. My advice is to press Y here if you're certain. Otherwise, use another disk.

This command is faster because you don't have to swap disks.

- ✔ If the target disk is unformatted, DISKCOPY formats it. If it's already formatted, DISKCOPY replaces the original contents with the copy.

- ✔ The DISKCOPY command is the only accurate way to duplicate a disk. Even the COPY command cannot always make a full copy of all the files on a disk.

- ✔ You may be asked to swap the SOURCE and TARGET disks a few times. This process can be maddening. If it bothers you, consider updating to MS-DOS 6.2, where they (finally) stopped the DISKCOPY disk-swapping madness.

- ✔ Use DISKCOPY to copy disks for only your use, not for friends — it's illegal to copy licensed programs for others.

Part III

The Non-Nerd's Guide to PC Software

The 5th Wave   By Rich Tennant

"I'M WAITING FOR MY AUTOEXEC FILE TO RUN, SO I'M GONNA GRAB A CUP OF COFFEE, MAYBE MAKE A SANDWICH, CHECK THE SPORTS PAGE, REGRIND THE BRAKE DRUMS ON MY TRUCK, BALANCE MY CHECKBOOK FOR THE PAST 12 YEARS, LEARN SWAHILI, ..."

In this part . . .

Software is what makes the hardware go. In a computer system, it's the software that's the brains. The computer hardware, even the admired microprocessor, is really nothing without the proper software in charge. A computer without software is like an orchestra without music. And those musicians can sit on stage for only so long before *that* gets really boring.

This part of the book is about computer software. Everything you do on your computer happens because of software. DOS may be the conductor, but your software is the music. And you, well, you're the patron. Or maybe you're the guy who coughs all the time during the quiet parts. Whatever. The following handful of chapters tell you everything you need to know about DOS and software.

Chapter 14

Basic Software Setup

. . . .

In This Chapter

▶ Locating software that works on your computer

▶ Installing software (generally speaking)

▶ Operating a new program and performing basic functions

▶ Finding out about a new program (the best way)

▶ Updating software

▶ Reading a command format

. . . .

*I*f you play your cards right, you never have to install any software on your PC. Someone else, someone who loves to do such things, will install the software for you. To install a program, you have to follow steps that are required only once. Making someone else do it for you can be a blessing.

This chapter is about using software for the first time. I give you information about selecting and installing a program, which can be pretty involved. I also cover a strategy for finding out about and using software for the first time — not that you would want to become an expert or anything.

Finding Compatible Software

Proud new computer owners — and enthusiasts — find it hard not to gravitate to the local software store. They come, they drool, they buy. For everyone else, the software store is like the fourth ring of hell — or an eight-mile-square auto-parts store with 10,000 guys named Bud who won't help you. Armed with the proper knowledge, however, you may be able to find what you want or at least find someone to help. Here's how to find the software that's right for you:

1. Know what you want to get done.

Software does the work, so finding software means that you first have to know what kind of work you need to do. For example, will you be writing? Then you need a tool to help you write — a *word processor*. Dozens of them — an overwhelming number — are out there. At least you've taken the first step, though, by narrowing down what you need. (Even if you think that it's a category which doesn't exist, ask someone. A software package may be available just for you.)

2. Find compatible software.

At this point, you know that you have a DOS computer. Therefore, you can buy only DOS software. Lots of technical details about software may limit which computer it runs on. For example, some software requires fancy graphics hardware; some requires a great deal of memory. If you know these details, you can compare what your computer has to the software's requirements, which are usually listed on the side of the box.

If you don't know what you have, ask the salesperson. Tell him or her that you're not sure what system you have and that you don't want to buy something that requires too much horsepower. (Besides, that stuff is expensive.)

3. Try that software.

Pick a few different packages to try out. Most software stores let you try before you buy. Let the salesperson set you up. Then play. Because you know what you want to do, this step shows you how easy some of the software is to use and how difficult it can be. Check for the level of so-called help offered in each package. Maybe one out there is just for you.

You should also find out what kind of support is available for the software. Does the company have a support line? Is it toll free? These questions are vital, and the answers may help you choose one package over another. You should also check the software store's return policy.

4. Maybe shop around.

If you don't like one store, go to another. If you don't like something in particular, be sure to be nasty and tell the store's manager. Also tell them where you're headed. Although you can price-shop if you want, most software stores offer great discounts anyway. If you find a store where a salesperson really knows the package you're interested in, however, it may be a good idea to buy the package there. Nothing beats someone to call on the phone for help.

5. Buy it.

Slap down your VISA card and buy the software! Don't buy too much at one time, though. A common mistake is to overwhelm yourself with too much software. Often, some packages gather dust while you concentrate on others. Just work on the issue at hand, solve one problem at a time, and don't overdo it.

Installation

No one really likes to install software. Well, I do (but I'm a nerd). I love the smell of a new software package. And, like everyone else I know who owns a computer, I take pride in trying to set the thing up without first reading the manuals. Of course, I don't think that you're this crazy.

Installation means copying the program you've just bought from floppy disks to your computer's hard drive. It also means more, typically configuring or setting up the program to work with your particular PC, printer, and the rest of that stuff. That is why installation is best left up to your local computer guru. If not, you can follow the outline in this section. Because each computer program installs itself differently, I cover this material in a broad sense. It gives you a general idea, though, of the task you're about to undertake.

Read me first!

Computer manuals and those national sweepstakes with you-know-who's picture on the envelope both have something in common: You get lots of little pieces of paper and instructions for the interesting things you must do. Computer manuals are easier to deal with. Seriously. You have no need to hunt through everything, fill out various forms, or paste Uncle Ed's picture inside the TV set. Just look for a sheet of paper somewhere that says "Read me first!" Read it, and you're on your way.

The installation program

You install a program by sticking Disk 1 into your PC's first floppy drive (drive A) and then running the installation program. If the disk doesn't fit in drive A, stick the disk into drive B and substitute B for A in the following instructions. The name of the installation program is usually Install, although Setup is also popular. Two steps are involved here. The first is logging to drive A. This topic is covered in Chapter 2, in the section "Changing Drives." Basically, after sticking Disk 1 into floppy drive A (and closing the drive door latch for a 5¼-inch disk), you type

```
C> A:
```

Typing **A** and a colon logs you to drive A. Press Enter.

Next, you enter the name of the installation program. This name is probably listed in the manual, on the disk label, or on the "Read me first!" sheet of paper, or else that paper tells you where to find these instructions. Be wary! Even though installing the program is the first thing you ever do with it, it's rarely the first chapter in the manual. (I've always wondered why that's the case.)

For example, if the name of the installation program is INSTALL, you type

```
A> INSTALL
```

Press Enter.

Sometimes, the installation program is called SETUP. If so, you type

```
A> SETUP
```

Press Enter here, too.

Don't forget to *read the information on the screen!* It's important, especially for an installation program. In fact, many "experts" usually screw up software installation by not reading the information screens. Follow the instructions closely.

The location

The first thing the installation program asks you is "Where do you want to put me?" Dumb question. You want to put the program on your computer.

The application needs its own workspace on your hard drive. This space is referred to as a *subdirectory*. Only advanced users may have some special scheme or plan in this instance. You should accept whatever suggestion the installation program makes — it's probably a good one.

Configuring a computer application

Configuration is the stupidest part of setting up a computer application. This part is where the program asks you information about your own computer: "What kind of printer do you have? What kind of display or monitor is attached? How much memory do you have? Do you have a mouse?" These questions are ridiculous! After all, the computer program is asking you those questions, and it's already inside the computer, where it can look around more easily than you can.

Still, you may have to tell the computer what it has (which, again, is like asking other people how old you are at your next birthday party). These questions can be difficult. If you don't know the answers, grab someone who does. Otherwise, guess. The *default* or *automatic selection* options tell the program to guess on its own, so if they're available, select them.

An important item to select is a *printer driver,* which is a fancy way of telling the application which printer is manacled to your PC. Look for your printer's name and model number listed. If it's not there, select *Dumb* or *Line* printer (and then go to your dealer and beat up the guy who sold you the printer).

READ.ME file

Finally, last-minute instructions or information are offered in a special file on disk. It's given the name README, READ.ME, README.TXT, or README.DOC. Good installation programs ask you whether you want to view this file. Say yes. Look through the file for any information that applies to your situation.

A utility is usually offered with a program to provide automatic viewing of the READ.ME file. If not, you can view it by using this DOS command:

```
C> MORE < READ.ME
```

That's the MORE command, a space, a less-than sign (<), another space, and the name of the READ.ME file. If the file is named just README, type it without a period in the middle.

✔ For information on pathnames and directories, see Chapter 17.

✔ For information on using the MORE command for viewing files, refer to the section "Looking at Files," in Chapter 2.

✔ A great way to view a README file is by using the DOS Editor, which is covered in Chapter 16.

Using Your New Software

After you run the install or setup program, you get to use new software. As a suggestion, after installing any new software, reset your computer. Press Ctrl+Alt+Delete or punch your computer's Reset button. (Some installation programs may do this part automatically.)

Do not reset your computer if you're using Windows! In that case, just close the DOS prompt window and start it up again to begin using your software.

To use the new program, type its name at the DOS prompt. The program's name should be in the manual or on a quick-reference card. (If nothing happens, see the section "Where Is My Program?" in Chapter 21.)

You're doing this step just to make sure that the program works as advertised. If something doesn't work, don't be too quick to blame yourself. Programs have bugs. Keep in mind that the features of a new program aren't immediately obvious.

If anything out of the ordinary happens, do the following: Check with your computer supervisor or local computer guru. Check with the software developer (its help number should be listed somewhere in the manual or in the material that came with it). Finally, you can check with your dealer. Although dealers try to be helpful, it's impossible for them to know the details of every piece of software they sell. They can, however, replace defective disks for you.

- ✔ For information on resetting, refer to the section "Resetting," in Chapter 1.
- ✔ Running programs (in a general sense) is covered in the section "Running a Program," in Chapter 2.

Running and Using Software

Using software to get work done is why, unfortunately, we need computers. Using software involves finding out about its quirks, however. Because that takes time, my first suggestion for finding out how to use any new software is to give yourself plenty of time.

Sadly, in today's rush-rush way of doing everything, time isn't that easy to come by. It's a big pain when the boss sends you down to the software store expecting you to come back and create something wonderful before the end of the day. In the real world, that's just not possible (not even if you're an "expert").

Most software comes with a workbook or a tutorial for you to follow. This series of self-guided lessons tells you how to use the product. It also tells you about the program's basic features and how they work.

I highly recommend going through the tutorials. Follow the directions on your screen. If you notice anything interesting, write it down in the tutorial booklet and flag that page.

Granted, some tutorials are really dumb. Don't hesitate to bail out of one if you're bored or confused. You can also take classes on using software, though they may bore you, too. Most people do, however, understand the program much better after completing the tutorial.

After doing the tutorial, play with the software. Make something. Try saving something to disk. Try printing. Then quit. Those are the basic few steps you should take when you're using any software program. Get to know it, and then expand your knowledge from there as required.

If you feel bold, you can take a look at the manual. Who am I fooling? Computer manuals are awful. Sometimes they help, especially if the manual is a reference, enabling you to quickly thumb to what you want, read it, and then get right back out (like this book). Never read the manual all the way through.

✔ Some businesses may have their own training classes that show you the basics of using the in-house software. Take copious notes. Keep a little book for yourself with instructions on how to do what. Take notes whenever someone shows you something. Don't try to find out anything; just note what's done so that you don't have to make a call if the situation arises again.

✔ If your computer is set up by using a menu system, your program probably has been added to the menu. Furthermore, additional automation may be offered in the form of *macros* or *templates*. These features simplify the operation of the program and make your life a heck of a lot easier (see the section "Black Box Program Rules," in Chapter 15).

Updating Your Software

Occasionally, your computer or your software may be updated. For computer updates, you may have to make modifications to your program, by telling it about the new hardware just installed.

For example, if Those In Charge change printers, add a network or new monitor, give you a mouse, or change anything else on your computer, you should ask your favorite computer wizard whether any of your software needs to be alerted to the modifications. Then, let the computer wizard make those changes.

Computer software is also updated frequently. New *versions* come out all the time. If you fill in your registration card, you're alerted to the new version and what it has to offer. Then, for a nominal or outrageous fee, you can order the new version. My advice: Order the update only if it has features or makes modifications you desperately need. Otherwise, if the current version is doing the job, don't bother.

✔ If you notice nothing different after changing hardware (all your programs run), you have no need to update anything. Just keep on (ugh) working.

✔ If you don't bother updating your software for several years, you may miss out on something. After a time, software developers stop supporting older versions of their programs, books about the subject go out of print, and it gets harder to find help. When that happens, you have to buy the new version.

About the Darn Command Formats

Whenever you see a DOS command listed in a book or manual, you often see its *command format*. It's perhaps the most cryptic part about using DOS. The command format tells you what to type, what's optional, what's either/or-ish, and what everything does. If street signs worked this way, people would ignore them.

The command format has three parts, though they're not separate:

- ✔ Requirements
- ✔ Options
- ✔ Switches

The *requirements* are items you must type at the command line. Take the FORMAT command. Here's what its command format may look like:

```
FORMAT drive:
```

FORMAT is the name of the command. It's required. Drive (and a colon) is also required, but it's in italics. The italics mean that you must type something there — something that means "drive" — what you type is up to you. In this example, *drive* means to put a drive letter (and a colon) there. This info would be explained in the command's description: Drive is required and indicates a disk drive letter. For drive, you would substitute A: or B:.

The following command contains an *option:*

```
VOL [drive:]
```

The VOL command is required. Whenever you see square brackets, however, it means that what comes between them is optional. In this example, drive (and a colon) appears in brackets, meaning that a drive letter (and a colon) is optional after the VOL command. Again, this stuff would be explained in the definition that follows the command format. It also explains what happens if you don't specify the option.

Note that you do not specify the brackets when you type the command at the DOS prompt. Brackets are only a visual clue in the command format. Here's an example:

```
VOL B:
```

In this example, the volume label of the disk in drive B will be displayed. B: is the optional [drive:] part of the command, as specified in the preceding example (and without the brackets).

Here is a command format for the DEL command, which deletes files:

```
DEL filename [/P]
```

DEL and filename are both required. Filename indicates the name of the file you want to delete, which can be any file on your disk. The /P (slash-P) is a *switch,* and it's optional, appearing in brackets. What /P does and why you would want to list it are listed in the instructions.

All switches start with either a slash or a dash, and most of them are optional. The typical switch is a single letter, and it can be either upper- or lowercase. Some switches are more than one letter, and some have options. Here's an example:

```
[/D=drive:]
```

That whole whatchamacallit is optional. The switch (/D) is followed by an equal sign and drive, which indicates that you must specify a disk drive letter (and a colon) in that spot. So /D is optional, although if you use it, you have to fill in a disk drive letter.

Finally, you get into optional either/or situations, in which you must specify either one switch or the other. These options are written as follows:

```
[ON|OFF]
```

In this example, the item is optional because it's in brackets. If you specify it, you must either use ON or OFF, not both. The vertical bar or pipe character (|) tells you to pick one or the other if you want this option.

✔ These command formats are used in the official DOS manual as well as in the DOS 6 online "help." For more information about online help, see Chapter 22.

✔ When a command requires a filename, it's often written in this format:

```
[drive:][path]filename
```

✔ The filename part is required, although specifying a drive letter (the drive-colon) or a path or both is optional. The drive enables you to specify on which drive the file lives; the path is used to identify the file's subdirectory. More information about paths is in Chapter 17.

Chapter 15

Software Mystery Grab Bag

*L*et's face it: There are two kinds of people in the world: computer enthusiasts and the rest of us. The computer enthusiasts use many different programs and love finding out how to use new ones. The rest of us have one, maybe two, programs we use often enough to feel comfortable with, and we sincerely hope that we never have to deal with a third.

If you ever do end up using a third (or fourth or . . . gulp), you should probably consider using some type of computer shell or menu system. It's a special program that takes care of running your computer. Like a seashell protects a soft, gooey underwater creature from being eaten by larger, predatory creatures, the computer shell protects you from DOS. No DOS prompt. No commands to memorize. Just press A for WordPerfect, and you're on your way.

This chapter discusses the use of DOS menu systems and shells. It also covers black box programs, which are things (macros, menu systems, dBASE, and batch files, for example) that someone else has set up for you to use on your computer. In case of disaster, always consult your guru first. Otherwise, turn here for help.

Black Box Program Rules

Before I begin with the popular programs, I need to explain what a black box program is.

A *black box program* is a program that runs itself so that you, the user, don't have to know how it works. The details are concealed inside a "black box."

For example, dBASE is a program that can run other programs for you, such as order entry, a customer list, or any number of database programs. These types of programs usually prompt you through the things you're supposed to do. Microsoft Windows (the original, up to version 3.11) is a single program that can run a number of other programs. Lesser kinds of programs, usually called *menu systems,* run all the programs on your computer from one handy menu. These are all black box programs, doing the DOS dirty work for you while you sit back and get work done.

What follows are rules for using a black box program, particularly those that supersede rules I've already pounded into your head elsewhere in this book. You can use these general rules in any black box program to get out of trouble.

Basic Black Box Information

Fill in the information in this section if you're using a black box program on your PC. If you don't know the answers, get the answers; force them from your PC guru at gunpoint, if necessary. (I'm not one to advocate the use of violence to get what's rightly yours, but this method has always worked for me.) Why get this information? Because when things go wrong, it helps you save yourself, maybe by looking in this book instead of having to wait for the guru to return from lunch or vacation.

Use the following information to locate the program if you ever "lose" it; see the section "Where Is My Program?" in Chapter 21 for your hunting license.

The formal name of your black box program: _____

How that name is pronounced: _____

The command you type to start your black box program: _____

Its drive and directory: _____

The following files are associated with the black box program, and you should never delete them:

Filename: **In English:**

_____   _____

_____   _____

_____   _____

_____   _____

_____   _____

Your guru's phone number: _____

Times when it's okay to call: _____

(Ask your guru that last question to be nice; feel free to call whenever you need him or her. Bring along a sack of Doritos, pizza rolls, or white chocolate almonds as a bribe.)

Note the names of programs you run. For example, in dBASE, you probably are running several "do" files. Write down their names here. If you're in Windows (whatever versions) you're running some programs that have *icons* (little pictures on the screen). Write down their names and what they do. The same holds true for whichever black box program you're running.

Program Name (Do File):   **What It Does:**

_____   _____

_____   _____

_____   _____

_____   _____

_____   _____

Exit from the black box program before turning off or resetting your computer. In a black box program, you can be at a DOS prompt that makes it look all right to reset or turn off your PC. However, that DOS prompt may just be part of the black box program — not a *real* DOS prompt.

If you're at a DOS prompt in a black box program, type the EXIT command:

```
C> EXIT
```

This action should return you to the black box program. From there, you should quit the black box program and return to the real DOS prompt. At that point, it's okay to reset or shut off your computer.

Using a Menu System

A *menu system* is a nifty little program that does away with the DOS prompt. (Well, as far as you're concerned, it's gone.) As long as someone nice has set things up, this kind of black box program comes right up when you start your PC. You see a menu of choices, each of which represents something you do on your PC:

A. Word processing

B. Lotus

C. Backup files

D. Crash the network

To select an item, press the proper letter or number key. It's that simple. You don't have to mess with DOS or remember commands. You do still have to know how to use your software.

✔ If you find yourself suddenly at the DOS prompt, try these two things to get back to your menu. First, type **EXIT** and press Enter:

```
C> EXIT
```

This action should return you to your menu program or to your word processor or other application. If not, try typing **MENU** and pressing Enter:

```
C> MENU
```

If this command doesn't work, then — and only as a last resort — reset your PC with Ctrl+Alt+Delete. If that doesn't work, call your guru. Chop some onions first so that you get more sympathy.

✔ Many popular menu programs are available. If you don't have one and find the notion intriguing, I suggest the product Direct Access, from Fifth Generation Systems. It's the DOS menu system everyone else tries to copy. (No, I don't get a kickback here; it's just worth recommending.)

✔ Even stolid old Windows is a menu system of sorts. Actually, Windows 3.11 is more of a shell because it doesn't really make things easier, just different.

Batch File Menu Systems

DOS has its own programming language — actually, two of them. First comes the QBASIC programming language, which you don't want to mess with. Then, it has the batch file programming language, which you may be curious about.

Batch files are nothing more than text files that contain DOS commands. DOS runs all the commands in the file one after the other, just as though you typed each line at the DOS prompt. The difference is that it all happens automatically. Also, you can use special DOS commands in the batch file, which makes it sort of programlike.

One of the advantages of a batch file program is that it's possible to create a home-brew menu system by using these batch files, plus a few magical flips of the wrist by a guru or other loving, yet knowledgeable, DOS user.

Here are the DOS batch file commands: CALL, CHOICE, ECHO, FOR, GOTO, IF, PAUSE, REM, and SHIFT.

dBASE — So Popular It's Scary

Often, you work on an application program that someone else has written in dBASE. Now, don't start chomping at your fingernails. dBASE, and other database programs similar to and better than it, is used to create PC software. That's its purpose — to provide a way to access information in a database. In fact, you may be using a program right now that was written in dBASE and not even know it.

If you're using a dBASE-like product, turn to this section whenever something goes wrong and you find yourself out of the prepared application, wishing that you knew how to get back in. On the other hand, you may need to use dBASE directly to look at your data or generate simple reports. I give you a few basic tips here.

(This discussion covers dBASE IV; if you can't find the Command Center and stuff like that, you probably have an older version, maybe dBASE III or even II. Most of the parts that don't refer to the Command Center work equally well in earlier versions, though. If you ask your programmer nicely, he or she can probably write in the equivalents in those earlier versions for you.)

Starting dBASE and running dBASE applications

If you're using an application (a program written in dBASE for you), the developer may have set it up to start automatically when you turn your computer on in the morning, or he or she may have given you explicit instructions for starting the program. If not, or if you somehow ended up at the DOS prompt (C>) and want to start dBASE, here's how.

You start dBASE by typing this command at the DOS prompt:

```
C> DBASE
```

If you're missing dBASE, it's usually found in the \DBASE subdirectory on drive C. Type

```
C> C:
```

and then

```
C> CD \DBASE
```

If you know the name of the prepared application, you can load it at the same time that you load dBASE; for example, to load a dBASE application called INVOICE, type

```
C> DBASE INVOICE
```

A logo screen and ominous-sounding licensing message are displayed as the program loads, demanding that you press Enter to accept the license. If you're using dBASE IV and you didn't specify the name of an application, you should next see the dBASE IV Control Center screen. If all you see is a blank screen with one line at the bottom and a single dot, don't panic. To get into the Control Center, type

```
ASSIST
```

To run an application from the dBASE IV Control Center, move the highlight to the application name in the Applications column and press Enter. When the prompt appears, asking whether you want to modify or run the application, choose Run.

What's the darn dot supposed to mean?

If you unexpectedly exit a dBASE application, you may find yourself not at the DOS prompt but at the *dBASE dot prompt,* perhaps the most horrid of any prompt in all of computerdom. To wit:

```
.
```

Yikes! That's just a period at the left of the screen with the blinking cursor next to it. No fun.

To run a prepared application for which you know the name (you made your programmer write it down for you earlier in this chapter, remember?), do this (suppose that the application name is INVOICE):

```
. DO INVOICE
```

The application loads, and you're back home.

dBASE IV database catalog

dBASE IV data and associated reports and applications are grouped into what is known as a *catalog.* When you start the Command Center, it opens the catalog that was in use the last time the program was run. To change catalogs, press Alt+C to activate the Catalog menu at the top of the screen. Choose the Use a Different Catalog option.

You can access the various data files, reports, and forms in the catalog by pressing the arrow keys to move the highlight to the item you're interested in and pressing Enter.

Canceling a command

The dBASE cancel key is Esc, which cancels almost any changes you make. The Esc key also backs you out of all menus and operations, such as browsing files or creating forms.

Undoing commands

When you're editing data in a form, you can undo changes to the data by choosing the Undo command from the Record menu, as long as you do it before moving to the next record. If you've already moved, you're out of luck — the changes are permanent.

The other thing you can undo in dBASE is record deletion. When you choose to delete a record, it's still there — the program just flags the data to signify that it's really not supposed to be there. Depending on how your copy of dBASE is set up, these marked records may disappear from your view of the data completely or they may show but indicate Del in the status line. Either way, you can undelete them with the Clear Deletion Mark option on the Record menu.

Getting help

You access online help in dBASE by pressing the F1 key. The help screen gives information about the particular operation you're working on at the time. You can use the window options to view related topics or a table of contents. When you're viewing the help table of contents, pressing F3 takes you to a more generalized list, and F4 displays a narrower group of topics.

General advice

The only thing you want to really be careful not to do in dBASE is something called *packing the database*. This action shows up as the menu option Erase Marked Records at various places in the system. Do not *ever* choose this option unless you know what you're doing. This process really erases the records that are only pretending to be erased when they're marked for deletion. After you choose this option, they are gone forever.

If you ever press the Esc key one too many times and end up back at the blank screen with the dot, remember to type **ASSIST** to get back to the dBASE IV Control Center. If you get to this point and really just want to get out of the program completely, type **QUIT**. *Never, never, never* exit dBASE by pressing Ctrl+Alt+Delete. dBASE files almost always get corrupted that way.

Chapter 16

Playing with the Editor

● ●

In This Chapter

▶ Using the DOS Editor

▶ Editing a file already on disk

▶ Printing a file

▶ Editing your CONFIG.SYS and AUTOEXEC.BAT files

● ●

*O*ne of the most useful tools available with DOS Version 5.0 and later is the Editor, which is called EDIT (because the word *Ed* was trademarked long ago by the *Mr. Ed* people). This program works like a word processor, enabling you to create and edit text files on disk. Although the Editor lacks the full-blown power of a major word processor, it does contain some nice features and can be used in a variety of situations when a word processor is just too clunky. For example, rumor has it that Elvis answers all his fan mail by using the DOS EDIT program.

This chapter covers the use of the DOS Editor program. It also contains information on editing your CONFIG.SYS and AUTOEXEC.BAT files. *What* these two files do is important, yet *how* they do it isn't crucial knowledge. How to edit the files, specifically the instructions for inserting special text, is described in this chapter in a — yes, I admit it — tutorial manner. You don't need to know why you're doing this; you don't even need to know what you're doing. When DOS tells you to edit your CONFIG.SYS or AUTOEXEC.BAT file, however, these instructions are the ones you need.

Using the DOS Editor

DOS comes with a program called EDIT. You use this program to create and edit text files on disk.

Although EDIT works like a word processor, it lacks many of the better features — such as fancy formatting, a spell checker, and the capability to create graphics. However, for just writing text — plain ol' English — EDIT is a fine and dandy thing to have. And you use it often in your DOS travels.

✔ A *text file* is a file that contains only text — no fancy information and no Greek or any other unorthodox or unreadable stuff. For example, files you can see by using the TYPE command are text files (see the section "Looking at Files," in Chapter 2).

✔ EDIT is available only with DOS Version 5.0 and later. You may need the QBasic program (QBASIC.EXE) installed with DOS for EDIT to work; if you delete QBASIC.EXE, you can't use the Editor.

Starting the Editor

You start the DOS Editor by typing **EDIT** at the DOS prompt:

```
C> EDIT
```

After pressing Enter, you see the Editor's start-up screen, similar to the one shown in Figure 16-1. Press the Esc key, and you're ready to start typing.

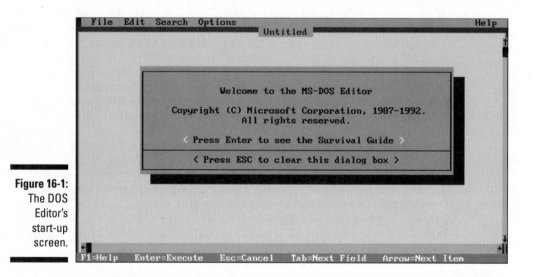

File   Edit   Search   Options   **Help**

Untitled

Welcome to the MS-DOS Editor

Copyright (C) Microsoft Corporation, 1987-1992.
All rights reserved.

‹ Press Enter to see the Survival Guide ›

‹ Press ESC to clear this dialog box ›

F1=Help   Enter=Execute   Esc=Cancel   Tab=Next Field   Arrow=Next Item

Figure 16-1:
The DOS
Editor's
start-up
screen.

✔ When you start the Editor with the EDIT command, you may see a box on-screen asking whether you want to use the Survival Guide, as shown in Figure 16-1. My advice is to press the Esc (Escape) key to skip it. If you press Enter, the Survival Guide appears, offering tips and such for using the Editor. Major yawner.

✔ Running DOS in Windows 95 or later does not display the Survival Guide. Instead, just start a-typin'.

✔ See the section "Editing text," later in this chapter, for tutorial typing tips.

✔ If you don't see the DOS Editor or you get a `bad command or file name` error message, it's time to contact someone else for help. Double-check the instructions here first. Also, make sure to tell the person that you've already tried to do it yourself. Even the most surly of computer wizards appreciates effort.

Starting the Editor to edit a file

If you know the name of the text file you want to edit, you can follow `EDIT` with that filename. For example, if you feel a burning desire to edit the text file BLORF.TXT, you type

```
C> EDIT BLORF.TXT
```

First comes `EDIT`, a space, and then the name of the text file you want to edit, `BLORF.TXT`, as shown in the preceding line.

If the file already exists, the Editor loads it from disk, displaying it on-screen and ready for editing. If the file doesn't exist, the Editor lets you create it from scratch. (Either way, no Survival Guide prompt — yeah!)

✔ Most text files end with the TXT extension. I use TXT when I create or save a text file because that part lets me know that a file is a text file. However, specifying a filename extension is optional when you load or save a file in the Editor. See Chapter 19 for more information about file-name extensions.

✔ If you do specify an extension on your text file, remember to specify it when you start the Editor.

✔ To quit the Editor, see the section "Quitting the Editor," later in this chapter.

✔ Another file to use with the Editor is README.TXT, the "read me" file included with most new software packages. You can easily view this type of file by using the Editor. Press PgUp or PgDn at your leisure or print the whole ding-dang-doodle.

Editing text

You use the Editor to either create a new file or edit a text file already on disk. This tutorial shows you how to create a new file on disk. Because you may be dry on ideas, I'm providing a sample file, though you should feel free to type anything you like (a list of suggestions is in the nearby sidebar "Suggestions for sample files to type").

Suggestions for sample files to type

Drumming up ideas for sample text files to type is the bane of the computer book author. I've seen some real losers in my time. To assist my fellow authors as well as budding DOS Editor enthusiasts, the following list contains some suggestions for li'l sample text files you can type. Only titles are offered; it's up to you to devise content.

Four famous-but-not-dead people I'd like to invite over for dinner

What clouds smell like

What if Bill Gates ran the afterlife?

Thoughts that Freud may have about the things I doodle when I talk on the phone

If I were in charge of building a VCR, what would I put on the knobs?

Why walking through a sandbox with wet socks on makes my skin crawl

Ten common household objects a two-year-old could stick in his ear

A promo for the new *Sports Illustrated* famous groin-injuries football video

Ten things you would find in an airplane lavatory

What Spam becomes after sitting unwrapped in the fridge for a week

Several convincing reasons that aliens would prefer to land in your state rather than anywhere else

Start by firing up the Editor to work with a sample file. The one I've created is called WORDS.TXT. Use the following DOS command to create the file WORDS.TXT in the Editor:

```
C> EDIT COLORS.TXT
```

Type the EDIT command, followed by a space and then the name of the file you want to edit, such as COLORS.TXT in this example. Press Enter.

If the COLORS.TXT file already exists, you see it on your screen. Otherwise, you have to type the file's contents with EDIT. The following is what I typed for my COLORS.TXT file:

```
Everyone's favorite colors
Jordan = Purple
Simon = Blue
Jonah = Red
Jeremiah = Green
Daddy = Brown
Mommy = Diamonds
```

Here are some general Editor typing and editing rules:

✔ Press Enter at the end of each line.

✔ No "word wrap" is available in the Editor.

✔ Press the Backspace key to back up and erase if you make a mistake.

✔ You can type long lines if you like, though they "scroll" to the right across the screen. Typing more than a screenful of text causes the Editor to scroll down.

✔ Lines of text in the Editor can be as long as 255 characters; the entire text file can be utterly huge — a size so boggling that you would have to be a pretty darned prolific writer to see the `Editor full` error message.

A list of Editor key commands, specifically those that move the cursor around, is shown in Table 16-1. Test out these commands. Press Ctrl+End to move to the end of your text, Ctrl+Home to move to the start, Ctrl+→ to move right a word, and Ctrl+← to move left — and so on. Play, play, play!

Table 16-1	Editor Key Commands
Key Command	**Function**
↑(Up arrow)	Moves the cursor up one line
↓(Down arrow)	Moves the cursor down one line
←(Left arrow)	Moves the cursor left (back) one character
→(Right arrow)	Moves the cursor right (forward) one character
PgUp	Moves up to the preceding page (screen)
PgDn	Moves down to the next page (screen)
Ctrl+←	Moves left one word
Ctrl+→	Moves right one word
Ctrl+↑	Scrolls the screen up one line
Ctrl+↓	Scrolls the screen down one line
Delete	Deletes current character
Backspace	Deletes preceding character
Insert	Switches between insert and overwrite editing modes
Ctrl+Home	Moves to beginning of file
Ctrl+End	Moves to end of file

✔ In addition to using the arrow-key commands shown in Table 16-1, you can refer to Table 10-1 for a list of other, bizarre key commands used in the Editor.

✔ You can also use the computer's mouse to position the cursor on-screen: Point the mouse where you want the cursor to be and click it once to move the cursor to that very spot.

✔ To save your all-important text file, refer to the section, "Saving Your Stuff to Disk," later in this chapter. ***Remember:*** Always save before you quit!

Playing with blocks

You can mark text in the Editor and treat that text as a single unit — a block, with which you can have lots of fun. For example, you can copy a block of text, cut and paste it, or just zap it all to kingdom come. You can mark a block in two ways:

✔ Use your mouse to *drag* over the text you want marked as a block.

✔ Hold down the Shift key and press the arrow keys to mark the block.

Either way, the marked block appears highlighted on-screen, typically shown with inverse text (such as blue text on a white background). After that block is highlighted, you can do the following things to it:

✔ Press Ctrl+C to copy the block, and then move the cursor to where you want to paste the copy and press Ctrl+V to paste it.

✔ Press Ctrl+X to cut the block, making it vanish from the screen. Move the cursor to where you want to paste the block, and then press Ctrl+V to paste it.

✔ In older versions of the Editor, Ctrl+Insert was the Copy command; Shift+Delete was the Cut command; and Shift+Insert was Paste.

✔ Delete a highlighted block by pressing the Delete key.

✔ It's much easier to access these commands from the Edit menu, by either clicking the mouse or pressing the Alt+E key combination. (See the section "Information about the Editor not worth reading," a little later in this chapter.)

Searching and replacing

To search for a specific tidbit of text in your document, press Alt+S,F. This move drops down the Search menu and chooses the Find command. A magical box then appears, in which you can type the text you're looking for. Type **Uganda** to find all references to that African nation. Press Enter to scope it out.

The Find command locates text from the cursor's position to the end of the document. If the text isn't found, Find then starts looking at the beginning of the document. If the text doesn't exist, a `Match not found` box is displayed. Sigh deeply and press the Esc key.

To find the next occurrence of your text tidbit, press the F3 key.

Information about the Editor not worth reading

The Editor uses drop-down menus to contain its commands. You activate the menu by pressing Alt and then the first letter of the menu you want to use. You can also press both the Alt key and the letter key at the same time; Alt+F drops down the File menu.

Each menu contains menu items, all of which pertain somehow to the title of the menu. For example, the File menu contains file commands. You select these commands by typing the highlighted letter in their name.

If you have a mouse, you can choose menu items with it. This method involves using a whole lot of mousy terms, which I don't really care to get into at this point in the book (but do get into in Chapter 10).

Printing with the Editor

To print your prose, use the Print command on the File menu. Start by making sure that your printer is turned on and all ready to print. Press Alt+F to get to the File menu; then press P for the Print command. You see a li'l box displayed on-screen. Press Enter to print your whole ding-dang file. Zip, zip, zip. It's done.

- If the printer isn't turned on or it's goofy or something, you see a `Device fault` error box. Fix the printer and try again.

- Chapter 11 has all the messy-messies on printing and using a printer.

Printing Any Text File without Having to Bother with the Editor

You can print any text file by using the DOS Editor to edit it and then choosing the Print command as described in the preceding section. You can also print any file at the handy DOS prompt by using this command:

```
C> COPY WORDS.TXT PRN
```

Yes, it's the typical COPY command, which in this case is used to print the text file WORDS.TXT. First comes COPY, a space, and then the name of the file you want to print. Follow the file's name with another space and then PRN. Make sure that your printer is on and ready to print, and then press Enter.

✔ You can use the COPY-PRN command to print any text file on disk, not just those created by the Editor. You can view these same files with the TYPE command. Refer to the section "Looking at Files," in Chapter 2.

✔ If you have a laser printer, you probably need to eject the page manually to see your work. Refer to the section "Forcing a Page Out," in Chapter 11, for more information.

✔ If the printer isn't ready to print (such as when you forget to turn it on), you probably see a Write fault error writing device PRN error. Gadzooks! Turn the printer on and carefully press **R.** That should do the trick. If not, press **A** and you're safely back at the DOS prompt. (Refer to Chapter 11 for printer help.)

Saving Your Stuff to Disk

Before you quit the Editor, you need to save your file back to disk. If you don't, all that work and your many precious words are not saved for posterity.

To save your stuff, press and release the Alt key and then press **F.** This action *drops down* the File menu at the top of the screen.

Press **S** to save the file.

If you're editing a new file, a Save box-thing appears, in which you can type the name of the file you want to save. Type as many as eight characters; be sure to use something memorable. Press Enter to save the file to disk.

✔ The file you save to disk is a text file, which means that it contains readable text as opposed to unfathomable stuff or information only the computer can digest.

> ✔ The Editor does not automatically give your file a TXT extension. You have to type it in the Save box if you want your files to end in TXT.

> ✔ See Chapter 19 for more information about naming files.

> ✔ If a box appears proclaiming that the file already exists, press **N** and select a different name. If you press **Y**, you overwrite the file that's already on disk. If that's what you want, okay. Otherwise, select another name because you may not be certain of what you're overwriting.

> ✔ Other application programs, text editors, and word processors can easily read the text files you create by using the DOS Editor. Unfortunately, the Editor can deal with only basic, no-frills text files. You cannot edit a document from your word processor by using the Editor unless you save it first in the *plain text, DOS text,* or *ASCII* format.

Quitting the Editor

You should quit the Editor only after saving your file to disk; refer to the preceding section for the details about this operation. After the file is saved, you quit the Editor so that you can return to DOS and spend more time enjoying life at the DOS prompt.

To quit the Editor, press and release the Alt key, and then press **F**. This action drops down the File menu.

Press **X** to select the Exit item. This action quits the Editor and returns you to the safe-but-not-warm-and-fuzzy DOS prompt.

> ✔ If you have changed the text in this session and haven't saved your file before quitting, a message box or window appears asking whether you want to save. Press **Y** in that instance; follow the steps listed in the preceding section about saving a file.

> ✔ Never, ever "quit" the Editor by pressing Ctrl+Alt+Delete or your PC's reset button.

"It Tells Me to Edit My CONFIG.SYS or AUTOEXEC.BAT File!"

One of the most puzzling DOS wild goose chases happens when a program says Put the following into your config.sys file or Edit your autoexec.bat file and add the following. To carry out these instructions, you're told to refer to your DOS manual. The DOS manual, on the other hand, says to refer to your application's manual. Herein we have the rumblings of any great bureaucracy: confusion and consistency in equal amounts.

Before diving into this stuff, you should know two things: First, you should always know what it is that you're adding to CONFIG.SYS or AUTOEXEC.BAT. The exact line of text you need to add should be specified somewhere. Never edit these files without a purpose.

Second, use this tutorial only as a last resort or when no other help is around. Especially in a business situation, someone should be in charge of the computers, and they should be updating these two important files. If you're at home or no one else is around to help, this section is where you turn. Beware: This stuff is funky.

You have no need to edit or update the CONFIG.SYS or AUTOEXEC.BAT files if you're running Windows 95 or later.

Hunting down the files

To get at CONFIG.SYS or AUTOEXEC.BAT, you must log to the root directory of your hard drive. Type this command:

```
C> C:
```

Press Enter. You're logging to drive C. Now type

```
C> CD \
```

That's CD, followed by a space and the *backslash* character (\) — *not* the forward slash (/).

The two commands you use here ensure that you're logged to the root directory of drive C, your boot disk. You're now ready to edit either CONFIG.SYS or AUTOEXEC.BAT. The next step is to determine which *text editor* you have.

> ✔ If you want to make a duplicate, safety copy of the file you're editing, refer to the section "Duplicating a File," in Chapter 4.
>
> ✔ For more information about logging, refer to the sections "Changing Drives" and "Changing Directories," in Chapter 2.
>
> ✔ The CD command is covered in Chapter 17, in the sections "Current Directory" and "Changing Directories."

Editing the file

If the instructions tell you to edit your CONFIG.SYS file, type

```
C> EDIT CONFIG.SYS
```

That's EDIT followed by a space and then CONFIG.SYS, which is the name of
the file you want to edit. This command starts the DOS Editor — the program
that edits files on disk.

If you're told to edit your AUTOEXEC.BAT file, substitute AUTOEXEC.BAT
for CONFIG.SYS:

```
C> EDIT AUTOEXEC.BAT
```

After pressing Enter, the DOS Editor appears on your screen. It looks something like Figure 16-2.

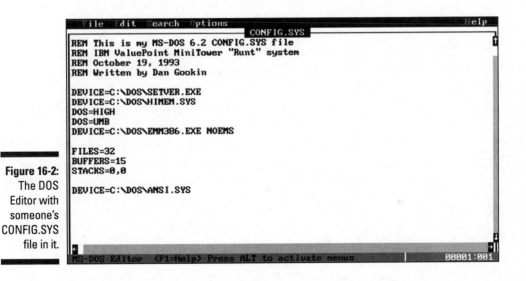

Figure 16-2:
The DOS
Editor with
someone's
CONFIG.SYS
file in it.

```
 File  Edit  Search  Options                                    Help
                              ┌─────────────┐
                              │ CONFIG.SYS  │
REM This is my MS-DOS 6.2 CONFIG.SYS file
REM IBM ValuePoint MiniTower "Runt" system
REM October 19, 1993
REM Written by Dan Gookin

DEVICE=C:\DOS\SETVER.EXE
DEVICE=C:\DOS\HIMEM.SYS
DOS=HIGH
DOS=UMB
DEVICE=C:\DOS\EMM386.EXE NOEMS

FILES=32
BUFFERS=15
STACKS=0,0

DEVICE=C:\DOS\ANSI.SYS



MS-DOS Editor   <F1=Help> Press ALT to activate menus           00001:001
```

Adding the new line

Because I'm not making any assumptions here, put the new line at the end of
the document, way down toward the bottom. If your instructions explicitly
tell you where to put the new line, follow them as best you can — if the
instructions say to put the line at the very tippy top, for example, do that.

To add the new line at the end of the file (which is where it goes if the instructions aren't specific), press Ctrl+End: Press and hold the Ctrl (Control) key and then press the End key. Release both keys. This action moves you to the last line in the file. (It doesn't matter which Ctrl or End key you use.) Then press Enter.

To add the new line at the start of the file, you . . . hey! You're already at the start of the file. Fancy that. (Press Ctrl+Home to move there if you aren't there already.)

Now type the line you need to add. For example, if you're adding the PROMPT command to AUTOEXEC.BAT, you type that command. If you're adding a command to CONFIG.SYS, type that command too.

After you enter the exact text of the command, double-check your work. Make sure that you typed exactly what you should have. After that's done, press Enter.

- ✔ The Ctrl and End key combination is often written as Ctrl+End. Refer to the section "Alt+S Means What?" in Chapter 10, for more information about key combinations.

- ✔ The first line of a document is called the "top," or the "beginning." If your manual says to add a line at the top of a document, you put that line first.

- ✔ The last line of a document is the "bottom," or "end."

- ✔ If you make a mistake while you're typing, press the Backspace key to back up and erase.

- ✔ Sometimes, commands in CONFIG.SYS require a full pathname in order to work properly. See the section "What Is a Pathname?" in Chapter 17, for information about pathnames.

Saving and quitting

Before saving your CONFIG.SYS or AUTOEXEC.BAT file back to disk, first double-check your work. Make sure that you typed everything exactly and that no stray characters appear unexpectedly. (This process requires a trained eye because, I admit, CONFIG.SYS and AUTOEXEC.BAT look like they have lots of sneeze marks in them.)

To save the file, press Alt+F to drop down the File menu. Press **S** to save the file. This action saves the file on disk, making your changes permanent.

To quit the Editor and return to DOS, press Alt+F to drop down the File menu again. Press **X** to exit and return to DOS.

> ✔ You can find additional information on saving and quitting earlier in this chapter.

Resetting

You're back at the DOS prompt, ready to continue working. Congratulations — your CONFIG.SYS or AUTOEXEC.BAT file is updated. Whew! Now comes the scary part.

You must reset your computer to see the results of any changes you've made to these files. This statement is true for only AUTOEXEC.BAT and CONFIG.SYS; any other file you edit or program you run doesn't require a reset. (I told you that this subject is funky.)

> ✔ You reset by pressing Ctrl+Alt+Delete or punching that big, red button on your PC. Refer to the "Resetting" section, in Chapter 1, if you feel anxious about doing it.

> ✔ Oftentimes, it's a good idea to run the MemMaker memory-management program after you update either CONFIG.SYS or AUTOEXEC.BAT. Refer to Chapter 8 for information about running DOS MemMaker.

> ✔ Whenever you add (or remove) a line from your CONFIG.SYS or AUTOEXEC.BAT file, you see (or miss) extra text displayed every time your PC starts.

> ✔ If you see any errors when the computer restarts, it means that you may have typed something incorrectly. Go through these steps again and recheck your work. Make sure that what you typed is exactly what was required. Then call for help.

Mired in the Past with EDLIN

If you have an old, old version of DOS — before DOS 5 — boy, do I feel sorry for you. You don't have access to the fancy Editor program. Instead, you're stuck with using DOS's old line editor, EDLIN. It's just the worst example of a text editor in the history of DOS. This program was written in 1981 — back when the only people using computers were puffy and pale Neanderthal nerds just rising from the primordial mud swamps of the slide-rule age. It makes me shudder.

Editing Your CONFIG.SYS or AUTOEXEC.BAT File with EDLIN

Follow EDLIN with the name of the file you want to edit. For example, when you're told to edit your CONFIG.SYS file, type

```
C:\> EDLIN CONFIG.SYS
```

To edit your AUTOEXEC.BAT file, substitute `AUTOEXEC.BAT` for `CONFIG.SYS`. After pressing Enter, you see

```
End of input file *
```

Yoikle! I shudder to think of the user hostility this program harbors. You see `End of input file`, which means God knows what, and then an asterisk on the next line. Is this like shaking hands with a snake or what?

To add a new line of text to a file, such as CONFIG.SYS or AUTOEXEC.BAT, you have to "move" to the end of the file. You do it by using the #I command. At the asterisk prompt, type a pound sign (#) and the letter **I** (no spaces!):

```
*#I
```

Press Enter. You see something like

```
13:*
```

You see a number, a colon, and an asterisk. The number is a line number, the last line in the file. The asterisk is EDLIN's friendly prompt. And no, you don't see anything on-screen. (Ugly editor. Ugly.)

Type the line you need to add. For example, if you're adding the PROMPT command to AUTOEXEC.BAT, you type that command. If you're adding a command to CONFIG.SYS, you type that as well.

After you enter the exact text of the command, double-check your work.

After you've made sure that everything has been typed correctly, press Enter. You see something like

```
14:*
```

The number is one higher than the new line you entered. At this prompt, press Ctrl+C: Press and hold the Ctrl (Control) key and, with that key held down, type a **C**. Release both keys. You see ^C displayed and then the main asterisk prompt two lines down.

You now have to save the edited file back to disk. In EDLIN, you do it by quitting the program with the **E** command, which stands for "Exit back to DOS." (I prefer that it stand for "Enough!")

Press **E** and then press Enter. Soon, you see the happy DOS prompt displayed.

✔ Note that EDLIN automatically makes a backup file: CONFIG.BAK for CONFIG.SYS or AUTOEXEC.BAK for AUTOEXEC.BAT. These files contain the original text you edited.

✔ If you've totally screwed up, you can quit EDLIN by pressing Q. EDLIN asks whether you want to `Abort edit?` Press **Y** to return to DOS and try again — if you dare!

Chapter 17

The Hard Drive: Where You Store Stuff

I've always been fascinated by hard disk management. Why isn't it *easy* disk management? Computers are supposed to make life easier, not harder. Yet computer nerds are fascinated by *hard* disk management. They've even come up with a whole row of verbal hurdles to leap over for anyone who attempts to understand hard disk management. Even considering that it's a hard disk you're managing, the subject could easily be called hard hard-disk management. Ugh.

All kidding aside, hard disk management is simply the way you use files on a hard drive. This concept involves some organization, and that's where the funky terms come into play. This chapter describes the ugly terms you encounter when you use a hard drive, what they mean, and why the heck you would ever want to use them. This stuff is really important. If you remember only one thing — how to find your way around a hard disk — it's worth the price of this book.

What Is a Subdirectory?

A *subdirectory* is workspace on a disk. It's almost like a disk within a disk. You can copy files and programs into a subdirectory or workspace, and you can use DOS commands. The advantage to subdirectories is that you can store information in a subdirectory and keep it separate from other files on the same disk. That keeps the disk from getting file-messy.

Any disk can have subdirectories, though they're used primarily on hard drives to keep files separate and your programs organized. Rather than let you suffer through a hard drive with bazillions of files all in one place, subdirectories enable you to organize everything by placing information in separate areas.

✔ Subdirectories could be called just *directories*. The prefix *sub* means "under," just as submarine means any large naval vessel a marine is standing on. All the workspaces on a disk are really directories. However, when you refer to one directory in relation to another, the term *subdirectory* is used.

✔ A subdirectory is the same thing as a *folder* in Windows 95 and Windows 98 terminology.

✔ If you want to create a directory to keep some of your files separate from other files, see the section "How to Name a Directory (The MD Command)," in Chapter 19.

✔ All the directories on your disk create or are organized into what's called a *tree structure*. For information, see the section "The Tree Structure," later in this chapter.

The Root Directory

Every disk you use under DOS has one main directory, called the *root directory*. The root directory (often just called *the root*) exists on all DOS disks; it happens naturally, created when you first format the disk.

The symbol for the root directory is the single backslash (\). DOS uses this abbreviation — shorthand — in reference to the root directory. This symbol also plays an important role in the *pathname*, which is covered later in this chapter.

Additional directories on a disk are subdirectories under the root directory. They branch off the root like branches of a tree. In fact, if you map out the directories on a disk and draw lines between each subdirectory, it looks like a family tree of sorts, as shown in Figure 17-1.

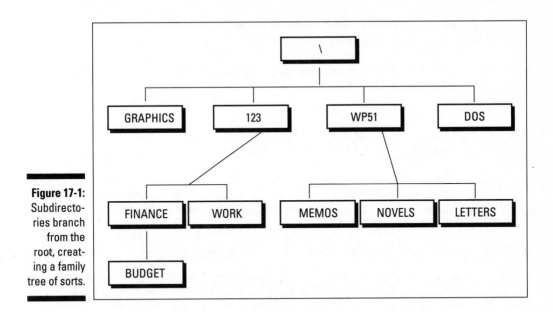

Figure 17-1:
Subdirecto-
ries branch
from the
root, creat-
ing a family
tree of sorts.

✔ The FORMAT command is used to prepare disks for use under DOS. In the formatting process, FORMAT also creates the root directory. For more information, refer to the section "Formatting a Disk," in Chapter 13.

✔ Whenever you're using a disk, you're *logged to,* or currently using, a directory on that disk. To change to another subdirectory, see the section "Changing Directories," later in this chapter; to change to another disk, refer to the section "Changing Drives," in Chapter 2. To see which directory you're currently logged to, see the section "Current Directory," later in this chapter.

You Are Not Required to Know This Stuff

Subdirectories are often called *child* directories. From a subdirectory's point of view, it has a *parent* directory. In Figure 17-1, for example, DOS is a subdirectory of the root directory (\ ). DOS is the root directory's child directory. The root directory is the parent of the DOS directory.

If you were logged to, or using, the 123 directory shown in Figure 17-1, its parent directory would be the root. The 123 directory also has two child directories — or two subdirectories — named FINANCE and WORK.

The visual representation shown in Figure 17-1 is only for your head; you *see* nothing of the sort as you use your computer. However, it's a good visual representation of the relationships between various directories on a disk. The TREE command, covered later in this chapter, enables you to see the representation in a different format.

That Funny <DIR> Thing

To find a subdirectory on a disk, you use the DIR command. Directories are listed there, along with other files. The way you identify a directory name is by the `<DIR>` thing shown after its name (where other files would list their file size in bytes).

For example, consider this output from the DIR command:

```
Volume in drive C is DOS HAPPY
Volume Serial Number is 16CE-9B67
Directory of C:\
123      <DIR>          03-18-96    9:33p
COMM     <DIR>          08-07-96    9:37p
DOS      <DIR>          09-20-97   10:52p
GAMES    <DIR>          09-22-97    5:18p
WP60     <DIR>          09-21-97    5:12p
AUTOEXEC BAT    574     09-05-97   10:04a
COMMAND  COM 54,928     08-11-93    6:20a
CONFIG   SYS    464     07-25-97   10:20a
WINA20   386  9,349     08-11-93    6:20a
         9 file(s)  65,315  bytes
        36,468,736  bytes free
```

The "files" 123, COMM, DOS, GAMES, and WP60 are actually directories on disk. At the top of the output in this example, `Directory of C:\` tells you that you're looking at a directory of drive C (that's the `C:`), the root directory (shown by the backslash). The `<DIR>` entries in the listing are all subdirectories of the root directory.

- ✔ Subdirectories appear in the DIR command's listing because they're part of your disk, just like files. In fact, directories are named just like files and can even have an extension like a file. For more information (if you're curious), see the section "How to Name a Directory (The MD Command)," in Chapter 19.

- ✔ For more information on the DIR command, refer to the section "DIR Command," in Chapter 2.

- ✔ For information about finding a lost directory on disk, see the section "Finding a Lost Subdirectory," in Chapter 19.

- ✔ The `C:\` is actually a pathname.

> ✔ Commas in big numbers appear only if you have MS-DOS 6.2 or later.
> Early versions of DOS don't use commas, which is just DOS's attempt to
> overwhelm you with large values.

What Is a Pathname?

A pathname is like a long filename. A filename is a name given only to a file; if
you're clever with eight characters, it also tells you something about the file's
contents. A *pathname,* on the other hand, tells you where a file is located — it
tells you on which disk the file has been saved and in which subdirectory.

A file's pathname is like a path to the file. It tells you how to get to a specific
file or subdirectory — an exact location. For example, the following is a pathname, a full pathname to a specific file on disk:

```
C:\WORK\CHAP12.DOC
```

The filename CHAP12.DOC identifies a file on a disk. In this example, the full
pathname says that it's a file on drive C, as shown by the `C:` at the beginning.
Furthermore, the file CHAP12.DOC is located in the WORK subdirectory. The
backslashes (\ ) in the pathname are provided as separating elements, to keep
the drive letter, subdirectories, and filename from running into each other.

This example breaks down as follows:

`C:`	Drive C
`C:\`	The root directory
`C:\WORK`	The WORK subdirectory
`C:\WORK\CHAP12.DOC`	The file CHAP12.DOC and its full pathname

Pathnames don't always have to end with a filename. They can also be used
to identify a subdirectory located somewhere on a disk. In that case, the
pathname tells you which drive it's on and all its parent directories on up to
the root. For example, consider this pathname:

```
C:\WP60\DATA
```

To break this line down, you have

`C:`	The drive letter, C
`C:\`	The root directory of drive C
`C:\WP60`	The WP60 subdirectory on drive C, a subdirectory of the root
`C:\WP60\DATA`	The DATA subdirectory under the WP60 directory

✔ The backslash is used as both a symbol for the root directory and a separator. A backslash always separates subdirectories from each other. A pathname has no spaces.

✔ A pathname that starts with a drive letter is called a *full pathname*. (Pathnames don't always need the drive letter.)

✔ The drive letter is optional in a pathname. However, I recommend using it because it's more specific.

✔ When you use the CD command by itself to locate the current directory, what it returns is a pathname; see the next section.

Current Directory

To find out which directory you're logged to, or using, type the CD command:

```
C> CD
```

The directory you're using is displayed on the following line. (What you see is a pathname of the current directory.) You can change to any other subdirectory on the same drive by using the CD command followed by that directory's pathname. See the following section for the specifics.

✔ CD has a longer form, CHDIR. Although both do the same thing, CD is quicker to type (and you can say "current directory" or "change directory" in your head rather than "chiddur").

✔ For more information about changing drives, refer to the section "Changing Drives," in Chapter 2.

✔ For more information about pathnames, refer to the section "What Is a Pathname?" earlier in this chapter.

✔ The PROMPT command can be used to tell you the current directory at all times. Refer to the section "Prompt Styles of the Rich and Famous," in Chapter 3.

Technical Background Junk about Disks and Drives

Whenever you use a computer, you're using or attached to some specific disk drive. Though your system may have several drives, you're using only one of them at a time. That drive is said to be the *currently logged drive*. (In computer lingo, "logged" means "using.") The same holds true with directories on a disk: You can use — or be logged to — only one directory at a time.

When you first use a disk, you're automatically logged to its root directory, the main directory on disk. After you've been using the computer for a while, you probably wind up elsewhere on the disk, such as in some sub-directory somewhere. To find out the pathname of that subdirectory, use the CD command as just described.

Changing Directories

To change to another directory, type the CD (Change Directory) command followed by the pathname of the directory to which you want to change. In computer jargon, this action *logs* you to that new directory.

Suppose that you want to change to the root directory. Type

```
C> CD \
```

That's the CD command, followed by a space and the root directory's name or symbol, the backslash.

To change to the \WP60 subdirectory, type

```
C> CD \WP60
```

Try to type a pathname that includes the root directory. This type of path-name always starts with a backslash, which indicates the root. If you know the full pathname of the directory, type it. Otherwise, you can refer to the section "Finding a Lost Subdirectory," in Chapter 19, to see about finding lost directories.

You can use the DIR command to find the name of a subdirectory to log to. If you find a name, a full pathname isn't needed. For example, if you use the DIR command and see the DATA directory (marked by <DIR> in the directory list-ing), you can log to (use) it by typing

```
C> CD DATA
```

Because DATA is a subdirectory, or child, of the current directory, you don't need to specify a full pathname.

You can take another shortcut to log to the parent directory:

```
C> CD ..
```

The dot-dot is an abbreviation for the parent directory — no matter where you are. This method is much quicker than typing the full pathname for the parent directory.

✔ You cannot use the CD command to change to a subdirectory on another drive. You must first log to that drive and then use the CD command. Refer to the section "Changing Drives," in Chapter 2, to find out how to log to another drive.

✔ If you see an `Invalid directory` error message, you didn't type a full pathname or you mistyped something. You may also not be logged to the proper drive. See the section "Finding a Lost Subdirectory," in Chapter 19.

✔ You can also use the CHDIR command, the longer form of the CD command. CHDIR stands for Change Directory, supposedly.

✔ Refer to the section "What Is a Pathname?" earlier in this chapter, for information about pathnames.

The Tree Structure

All the subdirectories on a disk make for a fairly complex arrangement. I know of no one, nerd or non-nerd, who actually knows exactly what's where on his or her system. To find out — to get a view of the big picture — you use the TREE command.

The TREE command is no longer available with Windows 95 and later. (And I bet that you thought Microsoft was against cutting down trees.)

Type this command:

```
C> TREE C:\
```

That's the `TREE` command, a space, C, a colon, and a backslash character. The `TREE` command is followed by a pathname; `C:\` means drive C's root directory. Press Enter, and the TREE command displays a graphical representation of your tree structure, how your subdirectories are organized for drive C. Early versions of DOS don't have graphical trees; they use a confusing text display instead.

The display scrolls off the screen for a time. If you want to pause the display, press the Ctrl+S key combination; to continue, press Ctrl+S again. You can also use this command:

```
C> TREE C:\ | MORE
```

That's the same command as before, followed by a space, the pipe character (|), another space, and the word `MORE`. This command inserts an automatic *more prompt* at the bottom of each screen. You press the spacebar to look at the next screen.

If you want to print a copy of the output, turn on your printer and type

```
C> TREE C:\ > PRN
```

That's the same TREE command described in the preceding example, a space, a greater-than symbol (>), another space, and the word PRN. Press Enter. If the printed output looks gross, try this variation of the command:

```
C> TREE C:\ /A > PRN
```

That's a slash-A in the middle of the command, surrounded by a space on each side. (As you make more demands on DOS, it gets more cryptic. At least your printed copy doesn't look so gross, though.) For more information about using a printer, refer to Chapter 11.

 For more information about Ctrl+S, refer to the section "Ctrl+S and the Pause Key," in Chapter 10.

"Is My Disk Okay?"

Computer disks are nothing like melons. You can't thump them to hear whether they're ripe. You can't see any soft spots. And you can't slice into them to find a soupy-black mush of maggots to realize that a disk is rotten. Instead, DOS gives you some disk-prodding tools that do the thumping, looking, and slicing for you — plus a bit of repair.

For almost everyone, the DOS disk fixer-upper tool is CHKDSK, the Check Disk command. CHKDSK was replaced by the ScanDisk command starting with DOS Version 6.2. This section sorts out the fruit.

Do not run CHKDSK or even ScanDisk from a DOS prompt in Windows, any version. Instead, use the Windows version of ScanDisk.

Checking the disk (the CHKDSK command)

To check out a disk, hard or floppy, by using CHKDSK, type **CHKDSK** at the DOS prompt, press Enter, and prepare to be overwhelmed:

```
C> CHKDSK
```

After pressing Enter, you see something like this:

```
Volume DOS HAPPY created 09-21-1984 1:26p
Volume Serial Number is 16CE-9B67
42366976 bytes total disk space
       73728 bytes in 2 hidden files
  110592 bytes in 52 directories
25837568 bytes in 879 user files
16345088 bytes available on disk
     2048 bytes in each allocation unit
        20687 total allocation units on disk
         7981 available allocation units on disk
  655360 total bytes memory
  637984 bytes free
```

Four chunks of information are listed. The first is trivia about your disk. The second, with five items, is more important. The first value tells you the size of your disk. It says that you have 42,366,976 bytes of *total disk space.* This value means that the drive holds about 40MB of stuff. The last value tells you how much space you have left. That's 16,345,088 bytes *available on disk,* which means that the drive has about 16MB of unused storage.

The third section is useless, with *allocation unit* sounding like something the government would say about every $35 billion it spends.

The final section tells you how much memory your computer has and how much is available for use by programs.

CHKDSK works on only one drive at a time. To use CHKDSK on another drive, first log to that drive and then run CHKDSK. Refer to the section "Changing Drives," in Chapter 2, for information about logging to another drive. You can also use CHKDSK on another drive by typing

```
C>CHKDSK A:
```

CHKDSK is often thought of as some form of cure-all for disk ailments. It's not; CHKDSK merely reports information the computer already knows about. If some computer weirdo says "run CHKDSK" to fix the problem, he probably doesn't know what he is talking about. One exception exists: See the following section.

If CHKDSK reports any errors, specifically `Missing files` or `unallocated clusters` or `lost chains` or something along those lines, it asks you a question. Press **N** for No and then see the following section.

✔ For more information about available memory, refer to Chapter 8.

"CHKDSK says that I have lost files in clusters or something"

The CHKDSK command is good at finding lost files on disk. These files aren't important ones you may have lost, but rather pieces of files that were blown to bits by DOS. Usually, these files are shattered when you reset your computer in the middle of something or when it goes bonkers; because CHKDSK typically finds nothing that's important, don't take its message as a bad omen.

When CHKDSK does report something wrong, you should fix the problem. To fix it, run CHKDSK a second time with its slash-F option. Type

```
C> CHKDSK /F
```

That's the CHKDSK command, a space, and then slash-F. Press Enter. CHKDSK discovers the same errors. This time, however, press **Y** when it asks you the question Convert lost chains to files?.

When you use slash-F and answer Yes to the question, CHKDSK gathers up all the pieces of the lost files it finds and places them on your disk. You really can do nothing with these files, so delete them. This command does the job:

```
C> DEL \FILE*.CHK
```

That's DEL, a space, a backslash, FILE, an asterisk, a period, and CHK. This file-name wildcard matches all the files CHKDSK creates in your root directory.

✔ For more information about deleting files, refer to the section "Deleting a Group of Files," in Chapter 18.

✔ For information about filename wildcards, see the section "Wildcards (Or Poker Was Never This Much Fun)," in Chapter 19.

Scanning the disk with ScanDisk

To make sure that your disk is in tip-top shape, you can use the ScanDisk command. This command takes a close look at your disk and, if it finds anything awry, fixes it on the spot. This capability is available only with MS-DOS 6.2.

To use ScanDisk, type the **SCANDISK** command at the DOS prompt, press Enter, and prepare to be overwhelmed:

```
C> SCANDISK
```

After pressing Enter, ScanDisk proceeds to smell, squeeze, and thump your disk, looking for any soft spots. You see an interesting screen with five tasks displayed and checked off as ScanDisk completes them, as shown in Figure 17-2.

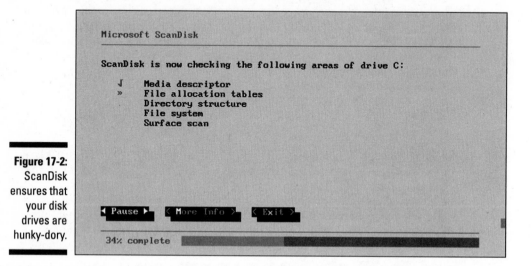

Figure 17-2:
ScanDisk ensures that your disk drives are hunky-dory.

Before doing the fifth task, Surface scan, you see a box displayed asking whether you want a surface scan. My advice is to press **N** for No and then press **X** to exit (quit) ScanDisk. Press Y only if you've been having problems with the disk, such as *read errors* or *write errors* or if you've noticed a general (beyond the normal) increase in disk mayhem.

If you press Y to perform a surface scan, ScanDisk takes a long, slow, careful look at your disk. Although this process is tedious, it's certain to find any errors and fix them. Because of the time involved, I recommend that you answer Y to the surface scan question only once a month or so.

ScanDisk works on only one drive at a time. To use it on another drive, first log to that drive and then run the SCANDISK command. Refer to the section "Changing Drives," in Chapter 2, for information about logging to another drive. You can also use ScanDisk on another drive by typing

C>SCANDISK A:

This command scans a floppy disk in drive A. Substitute your favorite drive letter for A: to scan that drive.

If ScanDisk reports any errors, it's a good idea to select the Fix It option. It directs ScanDisk to repair the disk. See the following section for details.

Having ScanDisk fix your disk

When ScanDisk finds something amiss with the disk it's scanning, a box appears on-screen. The box does its best to explain what's wrong and offers you several options for fixing the problem. Most of the time, when you're faced with this type of box, pressing Enter patches things up nicely. You should also write the changes to an *undo disk* — and it's a good idea to keep an undo disk handy next to your computer. I recommend this course: When ScanDisk gives you the Fix It option, press Enter, read the screen carefully, and shove in the undo disk as just described — the problem will be fixed.

A common disk boo-boo that ScanDisk locates is the old `Lost files or directories` error. You see a box with text that starts off something like this:

```
ScanDisk found xxxx bytes of data on drive X that may be one
             or more lost files or directories, but which is
             probably just taking up space.
```

Normally, you should select the Delete option to remove the excess files ("probably just taking up space"). The exception is when ScanDisk has been doing a great deal of repair work for you, in which case the Save option is a better choice.

To select the Delete option, press **L** or use your mouse to click the Delete "button." At this point you can stick your undo disk into drive A. Do so, and then ScanDisk continues to scan the disk. Before you quit, a summary screen is displayed to tell you what ScanDisk did.

If you've been using ScanDisk frequently to repair a misguided disk, select the Save option when faced with the preceding error message box. ScanDisk then gathers up all the pieces of the lost files it finds and places them on your disk. You can find the files in the root directory, named FILE0000.CHK, FILE0001.CHK, FILE0002.CHK — for as many files as ScanDisk has rescued.

You can examine the files with the TYPE command if you like. It helps you to see what was in the files, as shown in this example:

```
C> TYPE FILE0000.CHK
```

Or, you can use this command when the file is inexcusably long:

```
C> MORE < FILE0000.CHK
```

That's `MORE`, a space, the less-than symbol, a space, and then the name of the file you want to peer at.

As far as content goes, what's in the file is anyone's guess. If you recognize what's in there, however, rename the file to its original name (by using the REN command). Then copy the file to its proper location on disk. Kneel appropriately toward Microsoft headquarters and chant "Bill is good" several times in appreciation. (That's *good* with two *o*s, mind you.)

✔ When you're reading the ScanDisk fix-it screens, remember to press the down-arrow key to see any additional information that may be lurking beneath the box.

✔ If you select the Save option to save the files and, lo, they're full of a bunch of meaningless junk, delete them. This technique is 100 percent okay; rogue files seem to litter people's disks like beer cans after a rodeo. Use the DEL command as covered in Chapter 18.

✔ If you use an undo disk, keep it handy next to your computer. If the errors that ScanDisk detected turn out to not really be errors, sing "Whoomp, there it is" and put the undo disk back into drive A. Type **SCANDISK /UNDO** at the DOS prompt and follow the instructions on-screen.

✔ For more information about renaming files, refer to the section "Renaming a File," in Chapter 18.

✔ For information about viewing files (the "MORE <" thing), refer to the section "Looking at Files," in Chapter 2.

Backing Up

Backing up is the process of making a safety copy of your data, typically the data on your hard drive. You make a copy of all the files on your hard drive on a large stack of floppy disks by using one of the most lonely commands in DOS: the BACKUP command (or MSBackup if you're using DOS 6). Yes, the command is sad and lonely, but backing up is important and you definitely lead a life of woe and sorrow if you neglect it.

If you're using Windows (any version)as your PC's primary operating system, use the Windows backup programs. These programs understand some strange Windows things (primarily, how to deal with long filenames). DOS backup programs cannot do that. Besides, no DOS BACKUP program is included with Windows 95 or later.

DOS BACKUP (before DOS 6)

If you don't have a convenient third-party backup program or haven't yet upgraded to DOS 6, you can still use the DOS BACKUP command to back up your hard disk. Why not just use COPY? Well, you could do that if you need to back up only a few files that change regularly and if none of the files is bigger than a floppy disk. Backup programs can do what COPY can't: Break up a file and put half on each of two separate disks.

> ✔ If you have DOS 6, see the section "Running MSBackup," later in this chapter.

Backing up the whole dang hard drive

To back up your entire hard drive by using DOS BACKUP, the first thing you need is a stack of formatted disks. You should label each disk and number them sequentially, 1 through however many are in your stack. (I have no idea how many disks you need. Typically, a 40MB hard drive requires about 40 1.2MB disks; you can do the math for different-size hard drives and larger or smaller disks.) Third-party backup programs usually give you an estimate, but not DOS — oh no, that would be too easy.

If you have a stack of formatted and numbered disks nearby, type

```
C> BACKUP C:\*.* A: /S
```

That's the BACKUP command, a space, and then C:*.*, which means all files in the root directory of drive C. That's followed by a space, A: for drive A, another space, and then a slash-S. In the preceding example, you're backing up drive C. If you're backing up another hard drive, substitute its letter for C:. If your backup is to another floppy drive, put **B:** in the same spot A: is in.

Press Enter and follow the directions on-screen.

If you're using DOS 3.3 or earlier and you don't have a stack of backup disks, use this version of the BACKUP command instead:

```
C> BACKUP C:\*.* A: /S /F
```

The extra slash-F tells BACKUP to format any blank disks you may insert into the drive.

> ✔ Refer to the section "Formatting a Disk," in Chapter 13, for more information about formatting.

> ✔ Use the VER command, as described in Chapter 1, to see which version of DOS you have.

Backing up a single file

The BACKUP command can back up a whole hard drive, a subdirectory, or just a single file. Why would any sane person want to do that rather than just use the COPY command? The answer is that BACKUP is the only method you have of copying a very large file to a floppy disk (or to more than one floppy disk, as is usually the case). Here is the format:

```
C> BACKUP C:\WORK\LARGE.FAT A:
```

You see the BACKUP command, a space, and then the full pathname of the large file you want to back up. That's followed by a space and then the letter of the floppy drive you're backing up to, plus a colon. Press Enter and follow the instructions on-screen.

✔ See the section "What Is a Pathname?" earlier in this chapter, for more information about a file's full pathname.

Backing up today's work

You can back up the stuff you've worked on today, usually in one single sub-directory, by using this BACKUP command:

```
C> BACKUP C:\WORK\STUFF\*.* A:
```

Just type the BACKUP command, a space, and then the name of the subdirec-tory (work area) that contains your files — plus a backslash and the star-dot-star wildcard. That's followed by a space and then the drive letter of the floppy drive to which you're backing up plus the required colon.

✔ See the section "Using *.* (star-dot-star)," in Chapter 19, for information about that wildcard.

Backing up modified files

You can use a special type of backup command to back up files that have been changed or modified since the last *real* hard disk backup. This process is known as an *incremental* backup. The following BACKUP command per-forms an incremental backup of drive C:

```
C> BACKUP C:\*.* A: /S /M
```

The BACKUP command is followed by C:*.* for all the files on drive C. That's followed by a space and A:, meaning that you're backing up to drive A. Then comes a space, slash-S, another space, and finally a slash-M.

- ✔ If you're doing an incremental backup of another hard drive, substitute its letter for C: in the preceding example.
- ✔ If you're backing up to floppy drive B, substitute B: for A:.

Running MSBackup

MSBackup is a full-screen, pull-down menu, pop-up, graphical house of backup fun. If you're familiar with the old BACKUP command, stand back! Backups are faster and take fewer disks, and you don't even have to press the "any key" after inserting the next backup disk with MSBackup.

Start the MSBackup program by typing

```
C> MSBACKUP
```

If the MSBackup program hasn't been configured, it does so when you first run it. Follow the instructions on your screen (just press Enter during the appropriate lulls, and you'll be okay). You need two or more disks to assist with the configuring: Stick them in the drive when the program tells you to — this happens twice. Better still, let someone else do it because the configuration process is about as much fun as chewing on aluminum foil.

After MSBackup has been configured, you start it and see the main menu, as shown in Figure 17-3. To back up files, click the Backup button with the mouse or press Alt+B on your keyboard.

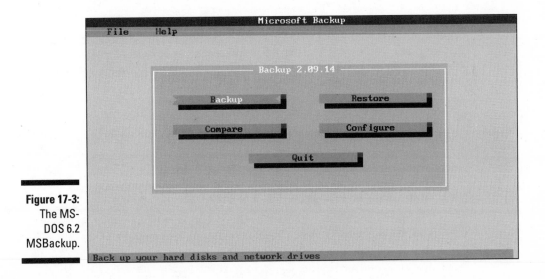

Figure 17-3:
The MS-
DOS 6.2
MSBackup.

✔ After you've configured MSBackup, you can reuse the one or two sample disks. The content of these disks is unimportant; reformat them with the FORMAT command if you like, as described in Chapter 13.

✔ To quit the MSBackup program, choose Exit from the File menu: Press Alt+F and then the **X** key. Or, if you're at the main screen (refer to Figure 17-3), press **Q** to quit.

✔ For information about the Restore option in MSBackup, see the section "Restoring from a Backup," in Chapter 21.

✔ If you use Windows 3.11, back up by using the DOS-based version of MSBackup over the Windows version. That way, if you ever need to restore your entire hard drive, the steps involved are less complex than if you had to restore the hard drive *and* restore Windows.

✔ You can use a mouse with MSBackup if you're well versed in mousy things. Refer to Chapter 10 for the jargon and such.

✔ Yes, MSBackup is a major pain in the ass.

Backing up the whole hard drive — all of it

Do this stuff at least once a month.

Start out by procuring a stack of formatted disks. Label these disks 1 through however many you have. On the first one, write Full Backup and maybe the date.

How many disks do you need? Typically, a 40MB hard drive requires about 40 1.4MB disks; you can do the math for different sizes of hard drives and larger or smaller disks. Don't worry about that, though; MSBackup tells you approximately how many disks it takes after it gets under way.

Start MSBackup by typing **MSBACKUP** at the DOS prompt:

```
C> MSBACKUP
```

Here are the steps for backing up an entire hard drive:

1. **At the main screen, press Alt+B to back up.**

   The next screen is the backup configuration screen, as shown in Figure 17-4. It's the second most complex screen in the program. (Don't worry — the first is coming your way.)

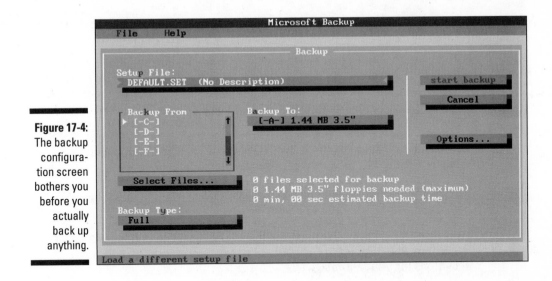

Figure 17-4:
The backup configuration screen bothers you before you actually back up anything.

2. **Press Alt+K to highlight the Backup From area of the screen. Press the up- or down-arrow keys to highlight the hard drive you want to back up. When the hard drive is highlighted, press the spacebar.**

   Don't be distracted by any surprise pop-up windows. It says `All files` by the drive letter after you press the spacebar.

   After you select the hard drive, you see in the lower right portion of the screen approximately how many disks the backup will take.

   You can choose from more than one hard drive (if you have 'em) by pressing the up- or down-arrow keys and pressing the spacebar when that hard drive letter is highlighted. I recommend this approach if you have more than one hard drive.

3. **Press Alt+Y. Make sure that the `Full` item is dotted. Press the up- or down-arrow key and press the spacebar to move the dot. Press Enter when `Full` has the dot by it.**

4. **Press Alt+S to start the backup.**

   (Then you get to see the most complex screen in the program, which isn't malevolent — just boggling.)

5. **Follow the directions on-screen: Insert your first backup disk. When you hear the beep, remove the disk from the drive and replace it with the next disk in the stack.**

   Keep going until all the disks are backed up or your arm gets sore.

6. **When you're done, you see a summary screen. Ogle over the statistics. Rubber-band your backup disks and keep them in a safe place.**

   Those disks come in handy if anything abominable happens to your hard drive.

Not required reading on setup files

Setup files are special files on disk that record your settings in the MSBackup program. They save you a wee amount of time because they record certain options you select on the backup configuration screen (refer to Figure 17-4 and Steps 2 and 3 in the preceding set of steps). If you want to save your own custom setup files, before you complete Step 4, press Alt+F,A and then give your setup file a name. Then, the next time you use MSBackup, press Alt+F,O and select your setup file from disk. Or, you can start MSBackup with the name of a setup file, as shown in this example:

```
C>MSBACKUP FULLHD
```

FULLHD is the name of a setup file, possibly one that backs up your whole hard drive. This file means that you don't have to go through Steps 2 and 3 every time you back up the whole hard drive; the setup file makes those selections for you "automagically."

Backing up modified files

You should back up modified files every day or at least once a week.

You can use a special variation of the MSBackup command to back up only those files that have been changed since the last backup. This process, called an *incremental backup,* takes less time than the full hard disk backup and fewer disks.

To perform an incremental backup, follow the same steps as outlined in the preceding section. The only difference is that after Step 3, you press the up- or down-arrow keys to highlight the word Incremental rather than Full. Press the spacebar to put a dot in the circle. You're cool now; press Enter. After that, everything works the same.

Backing up an entire subdirectory

This process is something you do to back up a work subdirectory. For example, at the end of every day, I back up the ELMO directory, which is where the files for this book are stored. (Write me if you want to know why it's called ELMO.)

To back up only a specific subdirectory, follow the same steps as outlined earlier in this chapter, in the section "Backing up the whole hard drive — all of it." Replace that Step 2 with the following:

2. **Press Alt+K to highlight the Backup From area of the screen. Press the up- or down-arrow keys to highlight the drive containing the subdirectory you want to back up.**

Press Alt+L. This action displays another overwhelming screen — pay attention to only the left side. There, you see a directory "tree." Press the up- or down-arrow keys to highlight the subdirectories you want to back up. To select a directory, press the spacebar. You can select more than one directory, if you like. Press Enter when you're done.

Continue with Step 3 from the section "Backing up the whole hard drive — all of it," earlier in this chapter.

✔ I recommend backing up your work directory every day. I do.

✔ You may want to save a custom setup file with your subdirectory selections. Refer to the section "Not required reading on setup files," earlier in this chapter.

Forget about Disk Compression

I do not recommend using *any* disk-compression software. Seriously, although these programs do work, they're not the true solution you need. If you're low on disk space, I heartily recommend that you buy a second hard drive or replace your hard drive with a larger, beefier model. This method is the best and safest way to go when disk space is low.

Dot to dot

How many times have you seen something like the following in the DIR command's listing?

```
   .     <DIR>      8-24-97    4:44p
   ..    <DIR>      8-24-97    4:44p
```

Doesn't that just bug you? A single period, or dot, isn't the name of a file, nor is dot-dot the name of a file. (Filenames, legal and illegal, are covered in Chapter 19, in the section "Use These Filenames — Go Directly to Jail!") By now, you know that both these dot-things are directories on disk. Where are they? What are they?!

The dot and dot-dot entries are abbreviations. "Dot," the first entry in this example, is an abbreviation for the current directory. "Dot-dot" refers to the parent directory.

You can use these abbreviations to refer to the current or parent directory in various DOS commands. This subject is an advanced and secretive one, however, best left up to the loftier books about using computers. If dot and dot-dot ever bugged the heck out of you, though, now you know what they represent.

Freeing up space on a hard disk

Disk-compression software isn't your only weapon in the battle of shrinking disk space. You can also help ease the hard drive space crunch by occasionally deleting files. No, not randomly; every hard drive has a few extra gross of files just lying around that aren't needed for anything and that can quickly vanish with deft use of the DEL command. The problem is knowing which files you can safely delete without fouling up your whole system.

Generally speaking, you can delete any of these types of files:

🖝 Backup files (ending with the BAK extension)

🖝 Temporary or junk files

🖝 Any files that start with a tilde (~) and end with the TMP extension (but only when Windows 3.11 is not running)

After deleting those types of files, you can free up disk space by doing what the nerds call *archiving.* In that process, you take old data files you don't need anymore but don't want to delete and copy them to floppy disks. For example, you may store all of last year's budget files and proposals in a specific place, copy them all to floppies, properly label the floppies, and then delete the old files from your hard drive. That way, you still have the files on floppy disks, and lots more room is made available on your hard drive. This technique usually frees up the most amount of space, and you can use the MSBackup program as discussed in this chapter to make the job easier.

You can also archive old programs, especially games, from your system. I found on my hard drive a copy of an old disk utility that was eating up 8 megabytes — and I hadn't used the program in more than a year!

Chapter 18

File Fitness (Stuff You Do with Files)

- -

In This Chapter

▶ Duplicating a file

▶ Copying a file

▶ Copying a file to the current directory

▶ Copying a group of files

▶ Deleting and undeleting a file

▶ Deleting a group of files

▶ Deleting a file that refuses to die

▶ Moving a file

▶ Renaming a file

▶ Printing a text file

- -

A file is basically a collection of stuff on disk, usually stuff you want to keep. One of DOS's main duties (right after confusing the heck out of you) is to work with files. For a file cabinet, this concept is obvious. Under DOS, it's not.

This chapter is about working with files — duplicating, copying, deleting, undeleting, moving, and printing them — everything you want to know about files.

Duplicating a File

Duplicating a file is done with the COPY command. You have to know the name of the original file and the new name you want to give the duplicate.

Suppose that the file you have is named MUSHY.DOC. You want to make a duplicate file named CRUNCHY.DOC. Here's what you type:

```
C> COPY MUSHY.DOC CRUNCHY.DOC
```

A common reason for copying a file is to make a backup file of an original. For example, if you work on CONFIG.SYS and AUTOEXEC.BAT:

```
C> COPY CONFIG.SYS CONFIG.BKD
```

In this example, the file CONFIG.SYS is duplicated and given the name CONFIG.BKD.

Both the original and the duplicate files have the same content but different names. The reason is that no two files in the same directory can be given the same name.

- ✔ If the operation is successful, DOS responds with the message 1 file(s) copied. If not, you most likely receive a File not found error message. That's okay. You probably just mistyped the original filename. Try again.

- ✔ To find out which files are on a disk, you use the DIR command. Refer to the section in Chapter 2 about the DIR command.

- ✔ For information on naming new files, see the section in Chapter 19 about naming files. Generally speaking, files can contain letters and numbers. A filename can be as many as eight letters or numbers long; you can specify an optional period and as many as three more letters or numbers if you like.

If the duplicate file already exists, DOS overwrites it. This overwriting happens without any notice. For example, if the file CRUNCHY.DOC already exists, DOS copies the original file, MUSHY.DOC, over it. Use the DIR command first to make sure that a file by that name doesn't already exist.

From MS-DOS 6.2 onward (including Windows 95 and Windows 98), the COPY command warns you before it commits wanton destruction of already existing files:

```
Overwrite C:CRUNCHY.DOC (Yes/No/All)?
```

This line means that the file CRUNCHY.DOC already exists. Rather than clobber it without so much as a thought, DOS is asking first. My advice is to press N here — N for "No thanks." (Press Enter after pressing N.) Then try the COPY command again and use another name for the duplicate.

Copying a Single File

Copying a file is handled by the COPY command. You have to know the name of the original file and the *destination,* the place where you want to put the copy.

For example, to copy a file to another drive, specify that drive's letter plus a colon:

```
C> COPY OVERTHAR.DOC A:
```

In the preceding example, the file OVERTHAR.DOC is copied to drive A. On drive A, you find an identical copy of the file OVERTHAR.DOC; both files have the same name and contents. To copy a file to another directory on the same drive, specify that directory's pathname, as shown in this example:

```
C> COPY OVERTHAR.DOC \WORK\STUFF
```

The file OVERTHAR.DOC is copied to the subdirectory \WORK\STUFF on the same drive.

To copy a file to another directory on another drive, you must specify the full pathname, which includes the drive letter and a colon:

```
C> COPY MENU.EXE B:\MAIN
```

The file MENU.EXE is copied to the MAIN directory on drive B.

As with using the COPY command to duplicate a file, if another file with the same name exists, current versions of DOS ask the `Overwrite (Yes/No/All)?` question. Press N and press Enter. (Refer to the preceding section's checklist for more information.) Early versions of DOS? Don't press your luck.

- ✔ If you want to copy a file to the same directory as the original, you must specify a different name. Refer to the discussion in the preceding section.
- ✔ For more information on pathnames and subdirectories, see Chapter 17.

Copying a File to You

A short form of the COPY command can be used to copy a file from another drive or directory to your current directory. In this format of the COPY command, you specify only the original file (which cannot already be in the current directory).

Copying? Duplicating? What's the diff and why should I care?

True, copying and duplicating a file are the same thing. In both instances, you have two copies of the same file, each containing the same information. The difference is only in the vernacular: A duplicated file is usually on the same drive in the same directory and has a different name. A copied file is usually created on another drive or in another directory.

Note that you can copy a file with a different name, which is like duplicating it, as shown in this example:

```
C> COPY SILLY.DOC A:DROLL.DOC
```

SILLY.DOC is copied to drive A — but it's given a new name, DROLL.DOC.

Suppose that the file DREDGE is located on drive A. To copy that file to drive C (your current drive), you type

```
C> COPY A:DREDGE
```

To copy the BORING.DOC file from the \WORK\YAWN subdirectory to your current location, you can type

```
C> COPY \WORK\YAWN\BORING.DOC
```

- ✔ Copying a file in this manner works only when you're not in the directory containing the file. After the COPY command, of course, the file is in the current directory.

- ✔ You cannot duplicate files by using this command; you can only copy them from elsewhere to the current directory. If you try this command and the file is in the current directory, you get a `File cannot be copied onto itself` error message.

- ✔ For more information on directories, see Chapter 17; information on the *current directory* is offered in the section about finding the current directory in that chapter.

Copying a Group of Files

You can copy more than one file with a single COPY command, by using *wildcards*.

The * wildcard replaces a group of characters in a filename.

The ? wildcard replaces a single character in a filename.

For example, if you want to copy all files with the DOC extension to drive A, you use this command:

```
C> COPY *.DOC A:
```

Here, the *.DOC matches all files ending in DOC: BABY.DOC, EYE.DOC, EAR.DOC, WHATSUP.DOC, and so on. Note that both the period and the DOC ending are specified after the asterisk. They are copied to drive A, as noted by the A:.

To copy all files, use the *.* (star-dot-star, which is less of a tongue twister than asterisk-period-asterisk) wildcard:

```
C> COPY *.* A:
```

This command is commonly used when you are copying all the files from the floppy drive to your hard drive:

```
C> COPY A:*.*
```

In this example, you're copying the files *to you* from the floppy drive. (Refer to the preceding section for the gory details.)

The ? wildcard is used to represent a single character in a filename. Assume that you have ten chapters in a book, named CHAP01.DOC through CHAP10.DOC. You can copy them to drive A by using this command:

```
C> COPY CHAP??.DOC A:
```

✔ For more information on wildcards, see the section "Wildcards (Or Poker Was Never This Much Fun)" in Chapter 19.

✔ See Chapter 17 for information on the current directory and pathnames.

Deleting a File

Deleting a file is done with the DEL command. You follow DEL with the name of the file you want to delete:

```
C> DEL SAMPLE.BAK
```

You get no feedback; the DEL command is like the midnight assassin, silent and quick.

If the file you're deleting isn't in the current directory, you must specify a drive letter and colon or a pathname. In this example, the file MEMO is deleted from drive A:

```
C> DEL A:MEMO
```

In the following example, the file XMASLIST.99 is deleted from the \WP51\DATA directory:

```
C> DEL \WP51\DATA\XMASLIST.99
```

✔ Never delete any file named COMMAND.COM. While you're at it, don't delete any file in your DOS directory. If you're using MS-DOS 6 and DoubleSpace, never, ever delete any file that starts with DBLSPACE.

✔ Do not delete any files in the Windows subdirectory (or folder). Those are files important to Windows and, whether you think they're needed or not, Windows needs them.

✔ Be careful with the DEL command! Delete files you've created, files you know about, and files you've copied. Don't go on a spiteful fit of vengeance and delete files whose purpose you don't know.

✔ The ERASE command can also be used to delete files. ERASE and DEL are exactly the same command and do the same things. (I know, it's redundant. But that's what you should expect from DOS.)

✔ If the file doesn't exist, you see a `File not found` error message.

✔ Information on using pathnames is covered in Chapter 17.

Extra Verbiage about Why You Would Want to Delete Files

Deleting a file with the DEL command seems like a drastic thing to do — especially when you've invested all that time in creating the file. But there are reasons to do so. The first is to clean up space. Some files may contain unnecessary copies of information; some files may be old versions or BAK (backup) duplicates. Deleting them gives you more space.

Zapping extra files is also a part of disk maintenance, or "housekeeping." If you've ever created a TEMP, KILL, or JUNK file, you would use the DEL command to delete them. (Oh, TEMP, KILL, and JUNK files may contain information you had to save to disk but no longer need — stuff like today's bets at the track, the rough draft of your letter to your congressperson, or that second copy of the books before the auditor comes.)

Deleting a Group of Files

To delete more than one file at a time — truly massive, wholesale slaughter — you use the DEL command with wildcards. This process can get nasty.

The * wildcard replaces a group of characters in a filename.

The ? wildcard replaces a single character in a filename.

For example, to delete all files with UP as their second part (the *extension*), you use the following command:

```
C> DEL *.UP
```

In this example, *.UP matches all files ending in UP, such as FED.UP, SHUT.UP, and THROW.UP. Note how both the period and the UP ending are specified after the asterisk.

As with deleting a single file, the feedback from this command is nil. Yes, even as a mass murderer, DEL makes no noise.

An exception to DEL's silence is when you use the *.* wildcard. Because this command deletes all files in the directory, something must be said:

```
C> DEL *.*
```

DOS heeds you with the following message:

```
All files in directory will be deleted! Are you sure (Y/N)?
```

Don't be too quick to press Y here. Ask yourself, "Am I certain that I want to ruthlessly destroy those innocent files?" Then, with a demented "Yes" gurgling from your lips, press **Y** and then Enter. Boom! The files are gone.

> ✔ For more information on wildcards, see the section "Wildcards (Or Poker Was Never This Much Fun)" in Chapter 19.

> ✔ You can also delete groups of files on other drives and in other directories. Wow! Run amok! But be sure to specify the proper locations for the files, disks, and pathnames as needed.

Some background stuff I shouldn't tell you about ATTRIB

The ATTRIB command is used to modify special features of a file that are called *attributes*. One of these attributes is the *read-only* attribute. When a file is marked as read-only, you can only read from the file. Any attempt to modify it, rename it, or delete it is met with an `Access denied` error message.

To make a file or group of files read-only, you use the ATTRIB command with a +R:

```
C> ATTRIB NOKILL.ME +R
```

In this example, the file NOKILL.ME is read-only-protected. The protection offered here is minimal, of course: Any dolt can use the ATTRIB command to remove the read-only protection and delete the file. Go figure.

The File! I Cannot Kill It!

Suppose that one day, when you're feeling rather spiteful, you decide to delete that useless BARNEY.LUV file. You type the following with wicked staccato fingers:

```
C> DEL BARNEY.LUV
```

After pressing Enter, you see that DOS tells you `Access denied`. Ha! Will that spoil your mood, or what?

Generally speaking, when you see `Access denied`, it means that someone somewhere doesn't want you to delete the file. Some very important files are on your system. Some may not have names that are obvious to you, so it's never a good idea to go out stomping on files like a kid through a flower bed. Tsk, tsk, tsk.

Shhh! (Whisper this next part if you're reading aloud.) If you really want to delete the file, you must first type the following line using the proper filename or wildcard:

```
C> ATTRIB BARNEY.LUV -R
```

That's the ATTRIB command, followed by the name of the file, a space, a minus sign (–), and then an R. You cannot have a space between the minus sign and the R.

By pressing Enter, you're removing the "access" protection from the file (or files). You can now delete it (or them):

```
C> DEL BARNEY.LUV
```

Need I mention it again? Files are protected for a reason. Use the ATTRIB and –R only when you badly want to delete a file.

Undeleting a File

One of the miracles of DOS (well, beginning with Version 5) is that it enables you to undelete a file you've just — whoops! — deleted. I'll be clear about this: Just because you can undelete a file doesn't mean that you should be sloppy with the DEL command. If you ever are sloppy (and who isn't?), though, you have the UNDELETE command to save you.

Suppose that you've just razed the BUBBLE.POP program. Upon realizing this grievous mistake, you type

```
C> UNDELETE BUBBLE.POP
```

Essentially, the UNDELETE command is the opposite of the DEL command. You simply substitute UNDELETE for DEL to snatch the file (or files) back.

After pressing Enter, DOS displays some interesting and complex statistics. I have no idea what all that means, but it sure is impressive. (Read it aloud over the phone to a friend, and he or she is certain to think that you're a computer genius.)

UNDELETE displays the file's name and whether it can be undeleted. If so, you're asked whether you want to undelete the file. Press **Y**. Furthermore, you have to supply the first letter of the filename.

You can also use the UNDELETE command with wildcards, as shown in this example:

```
C> UNDELETE *.*
```

You see the names of all recoverable files in the directory (or those that match the wildcard you've entered). Press **Y** to undelete each one as you're prompted. You have to specify the first letter of each filename.

And now for the sorry news: The DOS that comes with Windows 95 and Windows 98 *does not* have an UNDELETE command. In fact, if you delete a file at the DOS prompt, you cannot even use the Windows Recycle Bin to get it back. Be careful!

✔ If, for some silly reason, UNDELETE doesn't work, you should try the following variation instead:

```
C> UNDELETE BUBBLE.POP /DOS
```

✔ Retype the UNDELETE command as you did the first time, and add a space, a slash, and then **DOS** (similar to the preceding example). Press Enter, and UNDELETE should work as advertised.

✔ The sooner you undelete a file, the better. This situation has nothing to do with time; you can turn off your computer, wait a few weeks, power it back on again, and still be able to undelete the file. However, if you create any new files, copy files, or do any other disk activity, your chances of a full file recovery are remote.

✔ If you see a message that reads `The data contained in the first cluster of this directory has been overwritten or corrupted` — don't panic. That's the friendly DOS way of telling you that the file cannot be undeleted. Sorry, but it happens.

✔ You cannot undelete a file if you've copied over it with the COPY command.

✔ For more information on wildcards, see Chapter 19; for information on directories, see Chapter 17.

Additional, Skippable Information

A faster way to undelete files is by specifying the /ALL switch, as shown here:

```
C> UNDELETE *.* /ALL
```

In this example, the UNDELETE command attempts to rescue all the files (*.*) in the directory. The /ALL switch tells UNDELETE to go ahead and undelete everything — without prompting you with Y or N and asking for the first letter of the filename. Instead, each file is given the pound sign character (#) as its first letter. You can later rename each file on its own.

Moving a File

DOS didn't originally have a MOVE command. No, Microsoft must have thought it redundant. After all, you can use COPY to make duplicates of files and then use DEL to obliterate the originals. So why bother with a MOVE command? Well, guilt must have caught up with the company. Starting with MS-DOS Version 6.0, it has a MOVE command.

Oh, yes! There is a MOVE command!

To move a file from hither to thither, you use the MOVE command. To move the file BEKINS.VAN to drive A, you type

```
C> MOVE BEKINS.VAN A:
```

DOS copies the file BEKINS.VAN to drive A and then deletes the original. After all, that's what a move operation is: copy and then delete.

- ✔ The MOVE command's song goes like this: *Move this file to there.* You type the place where you're moving the file — the *destination* — last. Files can be moved to another disk drive or another subdirectory.
- ✔ If a file with the same name already exists and you have the pleasure of using MS-DOS 6.2 or later, the MOVE command displays a warning. For example:

```
Overwrite A:BEKINS.VAN (Yes/No/All)?
```

- ✔ This line means that a file with the name BEKINS.VAN already exists on drive A. Press N and then Enter, and the MOVE command won't stomp it.
- ✔ Remember: The MOVE command deletes the originals. If you want to copy a file, use the COPY command instead.

Moving a file in the pre-DOS 6 caveman days

When you come to think of it, moving a file is simply using COPY to make a duplicate and then using DEL to delete the original. That's basically a *move* (which would be sort of like paying the movers to move your furniture to the new house and then having them dynamite the old one).

The first step is to copy the file to the new location:

```
C> COPY BEKINS.VAN A:
```

In this example, the file named BEKINS.VAN is copied to drive A. Now delete the original:

```
C> DEL BEKINS.VAN
```

The original file is gone, although the copy still exists on drive A. That's moving.

- ✔ For more information on copying files, refer to the section "Copying a Single File," earlier in this chapter.

> ✔ For information on deleting files, refer to the section "Deleting a File," earlier in this same chapter.
>
> ✔ Renaming a file is like moving a file in the current directory; you make a duplicate with a new name and delete the original. See the section "Renaming a File," later in this chapter. Oh, I guess it's next.

Renaming a File

DOS enables you to plaster a new name on a file by using the REN command. The file's contents and its location on disk stay the same. Only the name is changed (like they used to do on *Dragnet* to protect the innocent).

For example, to rename CHAPTER1.WP to CHAP01.WP, you can use the following line:

```
C> REN CHAPTER1.WP CHAP01.WP
```

The old name is specified first, followed by a space and then the new name. No sweat.

If the file isn't in the current directory, you must specify a drive letter or pathname. However, the new filename doesn't need all that extra info:

```
C> REN B:\STUFF\YONDER THITHER
```

In this example, the file named YONDER is on the disk in drive B, in the STUFF subdirectory. It's given the new name THITHER by the REN command.

Renaming a group of files is possible — but tricky. No, the REN command cannot rename all files (*.*) individually. It can, however, rename a group of files all at one time. For example:

```
C> REN *.OLD *.BAK
```

Here, all files ending in OLD are renamed. They keep their original filenames (the first part), but each one is given the new second name, BAK.

> ✔ REN has a longer version, RENAME. Both are the same command; you can use either, though REN is quicker to type.
>
> ✔ For information on file-naming rules, see the section in Chapter 19 about naming a file.

✔ You can use wildcards with the REN command only when you're renaming a group of matching files. Generally speaking, the same wildcard must be used for both the original filename and the new name. For more information on wildcards, see the section "Wildcards (Or Poker Was Never This Much Fun)" in Chapter 19.

✔ In Windows 95 and Windows 98, you aren't restricted to the old DOS 8.3 file naming rule: A filename can contain up to 255 characters, including spaces. It cannot contain the following characters: \ / : * ? " < > | . Windows 3.11 does not support long filenames.

✔ When you're renaming a file with a long name or renaming a short-name file with a longer name, be sure to use double quotes to enclose the long name. For example:

```
C> REN TEMP.DAT "Temporary.DAT"
```

The file named TEMP.DAT is renamed with a longer name, Temporary.DAT. Especially if the long filename contains spaces, you *must* put it in double quotes.

✔ Information about accessing other disks and pathnames is covered in Chapter 17.

Worth reading only if you want to rename a subdirectory

The REN command enables you to rename files. If you want to rename a subdirectory, forget it! DOS is fussy with the REN command and does not enable you to use it to rename subdirectories. So just give up now. That is, give up with the REN command because it is possible to rename a subdirectory, but only with the MOVE command — yes, the MOVE command. Weird, but what did you expect?

To rename a subdirectory, use the MOVE command just as you would use the REN command. For example:

```
C> MOVE WP51 WINWORD
```

The MOVE command is followed by the name of the first directory, WP51. Then comes a space and the directory's new name, WINWORD.

With the DOS that's in Windows 95 and Windows 98, you *can* use the REN command to rename a subdirectory. It's as though Microsoft is saying, "Hey, we know that the REN command should have always been used to rename a subdirectory. So now that we've shoved DOS into a box, we finally get around to making it happen. Go figure. And, uh, hey: Everybody use Internet Explorer, okay?"

Printing a Text File

DOS has a command named PRINT, although that command is just way too weird to cover in this book. Instead, you can print any text file by using the COPY command. Yeah, it sounds odd — but it works. First, a few rules to follow in order:

1. **Try the TYPE command on the file first.**

   If you can read it, it prints okay. If you can't read the file (if it looks "Greek"), the same garbage you see on-screen is sent to your printer. That's probably not what you want.

2. **Before printing the file, make sure that your printer is connected, *online*, and ready to print.**

   If you need help, see the section in Chapter 11 about going online.

3. **Use the COPY command to copy the file from your disk to the printer:**

   ```
   C> COPY PRINTME PRN
   ```

   PRN is the name of your printer. After pressing Enter, DOS makes a copy of the file PRINTME (as shown in the example) on your printer.

4. **If a full page doesn't print, you need to eject the page from your printer. Type this command:**

   ```
   C> ECHO ^L > PRN
   ```

Cosmic drivel about ECHO ^L > PRN

The ECHO command is the DOS "display me" command. Anything you type after ECHO is echoed to the screen. This command is primarily used in batch files, which are quasi-programs written by advanced DOS users who think that they're really cool.

Ctrl+L is a special control character — actually, a single character you produce by pressing the Ctrl+L key combination. On-screen, this character may look like the ankh symbol, although every computer printer sees it as the direct command to toss out a sheet of paper. For laser printers, that's often the only way you can see your work.

The cryptic (very cryptic) > PRN is what's called *I/O redirection,* and it's leagues beyond what's in this book. Basically, the greater-than sign tells DOS to send its output (the Ctrl+L, in this case) to another device, something other than the screen.

The named device is PRN, the printer. In the end, the eject-page command (Ctrl+L) is sent to the printer (> PRN) via the ECHO command. And they all live happily ever after.

That's the ECHO command, followed by a space and then the Ctrl+L character (the eject-page command). You produce that character by holding down the Ctrl (control) key and typing an **L** — do not type ^L (the hat and L characters). Then type a space, the greater-than symbol (>), another space, and then **PRN**. Press Enter, and a sheet of paper magically ejects from your printer. Neat-o.

- ✔ Text files typically have names that end in TXT. The most common text file is named READ.ME or README. Some files ending in DOC are text files, although that's not always the case; type the file first to be sure.

- ✔ It's usually best to print a file by using the application that created it. DOS can print only text files.

- ✔ You can also print any text file by using the DOS Editor. Jaunt on over to Chapter 16 for information.

- ✔ For more information on the TYPE command and looking at files, refer to the section "Looking at Files," in Chapter 2.

- ✔ General information about using a printer with your computer is covered in Chapter 11.

Chapter 19

Files — Lost and Found

Did you know that the word *file* can be anagrammed into the word *life*? Aside from that, nothing's really interesting about files. Well, only two things: what you can and cannot name a file (which is much akin to getting a 14-letter last name on a vanity license plate) and that files, like certain socks, occasionally get sucked into some parallel universe since the last time you saw them. It's like the car-keys gremlin who goes around snatching up your keys for a few seconds. A file gremlin also steals files — even though you just saved them to disk.

This chapter contains instructions for defeating the file gremlin. Actually, this chapter contains tidbits of information about using files, naming files, and all that file stuff. It doesn't have information about copying, renaming, or deleting files, which is conveniently stored in Chapter 18.

Name That File!

When you create a file, you give it a name. The name should reflect what's in the file or somehow describe the file's contents. After all, that name gives you the clue to what the file is when you are looking at a directory listing. Rather than grant you poetic license to create highly accurate and descriptive filenames, however, DOS puts on blinders and gives you only so many letters to use. It's frustrating.

All filenames fit into a specific pattern, called the *eight-dot-three pattern:*

```
FILENAME.EXT
```

The first part of the filename can have as many as eight characters. This part can be followed by an optional dot (period) and as many as three additional characters. That's where they get the eight-dot-three (which really sounds like Mr. Spock calling out photon torpedo spreads).

The first eight characters of a filename are the descriptive part. These characters can be any numbers or letters. For example, all the following are okay filenames:

```
TEST
A
80PROOF
HELLO
1040
LETTER
KINGFISH
```

If you want to add an extension (a definition follows) to a filename, you must specify the dot (or period) and then as many as three more characters. Here is the same group of rowdy files with extensions added:

```
TEST.OUT
A.1
80PROOF.GIN
HELLO.MOM
1040.X
LETTER.DOC
KINGFISH.ME
```

The *extension* is normally used to identify file types; for example, whether a file is a word-processing document or a spreadsheet. Here are some common file extensions:

BAK	A copy of a data file as a backup
BAT	A special type of program; a batch file
COM	A command program or command file (program file)
DBF	A database file
DOC	A document or word-processing file
EXE	An executable file or another type of program
FON	A font file
GRA	A graphics file

PIC	A picture file
SYS	A system file
TXT	A text file
WKS	A worksheet file
YUK	A collection of jokes

Of course, the list goes on and on. None of this stuff is etched in stone anywhere, so feel free to give a file whatever extension you want — except for the dreaded COM, EXE, and BAT extensions (which are covered in the section "Significant Filenames," later in this chapter).

✔ Some programs supply their own extensions automatically; you simply type the first part of the filename, and the program adds the rest as it creates or loads the file.

✔ You can enter a filename in upper- or lowercase; DOS doesn't care. The DIR command displays filenames in uppercase.

Use These Filenames — Go Directly to Jail!

If you goof when you name a file, you usually get some pleasing error message or an idle threat. Generally speaking, as long as you stick to naming a file by using letters and numbers, you'll be okay.

You cannot, however, under any circumstances — even if the building were on fire and St. Peter appeared to you, winked, and said that it was okay just this once — use the following characters in a filename:

```
. " / \ [ ] : * | < > + = ; , ?
```

✔ The biggest boo-boo most users make is putting a space in a filename. A space! Heavens! Filenames cannot contain spaces.

✔ The period cannot be used, unless it's the separator between the filename and the extension.

✔ The special-characters asterisk (*) and question mark (?) are actually filename wildcards, covered later in this chapter.

✔ Because the colon (:) is used only after a letter of the alphabet to identify a disk drive, it cannot appear in a filename.

✔ Three special characters — less than (<), greater than (>), and pipe (|) — are all used by DOS for other, confusing purposes.

✔ Because the rest of the characters also have special meanings to DOS, using them offends your operating system. (It's not a nice thing to do to something that holds life-and-death control over your data!)

Long Filenames in Windows 95 and Windows 98

With Windows 95 and Windows 98, your DOS files can sport new, longer filenames. The names can be anywhere from 1 to 255 characters long and can contain spaces, dots, and a variety of interesting characters. You have to follow a few rules, of course:

If you're using a long filename at the DOS prompt, you must enclose it in double quotes, as shown in this example:

```
C> TYPE "LETTER TO THE BOARD.TXT"
```

If the long filename doesn't contain any spaces, you don't need the double quotes:

```
C> DIR HTML_FILES
```

or

```
C> COPY REPORT-JANUARY.18 A:
```

Feel free to go nuts.

✔ Yes, there still are characters you shouldn't use in a filename, even in a long one:

```
" * / : ? \ | < >
```

✔ Your typing must be accurate! Although a long filename is swell, if you make only one teeny typo, the whole thing is spewed back at you as Bad command or filename.

✔ Windows 95 and Windows 98 also maintain a short filename for every long filename created. The short name is an abbreviated form of the longer filename, one that fits into the traditional "8-dot-3" pattern. Just use the DIR command on the long filename to see what the shorter version looks like (the DIR command displays both names).

You can only use long filenames if you have Windows 95 or Windows 98. If you are using Windows 3.11 you are stuck with the old "8-dot-3" pattern.

Significant Filenames

Filenames that end with a COM, EXE, or BAT extension are special. Those are programs that do things on your computer. As such, please don't name any of your files with those extensions. Although you can use any other extension or three-letter combination you can dream up, COM, EXE, and BAT are for programs only.

How to Name a Directory (The MD Command)

Directories are given names just like files. They can contain numbers and letters, and they can have as many as eight characters plus an optional period and a three-letter extension. As a rule, however, directories usually lack extensions.

You name directories as they're created, by using the MD command. Here's an example:

```
C> MD JUNK
```

This command is MD, for Make Directory, followed by a space and the name of the directory to create. In this case, DOS creates a subdirectory named JUNK. (For more info about subdirectories, refer to Chapter 17.)

✔ You get no visual feedback for creating a directory.

✔ Creating directories is a job best left to someone else. However, you can create your own directories to store your favorite files, thus keeping them together. More information about subdirectories is offered in Chapter 17.

Using the DIR Command

The DIR command is used to see a list of files on disk. You just type **DIR** and press Enter:

```
C> DIR
```

The files are listed in a special format, shown with their size and date and time of creation or last update. Note that the special format separates the filename from the extension, padding the distance between them with spaces. Although this technique lines up the directory listing nice and pretty, it doesn't show you how to accurately type the filename.

To see a list of files on another drive, use the DIR command with the drive letter and a colon:

```
C> DIR A:
```

In this example, you see a listing of all files on the disk in drive A. If you want to look at drive B, substitute B: for A:.

To see a list of files in another directory on the same disk, specify that directory's pathname after the DIR command:

```
C> DIR \WP60\DATA
```

In this example, the DIR command lists all the files in the \WP60\DATA subdirectory.

To see a single file's information, just type that file's name after the DIR command:

```
C> DIR BLOOP.NOF
```

The DIR command is followed by the file named BLOOP.NOF. Only that single file (and its associated and miscellaneous information) is displayed.

To see only a specific group of files, follow the DIR command with the proper, matching wildcard:

```
C> DIR *.COM
```

In this example, DIR is followed by a space, an asterisk, a period, and then COM. This command displays only those files with the COM extension.

- ✔ For more information about subdirectories and pathnames, refer to Chapter 17.
- ✔ For more information about using wildcards, see the section "Wildcards (Or Poker Was Never This Much Fun)," later in this chapter.

The wide DIR command

When you long for the wide, open spaces of the Big Sky country, you can use this DIR command:

```
C> DIR /W
```

That's the DIR command, a space, and slash-W. Pressing Enter displays the directory listing in the wide format, with only the filenames marching across the screen five abreast.

If you want to display a wide directory of another drive or a subdirectory, sandwich the drive letter or subdirectory pathname between the DIR and the /W, as shown in this example:

```
C> DIR A: /W
```

or

```
C> DIR \WP60\DATA /W
```

Refer to the preceding section for more details.

Making DIR display one screen at a time

When the DIR command scrolls and scrolls, rolling up and up the screen and you cannot find the file — not to mention that you've completely forgotten about the Ctrl+S key combination mentioned in Chapter 10 — you can use the following DIR command at the next DOS prompt:

```
C> DIR /P
```

That's the DIR command, followed by a space and a slash-P. The P means *page* or *pause*, and DOS inserts a friendly press any key message after each screen of filenames. Press the spacebar to continue.

- ✔ To cancel the listing, press Ctrl+C. Refer to the section "Canceling a DOS Command," in Chapter 3.

- ✔ If you're just hunting down a specific file, follow the DIR command with that filename. Refer to the section "Using the DIR Command," earlier in this chapter.

- ✔ If you're looking for a group of files that can be matched with a wildcard, see the section "Wildcards (Or Poker Was Never This Much Fun)," later in this chapter.

- ✔ You can use this DIR command to see a directory listing of another drive or subdirectory. Just sandwich that drive letter or subdirectory path- name between DIR and the /P. Here's an example:

  ```
  C> DIR A: /P
  ```

  or

  ```
  C> DIR \WP60\DATA /P
  ```

Refer to the section "Using the DIR Command," earlier in this chapter, if you care to fondle the DIR command further.

Displaying a sorted directory

Have you ever gotten the impression that DOS just couldn't care less? It's true. When DOS displays a list of files, it shows them to you in any old order. To sort the files in the listing alphabetically, use this DIR command:

```
C> DIR /O
```

That's the DIR command, a space, and then slash-O. The O must stand for *Oh, sort these,* or maybe the word *sort* in a foreign language. (It may mean *order* — nah.)

Finding a Lost File

In some cases, losing a file is worse than losing a pet or a small child in the mall. Pets and children have legs and wander off. Files? Where do they go? (And would one expect to find them in the video arcade?)

The first step in locating a lost file is knowing its name. If you want to copy said file and are greeted with the happy File not found error message, you may have mistyped the name. (It happens.) Check your typing. Furthermore, you may want to check the directory listing to see whether the file is there. Type

```
C> DIR /P
```

The slash-P pauses the listing, enabling you to scan each entry. Even the author of this book has transposed filenames as he has saved them. (Here's a hint: The new files are usually listed at the end of the directory, though that's not a hard-and-fast rule.)

If the file still doesn't show up, use this command:

```
C> DIR \WHERE.AMI /S
```

That's the DIR command, followed by a space, and then a backslash and the filename. In this example, the filename, WHERE.AMI, is used. After the filename comes a space and then slash-S.

By pressing Enter, you tell DOS to search the entire hard drive for the file you've specified. If it's found, you see it on-screen:

```
Directory of C:\LOST\FOUND
WHERE AMI   574 08-01-98 10:04a
  1 file(s)   574 bytes
```

DOS has found the lost file in the subdirectory \LOST\FOUND. You then have to use the CD command to move to that subdirectory, and from there you can get at the file. The CD command is covered in the section "Changing Directories," in Chapter 17.

- ✔ If any additional matching files are found, they're listed too, along with their directory.

- ✔ When you find the lost file, consider copying it to the proper location or use the REN command to rename the file to the name you originally thought you used. Refer to the section "Copying a Single File," in Chapter 18, for information about the COPY command; refer to the section "Renaming a File," in Chapter 18, for information about REN.

- ✔ If the list scrolls off the screen, you can tack on the slash-P option. Here's an example:

```
C> DIR \WHERE.AMI /S /P
```

Everything else in the command remains the same.

- ✔ If the file still isn't found, it may be on another disk drive. Log to another drive, and then type the same DIR command again.

- ✔ If you still cannot find the file on any drive, you probably saved it under a different name. Because I don't know what that name is, it's up to you to scour your drive looking for it. Use the CD and DIR commands to move around and find the file.

Finding a Lost Subdirectory

A lost subdirectory is a little harder to find than a lost file, especially when you know that it's somewhere on the drive — but where? As with finding a lost file, the first step is to use the DIR command. Look for the telltale <DIR> in the listing. It shows you all the subdirectories.

If you don't find your subdirectory, you can use the DIR command to search for it. Type the following (this one is bizarre, so watch your fingers):

```
C> DIR \*.* /A:D /S | FIND "MORALS"
```

That's the DIR command, a space, and then a backslash and star-dot-star. That's followed by another space, a slash-A, a colon and D, and then a space and a slash-S. A space follows slash-S, and then the pipe or vertical-bar character, another space, the FIND command, a space, and then the name of the subdirectory you're looking for (MORALS, in this example). The subdirectory name *must* be in uppercase (all caps) and have a double quote character (") on either side.

Press Enter and DOS scours the drive, looking for your subdirectory. If it's found, it is displayed:

```
MORALS    <DIR>  09-23-97 7:23p
Directory of C:\LOST\MORALS
```

The subdirectory's name comes first — as it would in a directory listing. That's followed by the pathname. To change to that subdirectory, you type the pathname following the CD command. In the preceding example, it's

```
C> CD \LOST\MORALS
```

✔ If more than one subdirectory appears, you may have to log or change to each one in turn to find the one you're looking for.

✔ This command may not find your subdirectory. In that case, you can use the TREE command to view your hard disk's tree structure. Refer to the section "The Tree Structure," in Chapter 17.

✔ Refer to Chapter 17 for more information about the CD command and pathnames.

Wildcards (Or Poker Was Never This Much Fun)

Wildcards enable you to manipulate a group of files by using a single DOS command. The object, just like using wildcards in poker, is to specify wildcards in a filename in such a way as to match other files on disk. That way, you can wrangle a group of files — the whole lot of them — with only one command. This stuff is the convenience aspect of computers that they promise in the brochure.

For example, if you've named all the chapters in your Great American Novel with the DOC extension, you can treat all of them as a group by using a wildcard. If all your special project files start with PROJ, you can do things to those files en masse — even if the rest of the files are named something completely different.

DOS uses two wildcards: the question mark (?) and the asterisk (*), which are covered in the following two sections.

✔ Wildcards are generally used with DOS commands. You can seldom use them inside programs.

✔ Not all DOS commands swallow wildcards. The TYPE command, for one, must be followed by a single filename. Refer to the section "Looking at Files," in Chapter 2.

Using the ? wildcard

The ? wildcard is used to match any single letter in a filename. It can be used by itself or in multiples of however many characters you want to match. For example:

> The wildcard filename TH?? matches all four-letter filenames starting with TH, including THIS and THAT.

> The wildcard filename CHAP?? matches all files starting with CHAP and having one or two additional letters in their name. This name includes CHAP00 through CHAP99 and any other combination of characters in those two positions.

You can also use the ? wildcard in the second part of a filename:

> The wildcard filename BOOK.D?? matches all filenames starting with BOOK and having D as the first letter of their three-letter extension.

You can even mix and match the ? wildcard:

> The wildcard filename JULY????.WK? matches all files starting with JULY that have WK as the first two letters of their extension.

All these wildcard combinations can be used with the DOS file-exploitation commands: DIR, DEL, COPY, REN, and so on. Refer to Chapter 18 for more information about manipulating groups of files.

Using the * wildcard

The * wildcard is more powerful than the single-character ? wildcard. The asterisk is used to match groups of one or more characters in a filename. Here's an example:

> The wildcard filename *.DOC matches all files that have DOC as their second part. The first part of the filename can have any number of characters in it; *.DOC matches them all.

> The wildcard filename PROJECT.* matches all files with PROJECT as their first part, with any second part — even if they don't have any second part.

Beware! The * wildcard is rather lame when it comes to being used in the middle of a filename. For example:

> The wildcard filename B*ING matches all filenames that start with the letter *B*. DOS ignores the ING part of the name because it comes *after* the wildcard. I know. It's dumb. But that's the way DOS is.

Quirky yet easily skippable wildcard stuff

If you want to match all filenames that start with B, use this wildcard:

```
B*
```

This wildcard matches all files, whether or not they have a second part. True, you could use B*.*, but DOS matches the same files, so why bother with the extra dot-star?

The wildcard *. (star-dot) matches only filenames *without* an extension. This is the only time under DOS that a command can end in a period. Here's an example:

```
C> DIR *.
```

In this example, the DIR command shows only files without any extension (typically, only the subdirectories).

Using *.* (star-dot-star)

The most popular wildcard is the "Everyone out of the pool!" wildcard, *.*, which is pronounced *star-dot-star*. It means everything, all files, no matter what their name (but usually not directories).

Because star-dot-star matches everything, you should be careful when you're using it. This is that one rare occasion in your life when you can get everyone's attention. It's like this: You can't fool all the files some of the time, but you can fool all of them all the time with star-dot-star.

- ✔ The COPY *.* command copies all files in the directory. Refer to the section "Copying a Group of Files," in Chapter 18.

- ✔ The DEL *.* command is deadly; it ruthlessly destroys all files in the directory; refer to the section "Deleting a Group of Files," in Chapter 18.

- ✔ Using the REN command with *.* is tricky. You must specify a wildcard as the second part of the REN command; you cannot give every file in the directory the same name. Here's an example:

```
C> REN *.DOC *.WP
```

In this example, all files with the DOC extension are renamed to have a WP extension. That's about the most you can do with the REN command and wildcards.

Part IV
Yikes! (Or Help Me Out of This One!)

The 5th Wave   By Rich Tennant

POPOTAMUS MAN

MR. TWEETY
RAISED BY WILD
PARAKEETS

DIRECT FROM
AUSTRALIA!

GUY WHO BOUGHT OS/2 BECAUSE HE THOUGHT APPLICATIONS RAN A WHOLE LOT BETTER THAN UNDER DOS!

FREAK SHOW $1.00

In this part . . .

A certain level of fear is present when you use a computer. Don't worry — even the DOS gurus feel it. I used to think that it came from watching all those movies and TV shows where computers spontaneously blew up, spewing sparks and rubble every which way. That just isn't true anymore; today's computers are so powerful that they merely induce earthquakes and cause people to spontaneously combust.

Seriously, your computer won't explode. At times, it *will* do some unexplainable things that frustrate and annoy you. Don't take it personally! Although computers have their moments, it's still up to you to know what you can fix yourself and what requires the attention of an expert. The chapters in this part tell you the difference between the two situations.

Chapter 20

When It's Time to Toss In the Towel (And Call a DOS Guru)

● ●

In This Chapter

▶ Spotting computer problems and narrowing down the causes

▶ Detecting and dealing with software problems

▶ Fixing a broken battery (when the computer forgets the time)

▶ Locating a lost hard drive

▶ Determining when it's time to reset the system

▶ Knowing what to do after you've reset your computer (in a panic)

▶ Preparing to get help

▶ Dealing with some form of beverage spilled on the keyboard

● ●

Computers, like anything made by the human hand, aren't perfect. For the most part, they work flawlessly. But suddenly you feel that something is wrong — like when you're driving your car and it feels a little sluggish. Then, you hear *the noise*. Although computers don't usually make noises when they go south, they do start behaving oddly. This chapter tells you what you can do in those situations, and it gives you an idea of when it's time to yell out for a professional to deal with the situation.

"My Computer's Down, and I Can't Get It Up!"

You have a problem. Your computer isn't working the way it should. Something is definitely amiss.

The first step is to analyze the problem. Break everything down and find out what is working. Even if you can't fix the problem, you're better prepared to tell an expert about it and have him or her deal with it.

Check these items first:

✔ Is the computer plugged in? Seriously, check to see whether it is. If the computer is plugged in to a power strip, make sure that the power strip is plugged in and switched on. Furthermore, you may want to check other items plugged in to the same socket. Bad sockets happen. Check the circuit breaker too.

✔ Is everything else plugged in? Monitors, modems, and printers all need to be plugged in. Are power cords attached? Are they turned on?

✔ Note that most power cords on your computer have two connections: One end plugs in to the wall (or a power strip), and the other plugs in to the computer, printer, modem, and other devices. Believe it or not, *both* ends must be plugged in for the computer to work. One end is *not* built in to the computer the way it is on an iron or TV set.

Check these connections:

✔ Computers have a ganglia of cables attached. You have power-supply cables and data cables. A printer has two cables: a power cable and a printer cable. The power cable connects to the wall socket; the printer cable connects to the computer.

✔ Modems can have three or four cables attached: a power supply; a data line between the modem and the computer's serial port; one phone line from the modem to your telephone; and, often, a second phone line from your modem to the phone company's wall socket.

✔ Make sure that all the cables are connected to their proper ports on the PC's rump. You may have to trace each cable with your finger, seeing as how the back of a PC resembles the tail end of a squid. Also, serial and parallel ports look similar on some PCs. If your modem or printer isn't working, try swapping the plug around a few times (assuming, of course, that the device did work before).

✔ Keyboard cables can become loose, especially considering the unique design of most PCs, where the keyboard is connected to the back (which never made sense). Be careful here: Plug or unplug the keyboard connector only when the computer is turned off.

Here are some other things to check:

✔ Is the computer locked? Most PCs have a keyhole on the front. It must be turned to the unlocked or open position for you to use the computer.

✔ Is the monitor off or dimmed? Monitors have their own on/off switch; make sure that the monitor switch is on. Also, because monitors can be dimmed, check the brightness knob. Furthermore, some computers have *screen-dimming* programs. Try pressing the spacebar to see whether the monitor comes back on.

✔ Is your PC asleep? If you can see lights on the computer's front panel, the computer is probably asleep. Locate the crescent moon button and press it to bring the PC out of its coma.

✔ Have you had a blackout? If so, you can't use your computer. Sorry.

✔ Have you had a brownout? A *brownout* happens when the electric company isn't sending enough juice through the power lines. A computer doesn't turn on if the required number of volts isn't present. If the system is already on, a brownout forces the system to shut itself off. This situation is unusual because, during a brownout, the lights in the room and all your clocks may continue to work.

Buy your computer a UPS. No, not a big brown truck — an Uninterruptible Power Supply. This is a battery backup that lets you keep working in the event of a brownout or, in the event of a blackout, gives you time to shut down your computer in an orderly fashion. You can buy a UPS just about anywhere computers are sold.

The following list of items are all general things to look for and quick items to check if you're not a professional computer doctor. They're also all hard-ware items. If your problem is in your software, see the section "It's Just Acting Weird," later in this chapter.

✔ If possible, you can further narrow the problem to a specific part of your computer: the computer box, disk drives, keyboard, monitor, printer, or some other peripheral. If everything works okay except for one part of the computer, you've narrowed the problem far enough to tell the repair-person about it over the phone.

✔ Fixing this stuff isn't hard. Most repair places and computer consultants simply replace a defective part with a brand-new one. I'll go out on a limb, in fact, and say: Never trust anyone who claims to be able to fix what you have without needing to replace anything. I speak from experience here. Some bozo claimed (back in 1988) that he could fix my $4,000 laser printer. After $600 of his attempts, it ended up costing me only (relatively speaking) $1,000 to fully replace the defective part. It was an expensive lesson, but one worth passing on.

✔ For more information about ports, refer to the section "What Are Ports?" in Chapter 7. A general discussion of all types of computer hardware is offered throughout Part II of this book.

It's Just Acting Weird

Computers act weird all the time. Sometimes, however, they act more weird than usual. If you've read through the preceding section and have determined that your hardware works fine, what you may have is a software problem.

The best thing to check for with a software problem is any recent change made to the system, specifically your CONFIG.SYS and AUTOEXEC.BAT files. Adding new items or deleting old ones can drastically affect how the system works: You can lose disk drives; some programs don't find enough memory; and some applications refuse to work. To remedy the problem, undo the changes to either file (CONFIG.SYS or AUTOEXEC.BAT) or call someone else for help. For more details about editing CONFIG.SYS and AUTOEXEC.BAT files, refer to Chapter 16.

Frequently, weirdness occurs after a time. The longest I've been able to continuously run my word-processing software (without shutting the computer off) is about three weeks. (Okay, I slept a little every night.) After three weeks, mold must grow on the circuits because the computer suddenly stops working. The same thing happens to other programs too, but with different time periods involved. Resetting the computer seems to solve the problem.

Be wary of *memory-resident programs* (also called *TSRs*). If you notice your computer locking up tight, a memory-resident program may be to blame. Also, *popping up* a memory-resident program while your computer is in graphics mode may cause the screen to tweak — if not right away, then definitely when you return to graphics mode.

The mouse has been known to cause many problems, sometimes even with programs that don't use one. If you notice any random characters on your screen, they're probably caused by a misbehaving mouse. The only real cure for this situation is to turn off the *mouse driver,* which your local computer guru should do.

- ✔ Don't be surprised if you suspect a hardware problem and it turns out to be software. For example, losing your hard drive is really a software problem; the physical hard disk hasn't left your computer to go outside and frolic in the garden. Instead, DOS has mislaid its map of what equipment it has on board.

- ✔ Any program you're just beginning to use (including DOS) acts weird until it's used to you. In the first month you use a program intensively, you experience at least three confounding, unreproducible errors your guru never heard of — and then they never occur again. Try not to get too mad at the machine or the software.

- ✔ Refer to the "Resetting" section in Chapter 1, for more information about resetting your computer.

The Computer Has Lost Track of the Time

All computers sold today have battery-backed-up clocks inside. They keep the time no matter what, even if you unplug the PC. When you notice that the time isn't correct — or the computer thinks that it's January 1, 1980 (and Jimmy Carter is still in office!), you need to check your battery.

Replacing a computer's battery is as easy as replacing the battery in a clock or camera. If you don't particularly think that's easy, of course, make someone else do it for you.

✔ You have to run your PC's setup program to reset the clock. You may also have to reset other information in the SETUP program, which means that your dealer or a computer "expert" should perform this operation.

✔ Every once in awhile, you should type the word **DATE** at the DOS prompt, just to make sure that your PC hasn't drifted. It's annoying to look for files by date only to see that your computer has been date-stamping everything for 1951. Type **TIME** too and see whether it thinks that it's 1:15 in the morning.

Gulp! The Hard Drive Is Gone!

Hard drives do have a tendency to wander. Although normally no one would care, they do contain all sorts of important information, so concern over their whereabouts is justified.

A hard drive suddenly disappears for one of two reasons. The first is related to the computer's battery. In addition to maintaining the current time, the battery keeps a special area of memory active. In that area of memory, the computer remembers a few things about itself, including whether it has a hard drive. When the battery goes, the computer forgets about the hard drive. Oops!

To fix the battery problem, replace the battery. Because this procedure requires opening up the computer, it's okay to pay someone else to do it if the thought of opening up the computer makes you wince.

After the battery is replaced, you need to run your computer's hardware setup program. You have to tell the computer all about itself again: Give it the current time and tell it about its floppy drives and memory configuration and what *type* of hard drive is installed. Most hard drives are type 48 or 49, and fortunately most setup programs instantly recognize that, so you should be okay.

The second reason a hard drive suddenly disappears is age. The average PC hard drive can run flawlessly for about four years. After that, you start experiencing problems, typically Access, Seek, Read, or Write errors in DOS. These messages are a sign that the hard drive is on its last legs. If you see these ominous words, back up all your work and start hunting for a new drive.

Read This If You Care about Your Data

Buy a new drive when the old one starts to go. Sure, you can run special software utilities to fix those intermittent problems, but that's not going to do much for a hard drive that's truly on its way south for retirement at a reef off Florida. Look at it this way: An old, failing hard drive is like a bald tire. You need a new tire to replace it — not a toupee.

Keeping the old, worn-out hard drive around is also a bad idea. Even if it's only marginal, don't keep it for games or as a "temporary" files disk. That's like keeping your old bald tire as a spare.

A Record of Your Hardware Setup Program

Because your hardware setup program's information is so important, run that program right now and jot down the following important information. If the way you run the hardware setup program isn't obvious to you, get the information about diagnostics programs from Chapter 22.

Program name to run SETUP: _____

Keys to press to run SETUP: _____

First floppy drive: _____

Second floppy drive: _____

First hard drive (type): _____

Second hard drive (type): _____

Main (motherboard memory): _____

Extra memory: _____

Total memory: _____

Monitor/display: _____

Keyboard: _____

Serial port 1: _____

Serial port 2: _____

Printer port 1: _____

Printer port 2: _____

Math coprocessor: _____

Other stuff: _____

Other stuff: _____

Other stuff: _____

Note that not every computer has all these items. If any extra items are mentioned, write them down on the blank lines provided.

Steps to Take for a Locked-Up Computer

Although the Reset button is not a panic button, it's the next best thing. When your computer is all locked up and the programs seem to have flown to Orlando, try these steps:

1. **Press the Esc (Escape) key.**

   Or, if the program uses a different cancel key and you know what it is, press it. For example, the old WordPerfect program uses F1.

2. **Press the Ctrl+C (Control+C) or Ctrl+Break (Control+Break) key combination.**

   This step usually (and safely) cancels any DOS command.

3. **In Windows 95 or Windows 98, just close the DOS program's window.**

   Windows may balk and display a warning message. Whatever. Just close the window, and your problems should be gone.

4. **If none of these tricks works, try pressing Ctrl+Alt+Delete to reset your computer. If that doesn't work or if your keyboard is beeping at you, punch your Reset button.**

Note that you resort to resetting only after trying all the alternatives. Resetting is such a drastic measure that you should really run through your options before trying it. Never act in haste.

- ✔ If your system lacks a reset button and pressing Ctrl+Alt+Delete doesn't reset it, you have to turn off the PC. Refer to the section "Turning the Computer Off," in Chapter 1.

- ✔ Information on using the Ctrl+C cancel key is covered in Chapter 3, in the section "Canceling a DOS Command."

✔ Pressing Ctrl+Alt+Delete in Windows 95 or Windows 98 brings up a special Close Program dialog box. Avoid it! Press the Esc key to close the box.

✔ What does the Reset button do? It interrupts power to the main chip, which causes it to restart.

"I Had to Reset My Computer"

Okay. So you had to reset. I'm assuming that you've reset in the middle of something. Resetting at the DOS prompt is okay and generally doesn't do anything bad. Resetting in the middle of a program, however, isn't nice. Although it's not a sin, it's not nice (see the following for why).

After your system comes up again, get to the DOS prompt. This statement means that you should quit any automatic start-up program, such as WordPerfect or (especially) Windows 3.11. Then type the following line at the DOS prompt:

```
C> CHKDSK C: /F
```

That's the CHKDSK command, followed by a space and drive C: (C and a colon), and then another space and a slash-F. Press Enter. If you're asked the question Convert lost chains into files? or something similar, press **Y**.

After CHKDSK is done running, you need to delete some *garbage* files it created. Type this command:

```
C> DEL C:\FILE*.CHK
```

That's the DEL command to delete a file, followed by a space, C, a colon, a backslash, and the filename wildcard FILE*.CHK. You have to type this command only if you told CHKDSK (Check Disk) to convert the lost chains into files. Otherwise, you can skip this step.

✔ You may want to repeat this CHKDSK procedure for each hard drive on your system. If so, substitute the proper drive letter for C: in the first command listed here. Remember that you have to use the second DEL command only if CHKDSK says that it found lost clusters or files.

✔ Refer to the section "CHKDSK Says That I Have Lost Files in Clusters," in Chapter 17, for additional information about CHKDSK.

Now go back to your program, open the file you were working on, and see how much work you lost. (And they say that computers are time-saving devices!)

Running ScanDisk rather than CHKDSK

If you have MS-DOS 6.2 or later, you can run the ScanDisk program rather than CHKDSK to ensure that everything is hunky-dory after a reset. Type this line:

```
C> SCANDISK /ALL
```

That's the ScanDisk command, a space, and then slash-ALL. This command checks all your hard drives. Do a surface scan on each one. Obey the instructions in Chapter 17 if ScanDisk finds any missing files or clusters or whatever.

Freely skip this stuff on why you need to reset

When you reset in the middle of something, you often catch some programs with their pants down, so to speak. These programs may have created temporary files or may have some files that are "half open" on disk. Resetting leaves the files on disk, but not officially saved in any directory. The result is the lost chains or lost clusters that the CHKDSK command is designed to look for.

Running CHKDSK with its slash-F option (or SCANDISK /ALL) scours the drive and puts missing clusters and file fragments into real files on disk. They're named FILE0000.CHK, FILE0001.CHK, and on up through however many files were found. There's nothing most of us can do with these files, so they're okay to delete.

If you don't delete the files, nothing drastic happens. However, two negative things take place after a time: First, the files do occupy space on disk, even though they never appear in any directory. Over time, your disk gets full and you can't figure out why. The second long-term bad thing to happen is that your hard drive becomes very sluggish. Only by deleting these files do you speed things up.

When to Scream for Help

There comes a time when you must scream for help. When that happens, and when you've exhausted all other options mentioned in this book, be a good computer user and obey these guidelines:

- First, get mad. Get it out of your system.

- Know the problem. Be able to offer a full report on what you were doing, what you just did, and what happened. If you've narrowed down the problem, don't be afraid to say what you suspect it is.

- Be at the computer when you call for help. Tech-support people always ask you questions you can answer only while you're really at the computer.

- Tell the person you're begging for help from about anything new or changed on your PC. Always let him or her know whether you attempted to modify something or changed something yourself.

- In order of preference, contact the following people: your office computer specialist or MIS manager, a friend who knows something about computers (and is still willing to help you), your computer dealer, the manufacturer, the Almighty.

- If the problem cannot be fixed over the phone, take the computer to the shop. If possible, try to back up your data before you take the computer (refer to the section "Backing Up," in Chapter 17). Remember to bring along cables and any necessary peripherals. Ask the computer fix-it person what he or she wants you to bring in, just to be sure.

- Always opt for the diagnostic test first. Typical repair places do a look-see for about $30 to $60. Then, they should call you with an estimate. If they fix anything else "voluntarily" (for example, items not mentioned in the estimate or items they have not phoned you about), it's free. Although you should check with the laws in your state or county, generally speaking, repairing a computer is covered by the same laws that protect people at car-repair places.

- It's easier to replace something than to fix it. If possible, try to order a bigger, faster, and better version of the thing you're replacing.

"I Just Spilled Java on My Keyboard!"

I've added this special section because, believe it or not, many people spill things on their keyboards. Maybe not coffee (my personal favorite is lemonade), but something liquid that makes your eyes bulge out for a few comic moments.

Okay. Suppose that you've just spilled something on your keyboard. (If so, you're reading this section fast, so I'll type it as quickly as I can.)

Just turn off the computer!

Never, under any circumstances, should you unplug the keyboard with the computer still on!

Depending on the size of the spill, you may be able to save your information and quit the application; it's always better to turn off the PC at the DOS prompt. If not, it's okay to just flip the power switch. Try to pour out any excess liquid. Use a paper towel to sop up any remaining excess liquid.

Let the keyboard dry out. For coffee, the drying process should take about 24 hours. After that time, turn on your PC and refer to the section "'I Had to Reset My Computer,'" earlier in this chapter. Everything else should work as it did before.

If you've spilled something sugary on your keyboard, the dry-out time is still 24 hours. However, sugary stuff tends to create a sticky film. It doesn't interfere too heavily with the electronics, but it makes your keys stick. I've heard of people giving their keyboards a "bath" in a special solution. However, I recommend taking the keyboard to a pro for cleaning. In fact, it's a good thing to do regularly, considering all the cookie crumbs, chip fragments, and hair (ugh!) that ends up in your keyboard.

✔ If you have to unplug your keyboard, do it with the computer turned off.

✔ I've spilled liquid on just about every computer keyboard I've owned. Two of the keyboards, unfortunately, could not recover. I have no idea why, but they just stopped working. If that happens to you, you can buy a replacement keyboard, typically for $50 to $200, depending on what kind of features it has and who makes it.

✔ If you're accident-prone and you expect to spill other liquids on your keyboard from time to time, you can buy a clear, plastic cover molded to fit the keyboard's contour. You can still type and use the keyboard, but it's sealed.

Chapter 21

After You Panic, Do This

*I*f you're still in a panicky mode, refer to the preceding chapter. That's more of a panic-stricken chapter. This chapter is about what to do *after* you panic. The situation can always be resolved, no matter what. Even if the system is making popping noises and you see smoke, you have nothing to worry about (unless the drapery catches fire).

"Where Am I?"

Has this ever happened to you: You're driving your car and suddenly you realize that you've been under highway hypnosis? What happened during the last few miles? Where are you? Well, that's never happened to me. But sometimes I do wake up in the middle of the night screaming (if that makes you feel any better).

Getting lost is part of using a computer. If you ever find yourself lost, try one of these remedies:

✔ If you are using a familiar program and suddenly find yourself in the unfamiliar — but still in the program — try pressing Esc to *back out* (or press whatever the cancel key is, such as F1 in the old versions of WordPerfect).

✔ If pressing Esc doesn't work, check the keyboard. Press a few keys. If the keyboard starts beeping, the system is locked. You need to reset. Refer to the "Resetting" section, in Chapter 1.

✔ If you're suddenly out at the DOS prompt, see the following section.

✔ If you find yourself lost at the DOS prompt, use the CD command to find out where you are. Typing **CD** tells you the current drive and directory, and it may explain why the program you were trying to run doesn't work. Refer to Chapter 17 for more information.

✔ If you notice that your DOS commands aren't working or the display doesn't quite look right, you may want to check the DOS version. Type the **VER** command, and DOS dutifully tells you its make and model number. Refer to the section "Names and Versions," in Chapter 3, for more information.

✔ In Windows 3.11, Windows 95, or Windows 98, try closing your DOS program's window. Banish DOS!

✔ Finally, if nothing works, try resetting. Computers do, occasionally, pick up and go to Hawaii to watch the surf. Pressing the Reset button or Ctrl+Alt+Delete brings them back to reality.

"How Do I Get Back?"

Sometimes you may find yourself in a different place. Suppose that you are working in Lotus 1-2-3 and trying to save a worksheet when you suddenly find yourself at the DOS prompt. What happened? Or maybe you were at the DOS prompt just a moment ago, and now a strange program is on-screen.

In the latter case, you probably have just brought up a *pop-up* program by accident. This type of program is triggered by certain keypresses, and you may have stumbled across one of them. Press Esc to exit. This action should work and return you to the DOS prompt. (I've never seen a pop-up program that didn't pop back down after you press Esc.)

If you were just in a program and are now at a DOS prompt and you know that you didn't purposely quit the program, look at the screen. Do you see the MS-DOS copyright notice? If so, type

```
C> EXIT
```

This command returns you to your program. (If you're wrong, typing **EXIT** doesn't hurt anything.)

If you don't see the copyright notice, you've probably been dumped out of the program. To reenter the program, press F3 and then Enter. If you press F3 and don't see anything, try typing **MENU** or whatever command you normally type to use your computer (or the application you were so rudely ejected from).

Some programs require you to type two things when the program starts. For example, if you were running an accounting package in Basic, you may have to type something like this:

```
C> BASIC GL
```

or this:

```
C> QBASIC /RUN GL
```

dBASE also requires you to type two things to run a dBASE program. If you know the name of the program to run, put it after DBASE at the DOS prompt:

```
C> DBASE PAYROLL
```

In Windows 3.11, Windows 95, or Windows 98, you may have accidentally switched windows. Press the Alt+Tab key combination a few times to switch back to any window you may have accidentally exited from.

- ✔ Refer to the section "The F3 Key," in Chapter 3, for information.
- ✔ The "Running a Program" section, in Chapter 2, has a list of popular program names and the commands required to run them.
- ✔ Refer to Chapter 15 for more information about restarting dBASE, menu systems, and other black boxes.

"Where Is My File?"

If you just saved a file or are looking for one that you absolutely know exists somewhere, it may just be out of sight for now. Refer to the section "Finding a Lost File," in Chapter 19, for details on getting the file back.

"Where Is My Program?"

Programs are harder to lose than files, but it happens. The approach to finding a lost program depends on how you run the program.

If you run a program manually, you may just be lost on the disk. The manual way usually involves typing a CD command and then typing the name of the program at the next DOS prompt. If you type the CD command and get an Invalid directory error message, you're probably in the wrong place. Type this command:

```
C> CD \
```

It logs you to the root directory. Try running your program again. If it still doesn't work, try logging to the proper drive. To log to drive C, for example, type

```
D> C:
```

That's C and a colon. To log to any other drive, type its letter and a colon, and then type the preceding CD command. That should get you on the proper footing.

If you normally run your program by typing its name at the prompt and you get a Bad command or file name error message, DOS may not remember where it put your program. This situation usually happens because the *search path* has, somehow, been changed. I don't explain here how you can undo that; simply reset your computer to get the proper search path back: Press the Reset button or Ctrl+Alt+Delete.

- ✔ If you notice that DOS loses your files frequently yet resetting seems to bring them back, tell someone about it. Let that person know that some program on your system is "resetting the search path" and that you aren't particularly fond of it. He or she should be able to fix the problem for you.

- ✔ Refer to the section "I Had to Reset My Computer," in Chapter 20, if you do reset.

- ✔ Information about the CD command and your disk's directory structure can be found all over Chapter 17.

The Perils of DEL *.*

Yeah, deleting all your files can be a drastic thing. The DEL *.* command razes with abandon every file in a directory. However, a warning is displayed before this happens: DOS tells you that all files in the directory are about to be churned to dust and asks whether that's okay. You must type a **Y** to go on. Simple enough; you've been warned. Yet too many DOS beginners and experts alike are quick to press the Y key.

Before typing the **DEL *.*** command, make sure that you're in the proper directory. Use the CD command if the prompt doesn't display the current directory. (Refer to the "Current Directory" section, in Chapter 17, and to the section "Prompt Styles of the Rich and Famous," in Chapter 3.) All too often, you mean to delete all the files in one directory, but you happen to be in another directory when that happens.

If the files were accidentally deleted, they can be recovered by using the UNDELETE command. As soon as you've recognized your mistake, type

```
C> UNDELETE *.* /ALL
```

This command should bring back as many of your files as possible. Note that each may have a funky name, with the # character replacing the first letter. Use the REN command to rename the files one by one back to their original states.

> ✔ Refer to the section "Undeleting a File," in Chapter 18, for more informa-tion about the UNDELETE command; refer to the section "Renaming a File," in the same chapter, for information about REN.

> ✔ If a file cannot be recovered, it cannot be recovered. DOS knows about these things and doesn't push the subject any further.

"I Just Deleted an Entire Subdirectory!"

Neat. This result really requires effort on your behalf. You must not only delete all files in a subdirectory but also use the RD (or RMDIR) command to peel off a directory (or the wicked DELTREE command). That command isn't even covered in this book! Congratulations.

Now, the bad news: You cannot use the UNDELETE command to recover a lost subdirectory. Although the command should be able to achieve this result, it doesn't.

The only way to recover a subdirectory is to *restore* it from a recent backup. Depending on how recent your backup is and how new the files were in the subdirectory, you may or may not get a full recovery.

Restoring a directory by using MSBackup

Eight steps are involved in restoring a subdirectory. Most important, you must restore from a recent backup. Although older backups work, like those two guys trapped in the Time Tunnel, you miss a great deal of stuff that has happened since you last backed up. Still, it's better than having to retype all the stuff in the subdirectories or reinstall software.

To restore a subdirectory "branch" by using the MSBackup command, follow these tedious steps:

1. **Type the** MSBACKUP **command at the DOS prompt.**

2. **Choose Restore from the main menu; press** R.

3. **Select a recent backup catalog.**

    It's displayed in the area on-screen titled Backup Set Catalog. Odds are good that what's displayed there is the most recent backup. (The date of the backup is "hidden" inside the catalog filename in the last five characters. For example, 1214A means that the backup was made December 14.) If that's not the catalog you want, press Alt+K and select another catalog from the list.

4. **Select the Select Files option, or press Alt+L.**

5. **Look for the files you want to restore. In this case, look for the sub-directory you decimated. Press the up- or down-arrow keys to highlight that directory. Press the spacebar when that directory is highlighted, to select the directory and all its files.**

6. **Press Enter to lock in your selection.**

7. **Press** S **to select the Start Restore button.**

8. **Follow the instructions on-screen and insert your backup disks as they're called for.**

    (This step is where you're glad that you numbered the disks before you started the backup.)

No, this isn't a pleasant, happy task. But consider that without MSBackup, you'd never get a subdirectory back in any shape. While you're stewing over the swapping of disks, remind yourself to be more careful next time when you're deleting subdirectories.

If you're using Windows 3.11, remember to use the Windows Restore command, which is actually a part of the Windows Backup program. (You should be using Windows rather than DOS to back up anyway.)

Restoring by using the pre-DOS 6 RESTORE command

Ah, the cruddy old DOS RESTORE command. Those were the days: cryptic command lines, options, and switches, and one command did the job. None of that mouse stuff. Be thankful that you don't have to contend with the new MSBACKUP program. It's new! It's different! It makes opera seem enjoyable!

Suppose that, in a massive Freudian slip, you just deleted the directory C:\FAMILY\FATHER. To restore this directory from a recent backup disk set, place the first backup disk in drive A and type

```
C> RESTORE A: C:\FAMILY\FATHER\*.* /S
```

That's the RESTORE command, a space, the drive you're restoring from (A) and a colon. That's followed by a space and the name of the subdirectory you deleted — plus a backslash and star-dot-star. Then comes another space and finally a slash-S.

DOS scans your backup disks, asking you to remove each one and insert the next one in sequence. It does this until all the files are restored.

"I Just Reformatted My Disk!"

This is why disks are labeled: so that you know what's on them. Before you reformat a disk, check to see that it's empty. Refer to the section "Reformatting Disks," in Chapter 13. If you do reformat a disk, type this line:

```
C> UNFORMAT A:
```

If you're unformatting a disk in drive B, substitute B: for A: here. Press Enter and follow the instructions on-screen. Be patient: It takes a few minutes to unformat a disk.

Your disk may not be in the best shape after it's unformatted. For example, most of the files in the root directory may be gone. If they're found, they will probably be given generic names, as will any of your subdirectories. On the bright side, the data in your subdirectories, and all the subsubdirectories, will be totally intact.

Unformatting a disk works only if you use the UNFORMAT command on the disk before putting any new files on it.

Restoring from a Backup

Backing up is something you should do often. Your computer manager probably has you set up on some kind of backup schedule or, if you're on your own, you should back up your important stuff every day and do a full backup weekly or monthly, depending on how much you use your computer.

Rarely is the restore part of backing up done. It happens in only those few circumstances in which something goes wrong with the hard drive, you lose files or a subdirectory, or you need to recall an older version of a program.

How to restore by using the DOS 6 MSBackup utility

Here's how to restore a subdirectory you accidentally blew away:

1. **Your hard drive is gone. Weep bitterly.**

2. **Locate your MS-DOS 6 disks.**

3. **Reinstall MS-DOS 6 on your hard drive, all over again.**

4. **Type the** MSBACKUP **command at the DOS prompt.**

5. **Choose from the main menu; press** R.

6. **Select a recent backup catalog.**

   Look only at those catalogs whose filenames end in FUL. These files record your full hard disk backups, the best source for restoring the whole ding-dong hard drive.

   The catalog files are displayed in the area labeled Backup Set Catalog. It's usually a safe bet that what you see there now is what you want. If not, press Alt+K and select another catalog from the list that's displayed.

7. **Press Alt+I to highlight the Restore Files area. Press the up- or down-arrow keys to highlight the hard drive you want to restore — the one you blew away. Press the spacebar when that drive letter is highlighted to restore** *All files*.

8. **Press** S **to start restoring files to the hard drive.**

9. **Keep an eye on the screen and swap your backup disks out and in as they're called for.**

■ ✔ This technique works best when you back up often.

How to restore by using the pre-DOS 6 RESTORE command

If you need to restore a single file and you're fortunate not to have the DOS 6 MSBackup utility, use this command:

```
C> RESTORE A: C:\WORK\PROJECT\FILE1.DAT
```

In this example, A: is the drive containing your backup disk (or disks). You can use B: if the backup disks are to be placed in drive B. The full pathname of the file follows the drive letter, a colon, and a space. In this example, the file FILE1.DAT is to be restored. You must specify a full pathname, and the file can be restored to only that directory. Wildcards can also be used to restore a group of files.

If you need to restore a subdirectory, specify that directory's name plus a backslash (\ ) and star-dot-star:

```
C> RESTORE A: C:\MISC\*.* /S
```

In this line, A: indicates the drive containing the backup disk (or disks). Substitute B: if the backup disks will be placed in that drive. The drive letter is followed by a colon, a space, and then the full pathname of the subdirectory to restore. Do you see how star-dot-star is used here? It restores all files in the subdirectory. Furthermore, a space and a slash-S are added to the command.

I recommend that you use a third-party backup program. If you've been using the DOS Backup command anyway, use this command to restore your entire hard drive:

```
C> RESTORE A: C:\*.* /S
```

That's RESTORE and then A: to indicate the drive containing the backup disks (use B: if you're putting the disks into that drive). That's followed by a space, C, a colon, and star-dot-star, which indicates all files on drive C. If you're restoring to another hard drive, substitute its drive letter for C:. Finally, a space and a slash-S ends the command.

In all circumstances, you should start restoring by putting the first backup disk into the proper floppy drive. The RESTORE command tells you when to swap disks — that is, when to remove the current disk and replace it with the next disk in sequence. This process happens until all the files are restored.

✔ Backing up is covered in Chapter 17.

✔ Refer to Chapter 17 for more information about directories and path-names.

✔ Refer to the section "Using *.* (star-dot-star)," in Chapter 19, for information about using that wildcard.

Chapter 22

Diagnosing, Disinfecting, and Getting Help

● ●

In This Chapter

▶ Using a diagnostic program

▶ Scanning for viruses

▶ Using DOS's feeble online help

▶ Getting technical support

● ●

*T*his chapter covers a broad canvas but does it with color, style, and a boldness that even Bob Ross couldn't match. First come the majestic background diagnostic programs that tell you what's what inside your PC. These programs are followed by some bold foliage, the antivirus programs. The antivirus programs can help you fight the viral plague we're supposed to be having all the time (at least according to the media). Finally, I've added a waterfall and lots of "little friends" — the various ways DOS gives you help. There. I painted that whole thing without once using the words *titanium white* or *burnt umber.*

MS-DOS 6.0 and 6.2 are the only DOS versions that offer you the tools mentioned in this chapter. Otherwise, consider the information here only for enlightenment purposes.

Windows has its own set of tools for correcting and fixing various problems. If you're running DOS in Windows 3.11, use the special tools that come with it to fix things. Likewise, in Windows 95 or Windows 98, use the special disk fixing tools that come with those operating systems. Refer to your favorite Windows book for more information.

What's Up, Doc?

No matter how long you stare at a computer, you just can't tell what's inside it. This is the reason that the medical profession invented X-rays. Doctors just couldn't tell what was wrong inside you unless they cut you up and poked around. Then, after they found out, they would have to stitch you back together again and hope that you would live so that you could pay the bill. Then, along came X-rays and the ever popular MRI scan, and they could see inside you, well assured that you would live to pay the bill. Computers are different.

First off, computers can't be X-rayed unless you take them to the airport. I'm not going to drone on about how airport security people go all verclempt whenever they see a computer. Rule out X-rays. Second, computers can't talk. People can talk. "Doctor, my appendix is on my front side." Computers can barely muster "Hello, I'm now going to be rude to you" — so that's out too.

On the up side, though, computers are pretty self-aware. Given the right type of program, they can fill you in on all sorts of internal tidbits without your ever having to wield a screwdriver (or an MRI scanner). You get this information by using a program called a *diagnostic utility*.

Many diagnostic utilities exist in the DOS universe. Chances are that you already have one and don't even know it; both PC Tools and Norton Utilities come with diagnostics. More likely than not, however, you probably have the MSD, Microsoft Diagnostics, program that comes with both MS-DOS and Windows 3.11. Since that's the case, I ramble on at length about it here.

Diagnostic programs don't fix things so much as they tell you what's inside your PC.

Running MSD

You start MSD by typing **MSD** at the command prompt:

```
C> MSD
```

After you press Enter, the computer rummages around inside itself for a few tense moments (no need to step behind the lead wall here). Then it pronounces its prognosis on a screen that looks dreadfully like Figure 22-1.

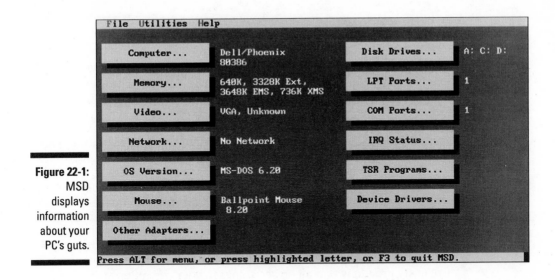

Figure 22-1:
MSD
displays
information
about your
PC's guts.

The first screen shows you only the basics: The Computer box tells you which microprocessor lives in your PC; the Memory box gives a cryptic memory summary; Video tells you about your display; and so on.

If you select a specific area, such as pressing **P** for Computer (or clicking that button with your mouse), you see more detailed information. Most of the stuff displayed is pretty nerdy, so proceed at your own risk.

To quit MSD, press the F3 key. You may have to press the Esc key a few times first to close any open windows or panels.

Okay, you really want to know which microprocessor you have?

A key thing to know about your PC is which *microprocessor,* or *CPU,* dwells within its off-white case. To find out, start MSD (see the preceding section) and then press **P** to activate the Computer screen-panel thing. There, you see a bunch of detailed information about your computer's basic bones. For example, some tech-support people may want to know your "BIOS version." There it is on-screen. The microprocessor info is found in the middle of the list — Processor. Press Esc to clean the screen away when you're bored with it.

More Than Bugs: Viruses

Protect your system against evil viruses. Wicked they are! Chances that you'll get one? Not as great as you fear. Although viruses are real, unless you're swapping a large number of disks that contain illegal or *pirated* software — especially games — you'll probably never see a virus.

We have the media to thank for the proliferation of virus phobia among computer users. The hype may be a bit heavy, yet sadly viruses aren't a myth. On the up side, you can do something about them. Many companies now sell antivirus software. These programs (utilities) go out and hunt for viruses infecting your files and painlessly remove them. Again, MS-DOS 6 — the "utility" DOS — comes with a program called Microsoft Anti-Virus, or MSAV. MSAV devours viruses quite nicely, and I ramble on about it here at length.

- ✔ What is commonly called a *computer virus* could really be one of a hoard of nasty programs that all do sad things to your computer, specifically the files you store on your hard drive. I have no need to go into detail or all the cutesy names given to these programs. Suffice it to say that you don't want one.

- ✔ In addition to Anti-Virus, DOS provides another program to aid in antivirus protection. The VSafe program is a TSR, sitting in memory and keeping a sharp eye on important parts of your disk. If any tampering occurs, VSafe lets you know instantly. The reason that VSafe isn't covered here is that it's somewhat of an alarmist, screaming "Wolf" once too often. The use of VSafe is covered in the DOS 6 manual (cough, hack!); also refer to the HELP command for more information about VSafe if you dare to use it.

Some common questions about computer viruses

What can I do to prevent viruses from invading my computer? Safe computing practices are listed in the sidebar "Steps to avoid nasty programs," later in this chapter. Most important among them is to never *boot* (start your computer) by using a strange floppy disk.

How can I tell whether my PC is infected with a virus? Don't be too quick to blame quirkiness on a "virus." Unfortunately, most viruses are specifically nasty and display appropriate messages telling you of your peril — *after* the damage is done. Before doing any damage, most viruses lurk inside your PC. The only way to be sure is to run a virus-scanning program.

I hear that my PC caught a virus in the Orient. Should I wear a mask while I compute? No, the bugs a PC catches are electronic. People don't "catch" computer viruses. Spray some Lysol around your computer room if it makes you feel good.

Will copying files from my friend's disk infect my PC? Probably not; however, it's a good idea to scan the disk with your antivirus software before you copy the files. Because most viruses infect your computer when you run an infected program, merely copying files doesn't have a risk. Running an infected program or — this is the most deadly way — booting from an infected floppy disk is what leads to infection.

How can I be sure that files I download with my modem don't have viruses? Run Anti-Virus on the files. If the files are contained in a ZIP file or other archive, "explode" them first and then run your antivirus software on the lot. You know in a matter of seconds whether the files are free from infection.

Can I get a virus from e-mail? Nope. Not unless the person sending you e-mail has "attached" a file, in which case the file may be infected. Then again, only if you run the file does it do any damage. To be sure, scan the file before you run it. And never accept random programs from people you don't know on the Internet.

How do I get rid of a virus? There are many techniques for virus removal, from "peeling" the virus from your disk to utterly destroying the infected file. Most antivirus software handles the removal process for you if any infected files are found. After that, you're safe from impending doom (unless your PC becomes infected again).

If my computer has a virus, should I restore from a backup to delete it? Generally speaking, no. The reason is that the virus may have been backed up, and restoring the file would restore the infection. You should first remove the virus and then do an immediate, full, hard drive backup.

It's said that a virus affects your computer's behavior, making it run slowly and often impeding your ability to get work done. If so, isn't Microsoft Windows a virus? No comment.

Running Anti-Virus

MS-DOS 6 comes with MSAV, or Microsoft Anti-Virus. To run it and scan your computer for viruses, type the following command at your DOS prompt:

```
C> MSAV
```

Type **MSAV** and press Enter. The program starts and displays all sorts of wondrous information, as shown in Figure 22-2. Pressing the F5 key makes the program look for and remove any virus-infected files on the hard drive.

```
┌─────────────────────────────────────────────────────────────┐
│ ─                    Microsoft Anti-Virus                    │
│  ┌──────────────────────────────────────────────────────┐   │
│  │ ─                     Main Menu                       │   │
│  │                                                      │   │
│  │   ┌ etect            ┐      ┌      Detect        ┐   │   │
│  │   Detect & Clean              • The Detect option scans the │
│  │   Select new drive               current drive for viruses. │
│  │                              • If any viruses are detected │
│  │   Options                       you have the option to clean │
│  │                                 the infected file, continue │
│  │   Exit                          without cleaning, or stop the │
│  │                                 scanning process.   │   │
│  │                                                      │   │
│  │   Microsoft                  Work Drive:        C:   │   │
│  │   ▶▶▶ Anti-Virus ───────     Last Virus Found:  None │   │
│  │                              Last Action:       None │   │
│  └──────────────────────────────────────────────────────┘   │
│  Help   Drive  Exit   Detect  Clean  Delete  Options  List  │
└─────────────────────────────────────────────────────────────┘
```

Figure 22-2:
Anti-Virus
(like Auntie
Em but not
as obsessed
with count-
ing chicks).

- ✔ If MSAV finds a virus, follow the instructions on the screen for virus removal. Then, phone up a friend and brag that you had a virus but MSAV saved your butt.

- ✔ I don't have any infected files; otherwise, I'd show you what the "I found one and would you like it removed?" screen looks like.

- ✔ Press F3 followed by Enter when you're ready to quit MSAV.

- ✔ Run MSAV as often as you like. Chances are, as long as you don't use illegal software or run programs somebody gave you "for free," you're safe from viruses.

Yes, You Can Believe It: DOS Has Lots of Help for You

No more can DOS be called uncivilized. Rude, perhaps, but definitely not as rigid and cold as in versions past. With DOS Version 5 and later, you get help. MS-DOS 6? Hey, you get perhaps the most helpful hand DOS has ever extended to a beginner. DOS offers not only online help with its many commands and utilities but also command-line help and a nifty full-screen help thing with examples and suggestions and, O, lots of fun.

Steps to avoid nasty programs

1. Never start your computer by using a strange or unmarked floppy disk.

   Even if a well-meaning friend gave you the disk (to examine some game or leer at some graphics files), never start your computer with it. It's the number-one way viruses are spread among PCs. (Also, these types of unmarked floppy disks are usually pirated copies of software, and their use is illegal.)

2. Avoid software that comes on unlabeled disks.

   Software you buy in the store should come in a shrink-wrapped box and be properly labeled. Some shareware software or free-bie stuff may come crudely labeled — but be careful; run MSAV on that disk as described in this chapter. Again, software on an unlabeled disk is probably pirated, and you shouldn't use it anyway.

3. Okay, enough beating around the bush: *Pirated* software, stuff that people copy and distribute illegally, is often rife with viral infections. Don't pirate; don't get a virus.

4. If possible, ensure that you're the only person who uses your computer.

   If your PC is out in the open, someone may happen by and ungraciously infect it for you. (Indeed, around my old office, computer pranks were popular to the point of memo-randum and condemnation by The Powers That Be.) When someone asks to borrow your PC, just say No!

5. Run virus-scanning and -removal software often.

   The Microsoft Anti-Virus program is a great tool for this purpose.

Help with DOS 5

DOS 5 was the first version of DOS to even think about offering help. You get not only the nifty /? command line help (covered in the following section) but also a program called HELP that lists all the DOS commands and can display more information about each of them. It works like this:

```
C> HELP
```

Type **HELP**. Avoid the temptation to type an exclamation point after that. Then press Enter. You see a list of all the DOS commands plus a brief description of what each one does.

You can also type HELP followed by a space and the name of a DOS command to see what that command does. Wow. Whodathot.

Keeping your antivirus software up-to-date

To scan for viruses, most antivirus software looks for what are called *virus signatures*. These telltale pieces of computer code identify viral infections. Most antivirus software can recognize hundreds of computer virus signatures. Unfortunately, the deviants are out there busily dreaming up new viruses whose signatures your software may not recognize.

Don't panic about it! As fast as they're churning out new viruses, the boys and girls who write antivirus software are working on solutions that recognize those new virus signatures. To obtain this new information, you need to either fill out and return the update coupon that came with your antivirus software or use a modem to access the software developers (or often their *forum* on CompuServe) and grab the new signature files. Using a modem to get the files can be easy, though I recommend that you have your guru do it.

The /? command-line switch

DOS command-line commands have the universal /? option, or *help switch*. You use this dealie after any DOS command to see a list of requirements and options for that command. The technotypes call it the *command format*. To see it, follow any DOS command with /? and no other options. Here's an example:

```
C> COPY /?
```

In this example, the COPY command is followed by a space and then a slash-question mark. Rather than copy anything (or display the "huh?" error message), DOS spits out a list of command options and formats for the COPY command.

The good thing about /? help is that it's there! It works with all DOS commands! The bad thing is that the help is no more useful than the DOS manual. Hey! It *is* the DOS manual! Right on the screen. How conve-e-e-nient.

✔ The information that /? displays is rather terse — not friendly at all. If you want something more friendly, see the following section, about the HELP command.

✔ What? The /? switch doesn't work? Then it's one of two things. First, you have DOS 4 or earlier. If that's not the case, what you probably have isn't a DOS command. Some third-party utilities work on the command line just like DOS commands. If /? doesn't work, most likely you've found one of those. Refer to its manual for the help you need.

✔ Refer to the section "About the Darn Command Formats," in Chapter 14, for more information about deciphering the darn command formats.

The F1 help key

DOS 6 has two types of commands. First are the traditional commands, such as COPY, MOVE, and REN. Then come commands that really should be called *utilities*. They include MSBackup, Anti-Virus, and a few others. For those commands — the MS-DOS 6 utilities — you can get helpful information by pressing the F1 key. This key is a standard help convention for most applications: Press F1, and you get help. Easy 'nuff.

The full-on, high-power, calmly desperate HELP command

Like DOS 5, DOS Version 6 has a HELP command. Unlike the pitiful DOS 5 help command, though, with DOS 6 you get what is essentially the manual — nerd meat and potatoes — right on your hard drive. Yet this command is better than having a real manual because it's very specific, provides lots of good examples, and doesn't smell as bad as the real manual.

Two ways to use the HELP command are available. First, you can just type **HELP** at the DOS prompt:

```
C> HELP
```

Do not follow HELP with an exclamation point. Just type **HELP** and press Enter.

When you type HELP by itself, you see a list of DOS commands plus some "topics" on which you can get extra help, as shown in Figure 22-3. Press the arrow keys or the Tab key to highlight the various help subjects, and press Enter to see the helpful information. You can also double-click the topics if you have a mouse.

When you need help with a specific DOS command, type **HELP** and then that DOS command. Here's an example:

```
C> HELP ANSI.SYS
```

Type **HELP**, a space, and then the DOS command or topic of interest. In the preceding example, HELP is followed by ANSI.SYS. After pressing Enter, you see oodles of information about ANSI.SYS and all that.

```
 File  Search                                                          elp
┌──────────────────────── MS-DOS Help: Command Reference ──────────────────┐
│ Use the scroll bars to see more commands. Or, press the PAGE DOWN key. For │
│ more information about using MS-DOS Help, choose How to Use MS-DOS Help    │
│ from the Help menu, or press F1. To exit MS-DOS Help, press ALT, F, X.     │
│                                                                           │
│ <What's New in MS-DOS 6.2?>                                               │
│                                                                           │
│ <ANSI.SYS>              <Exit>              <Nlsfunc>                      │
│ <Append>               <Expand>            <Numlock>                      │
│ <Attrib>               <Fasthelp>          <Path>                         │
│ <Batch commands>       <Fastopen>          <Pause>                        │
│ <Break>                <Fc>                <Power>                        │
│ <Buffers>              <Fcbs>              <POWER.EXE>                     │
│ <Call>                 <Fdisk>             <Print>                        │
│ <Cd>                   <Files>             <Prompt>                       │
│ <Chcp>                 <Find>              <Qbasic>                       │
│ <Chdir>                <For>               <RAMDRIVE.SYS>                  │
│ <Chkdsk>               <Format>            <Rd>                           │
│ <CHKSTATE.SYS>         <Goto>              <Rem>                          │
│ <Choice>               <Graphics>          <Ren>                         │
│ <Cls>                  <Help>              <Rename>                       │
│ <Command>              <HIMEM.SYS>         <Replace>                      │
│<Alt+C=Contents> <Alt+N=Next> <Alt+B=Back>                 00006:002       │
└───────────────────────────────────────────────────────────────────────────┘
```

Figure 22-3:
HELP as
MS-DOS 6.2
dishes it up.

✔ To quit HELP, press Alt+F,X. This action chooses the Exit item from the File menu and returns you back to the cozy DOS prompt.

✔ As you read the helpful information, two items are at the top of the HELP screen, just below the menu bar. The items are two of the following: Syntax, Notes, or Examples. The Syntax item displays a screen that de-scribes the command's format and options; Notes displays information about using the command, plus tips; and Examples shows you how the command can be used and what it can do. Always look to the Examples screen. In most cases, what you're looking for is illustrated right there.

✔ You move around in the HELP program by pressing the Tab key. Press Tab to highlight an item on the screen; press Enter to see more information. Other key combinations are displayed at the bottom of the screen.

✔ Lamenting the loss of the DOS 5 timid HELP command? It's still around. Type **FASTHELP** at the prompt.

✔ HELP's Find command can be used to find itsy-bitsy information about specific subjects. For example, if you see the STACKS=0,0 thing in your CONFIG.SYS file, you can type the HELP command and press Alt+S,F to bring up the Find box. Type STACKS in the Find What box and press Enter. DOS scours the HELP command's archives for matching information and displays it right there on-screen.

Your Last Resort: Calling for Technical Support

No rule says that a company must offer you phone support for your computer or its software. However, some companies are nice and offer it to you — sometimes for free — when you need it. For this, you should be thankful.

Never use tech support as a first resort.

Support lines are often flooded with people asking lame questions, which bogs down support for those people who are really in a bind. This book contains the answers to most of your questions and helps you piece together quite a number of PC puzzles. Still, when the time comes and you feel the urge to call technical support, do those folks a favor and run through this list first:

1. **Look up your question in this book or your software manual.**

   Use the index. Refer to the table of contents. Don't be lazy and just read the first few sentences or just pieces of paragraphs. In this book, related information is always listed in the check marks that conclude each section.

2. **Ask your guru for help.**

   If it's your office, then that's what they pay the gurus for. At home, call your crazy neighbor Earl and see whether he's still willing to help you.

3. **Check the online help.**

   Most modern software gives you help by pressing the F1 key. In DOS, you can use the HELP command, as discussed earlier in this chapter. Don't neglect scoping out the "examples" in the HELP for DOS 6.

4. **Refer to the README file.**

   Almost every software program sold today comes with a lengthy README.TXT file, which you're usually exposed to right after installation. Refer to it again if you need to — especially for hardware (computer or printer) problems. Lots of specific information is in there.

5. **Try the situation again and take notes.**

   If you've been diligent to this point, try the operation again. For some dumb reason, it almost always works the second time. If not, take some notes. Write down any error messages or numbers. Also, recall the last thing you did to your PC. I have a friend whom I won't name (okay, it's Tom), and he always messes with his PC and then seems surprised when things foul up afterward. If you mess, expect weirdness. The two *are* related.

6. **Run a diagnostic program.**

   This step doesn't solve any problems. Instead, the diagnostics come in handy when you're telling tech-support people what's where inside your

PC. (Don't forget the MSD program that comes with most versions of DOS and Windows 3.11.)

7. **Dial tech support.**

- Most software manuals bury the tech-support numbers. If so, write them down on the blank pages provided in the back of this book.

- Note that often several ways exist to get tech support. The best is to call up and talk to a real, live human. However, some automated tech-support systems ("voice menus") are quite good. Consider calling them first because the lines aren't as busy as the real human type of tech support.

- Tech-support calls come in three types: Free 800-number lines; toll calls (you pay for the phone call); and expensive calls, where you pay for the call *and* for the person's time on the other end of the line.

- Printer problem? Call your printer's tech-support people. DOS problem? Call whomever sold you DOS. Word-processor problem? Call the word-processor developer.

- Pay attention when you call! Be at your computer with it turned on and ready to go. The tech-support people can help you best when you're helpful to them as well.

- Be careful when you're dialing any 1-900 tech-support numbers. If you misdial, you may get the 1-900 Tech Guy Party Line or the Psychic Nerds Network.

- Tech-support hours are usually from Monday though Friday (but not on holidays) during business hours. Check to see whether the times are Eastern, Central, Mountain, or Pacific.

- Modem support is available from the majority of computer companies. You can download files or pose questions online. Many developers also have forums on CompuServe, and you can get help from newsgroups on the Internet. Companies also have fax lines for tech-support questions, as well as fax-back lines, where the other computer calls your fax machine and sends you the information you requested.

- Software companies often sell more than one product. Make sure that you're calling the right number for that product. Also, Microsoft sells both DOS and Windows. Call those support lines only with your specific DOS and Windows questions. If you're having a problem with a Lotus or Borland product, call them instead.

- For heaven's sake, don't call up and play "Stump the support guy."

- Don't forget to have your serial number handy! Many places ask for a product's serial number before you get support.

Chapter 23

DOS Error Messages (What They Mean, What to Do)

● ●

In This Chapter

▶ Abort, Retry, Fail?

▶ Access denied

▶ Bad command or file name

▶ Bad or missing command interpreter

▶ Divide overflow

▶ Drive not ready error

▶ Duplicate file name or file not found

▶ File cannot be copied onto itself

▶ File creation error

▶ File not found

▶ General failure

▶ Insufficient disk space

▶ Internal stack overflow

▶ Invalid directory

▶ Invalid drive specification

▶ Invalid file name or file not found

▶ Invalid media, track 0 bad or unusable

▶ Invalid number of parameters

▶ Invalid parameter

▶ Invalid switch

▶ Non-system disk or disk error

▶ Not ready, reading drive X

▶ Overwrite filename

▶ Write protect

● ●

The list of possible error messages you may see DOS display is massive — truly huge. The reason isn't that DOS is riddled with mistakes; the reason is that DOS is so vast. When you consider the bonus programs included with DOS 6 — such as DoubleSpace, MSBackup, and Anti-Virus — the potential for error messages is staggering. Rather than have you stagger about, though, this chapter contains 20-something common error messages you may see while you're running your PC. Each error message is explained according to its meaning and probable cause, with a suggested solution for each one. Nothing here is really fatal, though a few of the error messages will scare the bejesus out of you. Never fear — a solution is always at hand.

Note that DOS error messages tend to be kind of vague. The reason is that neither DOS nor the PC hardware is built to perform the kind of defaulted diagnostics that would result in messages like "There's no disk in drive A; please put one in," or "Press A to cancel that last command." Oh, well.

You can find extended discussions of some issues or solutions in other chapters. I've cross-referenced them here.

Abort, Retry, Fail?

Meaning: The latest missile launched by the air force is careening out of control toward Moscow. Actually, this is a generic response to a variety of what DOS calls *fatal errors*. DOS has taken its best stab at doing something and just can't figure out what's wrong.

Probable cause: This message is typically preceded by a line of text explaining what DOS tried to do: Read from a disk, write to a disk, or touch its toes, for example. Nine times out of ten, you see this message when you attempt to access a floppy disk in drive A or B and the drive door is open or no disk is in the drive.

Solution: If you can remedy the situation, such as by closing the drive door or putting a disk in the drive, do so. Then press **R** to *r*etry. If nothing can be done, press **A** for *a*bort (which means cancel, although most programmers don't know whether *cancel* has one or two *l*s in it).

You can press **F**, the *f*ail option, in a few rare circumstances. Suppose that you type **A:** to switch to drive A and no disk is in there. When that happens, the `Abort, Retry, Fail` error message appears and you never see a DOS prompt again — unless you type **F** to fail. Then, you see `Current drive is no longer valid`. Okay. Type **C:** to log back to drive C.

Tales from real life you don't have to read

Most often I get the `Abort, Retry, Fail` error message when I type **A:** rather than **B:** and no disk is in drive A. My solution is to have handy a formatted disk (any disk will do). I slip that disk into drive A and then press **R** to retry. After the DOS command is done (or whatever), I retype the command again and specify **B:** or whichever letter I originally meant to type.

Skip this section only if you don't take the hard drive seriously

When you get the `Abort, Retry, Fail` message and the error DOS displays seems more drastic, it's time to worry a bit. Situations such as a `read error`, `write error`, or `seek error` could be the rumblings of a major disk disaster (especially if the disk you're trying to access is the hard drive). If the errors are consistent, refer to the nearest PC-knowledgeable person and scream "Help" quietly into his or her ear.

Access Denied

Meaning: You've tried to change a file that DOS is not allowed to change.

Probable cause: The file you've specified, or one of several files in a group, has its read-only file protection set. You cannot rename the file with REN; you cannot delete it with DEL; and you cannot use any applications to change the file's contents. This error may also occur if you've specified a subdirectory name in a command that normally manipulates files.

Solution: Just ignore the file. Chances are that the file's not meant to be touched anyway. (If you're desperate, you can refer to the section "The File! I Cannot Kill It!" in Chapter 18.)

Bad Command or File Name

Meaning: DOS doesn't understand the command you just typed.

Probable cause: You mistyped a command name or misspelled the name of a program on disk or DOS cannot find the named program. It's also the typical DOS response when you type a dirty word or hurl an insult via the command line.

Solution: Check your typing. You can also refer to the section "Where Is My Program?" in Chapter 21, if you're certain that the program worked before.

Bad or Missing Command Interpreter

Meaning: DOS cannot locate the file named COMMAND.COM, which contains its basic operations, and so it cannot proceed. Sounds worse than it is.

Probable cause A: One of two categories is usually the culprit. If you were exiting a program to return to the DOS prompt and you saw this message or a similar one referring to an inability to locate COMMAND.COM, it just means that DOS has gotten confused, probably because your program decided to drop DOS off at a different drive than DOS was expecting (like the A, B, or D drive when the C drive is the one that has the COMMAND.COM program on it).

Solution A: Just reboot, reset, or push the Reset button. Everything should be fine at this point because the program was exiting normally anyway.

Probable cause B: This one happens when you're starting your computer. It may mean that you left a disk in drive A; you don't have a disk in drive A and the hard disk hasn't been set up to start DOS; or COMMAND.COM isn't in the root directory of your hard drive where it's supposed to be because it has been moved or deleted (a major no-no).

Solution B: If a disk is in drive A, take it out and push the Reset button. If that's not the problem or it doesn't work, get help from a knowledgeable user. This user will probably dig out your original DOS floppy disk and copy COMMAND.COM back on the hard drive's main directory where it belongs. This assumes that you have a *bootable* copy of the DOS disks around. Just stick your DOS Setup Disk 1 into your drive A and press the Reset button. When the Setup program runs, press F3 twice to quit, and then copy COMMAND.COM back to the drive C root directory. An easier solution is to make a bootable disk just for these types of emergencies. Make a bootable disk by putting a fresh floppy in drive A and typing

```
C> FORMAT A:/S/U
```

The S stands for *system*, which is what COMMAND.COM is part of — the DOS system file group. If FORMAT burps and doesn't do its job or you have only a low-density floppy in a high-density drive, refer to the section in Chapter 13 about formatting a disk.

Divide Overflow

Meaning: A program — not necessarily DOS — has tried to divide some number by zero. On a calculator, it produces the infamous E error. On your PC, it's called *divide overflow*.

Probable cause: The program screwed up. Yeah! It isn't your fault. In fact, it's usually a sign that the program wasn't very well written or tested. Another cause could be computer fatigue; these things happen more often if the PC has been on for a long, long period of time.

Solution: Because this error message usually is followed by a DOS prompt, it means that you can try to run your program again. If you care, see whether you can duplicate the error and then proudly call up the software developer to report a *bug*. (This is really advanced user stuff — your guru will be jealous.) Sometimes a reset solves the problem, especially if it's due to computer fatigue.

Drive Not Ready Error

See the section "Not Ready, Reading Drive X," later in this chapter.

Duplicate File Name or File Not Found

Meaning: You've used the REN command to rename a file and something went wrong.

Probable cause: You've specified a new filename with improper characters in it; you've specified the new name and that file already exists; or the file you want to rename doesn't exist.

Solution: Try the command again. Check to see that a file with the new name doesn't already exist. (Refer to the section "Renaming a File," in Chapter 18, for more information.)

File Cannot Be Copied onto Itself

Meaning: You've forgotten something with the COPY command. This message isn't a major boo-boo. In fact, nothing bad has happened (which is ironic, considering the insincere nature of the COPY command).

Probable cause: You've used the COPY command to duplicate a file and given the duplicate the same name as the original. Although COPY overwrites a file that already exists, you cannot use COPY to overwrite the source file. For example, you probably typed something along the lines of

```
C> COPY MYSELF MYSELF
```

when what you meant to type was

```
C> COPY MYSELF B:
```

and you left off the B:.

Solution: Don't specify the same name twice. Refer to the section "Duplicating a File," in Chapter 18, for the proper ways and means.

File Creation Error

Meaning: For some unspecified reason, DOS does not make a new file.

Probable cause: Using the COPY command to copy or duplicate a file and the filename is already used by a directory; or if a file already exists by that name, but it's a read-only file; or if the disk or directory is full and can't contain any additional files. This error can also be produced by any program as it saves a file, though File creation error is an error message specific to DOS.

'Nother cause: You tried to name a file with the > or | symbols, which is a no-no.

Solution: If the filename is already taken by a directory or some other file, try creating the file by using a new name. If the file is read-only, refer to the section "The File! I Cannot Kill It!" in Chapter 18. If the disk is full, delete some superfluous files or try using another disk or making a subdirectory.

File Not Found

Meaning: DOS is unable to locate the file you've named.

Probable cause: You mistyped the name or the file isn't on that drive, in the current directory, or on the path you've specified.

Solution: Check your typing. Refer to the section "Finding a Lost File," in Chapter 19.

General Failure

Meaning: DOS has lots of specific error messages. When it tosses `General failure` at you, it means that something bad has happened but DOS has nothing specific to say about it. It's like DOS saying, "All hell's breaking loose," but it's not that serious.

Probable cause: Typical things that cause DOS to report a `General failure` message include an incompatible floppy disk; the floppy drive door's being left open; an attempt to read from an unformatted disk; or the absence of a disk from a floppy drive.

Solution: Check to see whether a disk is in the drive or the drive's door latch is open. Try again by pressing **R** for *re*try. If a disk is present, it's not properly formatted; press **A** for *a*bort. Use the FORMAT command to format the disk — but make sure that the disk is formatted to its proper size and capacity. Refer to Chapter 13 and the sections "What Kind of Disk Is This?," "Formatting a Disk," and "Formatting a Low-Capacity Disk in a High-Capacity Drive."

Insufficient Disk Space

Meaning: The disk is full. No more room is left to create or copy any files.

Probable cause: You've used the COPY command to copy too many files to the disk. Various other DOS commands and programs may produce this error.

Solution: Use a different disk, or delete some unneeded files, or start copying to another disk. If you notice that the disk still seems to have ample space available, you've simply filled up the root directory. Delete a few files (or copy them to another disk), and then create subdirectories for the extra files. Refer to the section "How to Name a Directory (The MD Command)," in Chapter 19. Run ScanDisk, as explained in Chapter 17, to see whether your disk is filled with loose fragments that take up space but don't do any good. Also refer to the sidebar "Freeing up space on a hard disk," at the end of Chapter 17.

Internal Stack Overflow

Meaning: Hey! What's that stuff leaking from the computer? No, this message means that one of DOS's internal storage areas — the *stack* — is full and needs more room. Everything grinds to a halt.

Probable cause: You have the command STACKS=0,0 in your CONFIG.SYS file. Either that, or the two values just aren't large enough.

Solution: You have to bribe your guru to fix this one. If you want, refer to Chapter 15 and edit your CONFIG.SYS file. Look for the line that says STACKS=0,0 and delete it. If that task is beyond you — or it doesn't solve the problem — get on your knees and plead for help.

Invalid Directory

Meaning: You've specified a directory that doesn't exist. (DOS is big on using the term *invalid*, which it takes to mean "illegal.")

Probable cause: You used the CD command to change to a directory you don't have. If not that, then you may have specified a full pathname to a file or directory and something in the pathname isn't right.

Solution: Check your typing. Refer to the section "Finding a Lost Subdirectory," in Chapter 19, to find out how to hunt down lost directories.

Invalid Drive Specification

Meaning: What the hell kind of drive is that?

Probable cause: You've typed a drive letter that isn't assigned to any disk drive on your system. For example, if you have drives A, B, and C and you type **D:**, you see this message.

Solution: Check your typing. The colon (:) is a sacred character under DOS. It only follows a drive letter, which can be any letter of the alphabet. If that drive doesn't exist, DOS spits back a variation of the Invalid drive specification error message. P.S.: If DOS gives this message when you try to log (switch) to drive C, it means that DOS has lost track of your hard drive. Oops. See the section in Chapter 19 called "Gulp! The Hard Drive Is Gone!"

Invalid File Name or File Not Found

Meaning: You've specified a filename with an illegal character, one that DOS cannot find.

Probable cause: You've used the REN command to give a file a new name that has an illegal character in it. This error message also appears when you try to use the TYPE command with a wildcard filename; you can view only one file at a time by using the TYPE command. (Refer to the section "Looking at Files," in Chapter 2.)

Solution: Check your typing. Refer to the section "Use These Filenames — Go Directly to Jail!," in Chapter 19. Also refer to the error message section "Duplicate File Name or File Not Found," earlier in this chapter.

Invalid Media, Track 0 Bad or Unusable

Meaning: The FORMAT command cannot format the disk. At least, it cannot format it to a specific capacity.

Probable cause: You're trying to format a disk at the wrong capacity; for example, a 360K disk to 1.2MB or a 1.2MB disk at 360K. Or, you may have successfully formatted a high-capacity disk at low capacity and now are attempting to reformat it to high capacity. Or you have a bad disk.

Solution: You can try the FORMAT command again, but add the slash-U (/U) option. If that doesn't work, try taking a bulk eraser, one you may use to erase a videotape, and erase the disk. That technique may enable the disk to be formatted — but always format disks to their proper capacity. Refer to Chapter 13.

Invalid Parameter, Invalid Switch

Meaning: You typed something improperly at the DOS prompt, left something required out of a command, or mistyped an option.

Probable cause: Usually a typo. If one of these error messages pops up, you're on the right track, although you may need to check the format of the command again.

Solution: Check your typing. You may have forgotten a space. If you've forgotten an option with some DOS command, enter the command again but with its help switch, slash-?, supplied instead. Here's an example:

```
C> FORMAT /?
```

Or type

```
C> HELP FORMAT
```

Either method displays all the options and requirements of the command. Check for the one you want, and then specify it properly. Refer to the section "About the Darn Command Formats," in Chapter 14, and to the section "The full-on, high-power, calmly desperate HELP command," in Chapter 22, for more information.

Non-System Disk or Disk Error

Meaning: You're trying to start the computer from a nonbootable disk. Although the disk may be formatted, no copy of DOS is on the disk.

Probable cause: You've left a floppy disk in drive A while starting your computer.

Solution: Make sure that drive A is empty, or open the drive door latch. Press the spacebar to enable DOS to boot from the hard drive.

Other versions of DOS, some third-party utilities that have their own disk formatting programs, and disks that come preformatted put subtly different error messages on their disks. The general gist here is Non-System Disk. What you see on-screen may be different from the title of this section.

Not Ready, Reading Drive X

Meaning: You've tried to access or log to either of your floppy drives, and DOS found only air where it expected a disk.

Probable cause: No disk is in the drive, or the drive door latch is open.

Solution: Stick a disk in the drive or close the drive door, and then type **R** to retry.

Overwrite FILENAME.HEY (Yes/No/All)?

Meaning: You've tried to copy a file over one that already exists. DOS is asking you whether you want to overwrite the file that's already on disk.

Probable cause: Betcha didn't know that a file by that name was already there?

Solution: Press **N**. Try again with another name. Only if you're *really* certain that you want to overwrite the file should you press **Y**. Pressing **A** (for *a*ll) means that you want to overwrite *every dang doodle* file for a gang-copy operation. Bad news if you do.

Write Protect

Meaning: You've attempted to write to or alter a disk that's been tagged as write-protected.

Probable cause: The disk has a write-protect tab on it, or the 3½-inch disk has its little tile off the hole. It prevents any information from being written to the disk or information on the disk from being changed.

Solution: Answer **A** for *a*bort. If you really want to change the information, remove the disk's write-protection and try again (press **R** for *r*etry rather than **A** for *a*bort). Refer to the section "Write-Protecting Disks," in Chapter 13, for additional information.

Part V

The Part of Tens

"A CONSULTANT TOLD US THAT POLYESTER CAN CAUSE SHORTS IN THE SYSTEM, SO WE'RE TRYING AN ALL LEATHER AND LATEX DATA ENTRY DEPARTMENT."

In this part . . .

When I wrote the original ...*For Dummies* book, *DOS For Dummies,* back in 1991, I wanted to end it with a bunch of, well, *random* information that just didn't fit anywhere else in the book. My inspiration for The Part of Tens came from *The Book of Lists* — not, as many have claimed, from David Letterman's Top Ten lists. After all, these are just lists of items where one is not really more important than the other. For example, "Ten horrible ways to pronounce *ASCII*" would present ten horrible pronunciations, any one of which could be number one in someone's mind.

This part of the book presents several lists of tens for you to follow as you work with DOS and your computer. There are good lists and there are bad lists. Just heed the instructions herein, and you should be okay, or at least moderately content, for all your computer needs.

Chapter 24

Ten Things You Should Do All the Time

*T*he rest of the lists of tens in this book are all fairly negative things, so why not start on an upbeat note? You may not have to do these things every second of the day, but keep each of these things in mind as you use your PC. Some of these items are elaborated on elsewhere in this book — that is duly noted here.

Care for Your Files

You should do three things to ensure that you, your PC, and the files you create always live in harmony: Back up, check your disk, and check for viruses. Refer to Chapter 17 for information about backing up. Information on checking the disk (using CHKDSK or ScanDisk) is also in Chapter 17. Checking for viruses is covered in Chapter 22.

Always Quit a Program Properly and Return to DOS

You have no reason to quit a program by punching the Reset button — or worse, by turning the computer off and then on again. Just as in social circles, there's always a proper method of exiting any situation. Know what it is and use it to quit your programs. Believe it or not, it's faster to quit back to the DOS prompt than to reset anyway.

Keep Your Disks Away from Magnets

A magnet erases a disk faster than looking at Medusa turns you to stone. Magnets are everywhere, so be careful. For example, the mouthpiece on most phones and phone handsets has a big magnet in it; rest the phone down on your desktop and THWOOP! the data on the disk is gone.

Other popular desk items that contain magnets are shown in this list; please try to keep your disks away from them:

- Modems
- Paper-clip holders
- Compasses
- Those things that pick up cars at the junkyard
- The planet Jupiter

Keep Your PC in a Well-Ventilated Place

PCs need to breathe. The internal fan needs to suck air in through the front of the computer box, and it needs to wheeze that air back out again through the rear of the box. Make sure that nothing covers the front of the computer (where it breathes in) or the back of the computer (where it coughs it back out).

The purpose of the fan is to keep the computer cool. Just like men in the Kinsey report, electrical components perform better under cold conditions than hot, so it may be a good idea to keep your computer out of direct sunlight — and keep your meltable disks out of the sun too. Even for security reasons, try not to place computers directly beneath a window. (I've seen too many computers disappear from various offices thanks to the old smash-'n'-grab.)

Buy Formatted Disks

So you were cheap and bought nonformatted disks. Furthermore, you didn't format those disks and now you need a disk on which to store a file but you don't have any formatted. You have no way around that problem. In fact, I've even driven to another location just to format a disk so that I could take it back to the office and use it. The only way to avoid this problem is to buy your disks preformatted or just format the whole box of disks after you buy it. Yeah, that takes time. But so does driving seven miles to format a disk.

Label Your Disks

I'm in the habit of sticking a label on a disk after it has been formatted. I may just label it with the date or the word *Formatted*. Later, as the information on the disk changes, I change the name to reflect its contents. You can label some disks to reflect their purpose, such as Work to Home or Today's Stuff. The purpose is to help you keep track of your disks and the information on them. (Refer to Chapter 13 for more information about formatting disks.)

Wait at Least 30 to 40 Seconds before Turning the Computer On Again

Nothing screws up a computer faster than rapidly flipping the On–Off switch a few times. Computers should be allowed time to *power down* (which is a term the Sunday Paper Grammarians love to harp on). You should allow the fan to stop spinning and those torrentially turning hard drives to gracefully wind down to silence. Only then is it 100 percent okay to turn the system back on again.

Change Your Printer's Ink Source When It Gets Low

In the Hall of I'm Too Cheap, near the Display of Irony, is a plaque devoted to those who pay $900 for a decent laser printer but are too cheap to go out and buy a new $90 toner cartridge when one gets low. Don't do that. If your printing starts to fade, buy a new printer toner cartridge or ribbon. In most cases, using an old one has a negative effect on both the printer and your hard copy. This area is something you shouldn't neglect.

Buy Supplies

In the same vein as changing a printer ribbon, you should always keep handy plenty of supplies for your computer — including disks, labels, printer ribbons or toner cartridges, paper for the printer, and other goodies you can find hanging from the racks at any software store.

Buy More Books

Speaking from experience and as an author of several computer books, I can't recommend anything better. Seriously, keep a sharp eye out for computer books. Definitely give the computer and software manuals a try before you buy a computer book on the subject. Some books are long-winded rewrites of the manual. Avoid them. Instead, try to find books with personal insight and plenty of tips and that are written in a language you understand. The computer press reviews books but rarely keeps those items in mind. Be your own critic.

Chapter 25

Ten Common Beginner Mistakes

In This Chapter

▶ Assuming that it's your own fault

▶ Mistyping commands

▶ Buying the wrong thing

▶ Buying too much software

▶ Assuming that it will be easy (just because the program says so)

▶ Incorrectly inserting disks

▶ Logged to the wrong drive or directory

▶ Pressing Y too quickly

▶ Reformatting an important disk

▶ No organization or housekeeping

Golly, if there really were only ten common beginner mistakes, life would be so much easier with computers. Sad to say, this chapter only highlights a few common beginner faults, although there's nothing that can't be cured. Review this list and reduce your problems.

Assuming That It's Your Own Fault

The first thing most beginners assume is that when something doesn't go right, it's their own fault. Usually, it isn't. Computers don't always work as advertised. If you type a command exactly as it's listed in a book or manual and the command doesn't work, the manual is wrong, not you. How do you find out what is right? You can check the program's README file, or you can call the developer for technical support. Or experiment, especially if it's your own computer (so that you delete your own files and not your coworker's).

Mistyping Commands

Making typing mistakes is a common problem for all computer users. Beginners typically forget spaces on the command line, sandwiching separate parts of a DOS command together, which doesn't make sense to DOS. The result: You get an error message. Also, never end any DOS command with a period. Even though the manual may have a period after the command (in obeisance to English grammar), few, if any, DOS commands ever end with a period. And be aware of the differences between the forward slash (/) and the backslash (\ ) as well as the colon (:) and the semicolon (;).

Buying the Wrong Thing

Hardware and software must be compatible with your computer. In particular, software must run *under DOS*, and your computer must have the proper innards to support the software. The problem exists primarily with PC graphics and memory. If you don't have enough or the proper type of either, some software may not work. Don't try too hard to save money by buying bargain hardware from remainder catalogs if you don't know enough about computers to tell the difference.

Buying Too Much Software

It's fun to go crazy in a software store, wielding your VISA card like a samurai sword. Bringing home all those applications and getting started with them takes time, however. Don't give yourself too much to do, or you may neglect some of the programs you've bought. Start by buying software with the basics — maybe one or two packages. Get comfortable with using those, and then expand with other programs as needed. Your brain and your monthly VISA bill will be easier to live with.

Assuming That It Will Be Easy (Just Because the Program Says So)

This mistake goes right along with buying too much software. You need time to find out how to use a program, get comfortable with it, and become productive with it. With today's overwhelming applications, you may never master everything (no one does). Still, give yourself time to learn. You can get your work done much more quickly if you take those extra few days to experiment and play with the software, work the tutorials, and practice. (Be sure to tell the boss about that.) Most of all, don't buy software on deadline. I mean, don't think that you can buy the program on Monday, install it on Tuesday, and produce the divisional report that's due on Wednesday. Programs save time only after you've found out how to use them — until then, they eat time.

A corollary to this rule is "Don't expect to understand how to use the program if you refuse to look at the manual (or a book about the program)." There's no such thing as an intuitive program, no matter what they say. At least take the introductory tutorial.

Incorrectly Inserting Disks

The handy 3½-inch disks can fit in a floppy drive in only one way. Even though you have potentially eight ways to insert a disk, only one of them meets with success. The 5¼-inch disks are different. You can fit them into a drive on any of four sides both right side up and upside down. The correct method of inserting both types of disks is with the label up and toward you. The notch on the 5¼-inch disk is to the left, and the oblong hole on the disk goes in first. Nothing heinous happens if you insert a 5¼-inch disk the wrong way — it just doesn't work.

Logging to the Wrong Drive or Directory

As you work with a computer, you're always using, or *logged to,* one directory on one disk drive. Never assume that you know where you are. If you do, you may delete files you don't want to delete or be unable to find files you expect to be there. Refer to the section "Current Directory," in Chapter 17.

Another common variant of this mistake is logging to a floppy drive that doesn't have a disk in it. If you do that, you see a `General failure` error message; put the proper disk into the drive and then press **R** to retry.

Pressing Y Too Quickly

DOS asks a Y/N (yes or no) question for a reason: What's about to take place has serious consequences. Are you *sure* that you want to go ahead? Press **Y** only if you really do. If you're uncertain, press **N** or Ctrl+C and reexamine your situation. This question happens more often than not with the DEL*.* command; make sure that you're logged to the proper directory before typing DEL*.* to delete all the files.

Reformatting an Important Disk

Eventually, like all computer users, you accumulate some 10,000 or so floppy disks, which you keep in a drawer, on a tabletop, tossed on a shelf, or in cityscape-like piles on the floor. Grabbing one of these disks and reformatting it is cheaper than buying a new disk. Make sure, though, that the old disk doesn't contain anything valuable first. How do you do that? Label the disks properly and run the DIR command to see what's there before you format.

No Organization or Housekeeping

Organization and housekeeping are two duties that intermediate-to-advanced DOS users take upon themselves. It's routine stuff, actually part of the larger picture of hard disk management. Not performing housekeeping or being unorganized are things beginners are good at. Over the long run, however, picking up after yourself now can save you massive problems in the near future.

Unless you want to pick up a good book about hard disk management (which implies taking that first step toward computer nerdhood), my suggestion is to let your favorite computer expert have a crack at your computer. Tell him or her to check out the system, organize things, and clean up your hard drive. (But tell him or her not to get too fancy — you don't want to plow through six layers of subdirectories to find something.) The result is a faster system — and maybe even some more disk space. That's a plus, although getting more disk space isn't something beginners need to concern themselves with.

Chapter 26

Ten Things You Should Never Do

. . . .

In This Chapter

▶ Don't switch disks

▶ Don't work from a floppy disk

▶ Don't take a disk from the drive when the drive light is on

▶ Don't turn off the computer when the hard drive light is on

▶ Don't reset to leave an application

▶ Don't plug anything into the computer while it's on

▶ Don't force a disk into the drive

▶ Never format a disk to a different capacity

▶ Never load software from an alien disk

▶ Never use these DOS commands: CTTY, DEBUG, DELTREE, FDISK, FORMAT C:, RECOVER

. . . .

*U*h-oh. Here is a list of ten big no-nos. Actually, you can do many bad things to a nice computer. For some of them, I'm hoping that you don't need a written warning. For example, it's a bad idea to attempt to fix your own monitor. Although you can, conceivably, upgrade your computer, being able to do something and wanting to do it are two different things.

Here, then, are ten unhealthy things you don't even want to consider doing.

Don't Switch Disks

This warning isn't that obvious. Basically, it means that you don't switch disks while you're still using the one in the drive. Suppose that you're working on a file in drive A and you haven't yet saved the file back to disk. Then, for some reason, you switch disks and try to save the file on the second disk. The result is that you've ruined the second disk and not truly saved your file.

Always save a file on the same disk from which you've loaded it. If you want a second copy of the file on another disk, use the COPY command after you've returned to DOS. Refer to the section "Copying a Single File," in Chapter 18.

Don't Work from a Floppy Disk

I am often amazed that people whose computers have nice, big, fast hard drives do their work on floppy disks. It's almost impossible to find a program anymore that can be run from a floppy. And, for heaven's sake, don't start your PC from a floppy disk when you can do it by using the hard disk. This technique leads to nothing but trouble.

Floppy disks are still useful. You can read and write files on a floppy, send work back and forth between two distant computers, and so on. Using floppies is slow, and floppies are less reliable than hard disks, but they work. Back up your data files to your floppies, and use the floppies to move files to another machine — but do your day-to-day work on your hard drive.

Don't Take a Disk Out of the Drive When the Drive Light Is On

The drive light is on only when the computer is writing to or reading from the disk. As with humans, the computer becomes annoyed when you remove its reading material before it's finished reading it. The result could be a damaged disk or lost information.

If you remove a disk before the light goes out, the computer displays a "What's going on?" error message. Replace the disk and press **R** to retry the operation.

Don't Turn Off the Computer When the Hard Drive Light Is On

The only safe time to turn off the computer is when you're at the DOS prompt. If the hard drive light is still on, however, it means that the computer is accessing the hard drive. It's safe to turn off the system only when the hard drive light is off, meaning that the computer is done writing to disk. (You should also refer to the section "Turning the Computer Off," in Chapter 1, and the section "Black Box Program Rules," in Chapter 15.)

Don't Reset to Leave an Application

This advice goes along with not turning off the PC in the middle of something. Always properly quit a program and return to the DOS prompt. From the DOS prompt, you can quickly run your next program. You can reset, of course, if the program has run amok and pressing Ctrl+C or Esc doesn't stop it.

Don't Plug Anything into the Computer While It's On

Connect any external goodies to your computer only when your computer is off, especially the keyboard, monitor, and printer. Plugging in any of those items while the computer's power is on can "fry" something you've paid a great deal of money for. It's best to turn off the computer, plug in your goodies, and then turn the computer back on again.

Don't Force a Disk into the Drive

If the disk doesn't go in, it's probably pointed in the wrong direction. Or, worse, what you're sticking the disk into is probably not a disk drive or a disk is already *in* the drive. Refer to the section "Changing Disks," in Chapter 2, for the details.

Never Format a Disk to a Different Capacity

Oh, you can try. The results are usually a disk riddled with errors or a disk that fails miserably over time and loses lots of data. It works both ways: Don't format a low-capacity disk to high capacity, and never format a high-capacity disk to low capacity. The first example is bad physics. The second example is just a waste of money.

Never Load Software from an Alien Disk

Buy software only when it's *shrink-wrapped* from a reputable computer dealer. Any other program you get, especially those on cheaply labeled disks, is suspect. Don't trust it! This is how computer viruses are spread, so it's best not to load anything from an alien disk. And, for Pete's sake, never boot from that type of disk.

Never Use These Dangerous DOS Commands

The following commands serve special purposes way beyond the reach of most beginning computer users. Although it's okay to let someone who knows what they're doing use these commands, you should never try them yourself. The consequences are just too horrible to think of.

Command	What It Does
CTTY	Unhooks DOS from the keyboard and screen. Don't try it.
DEBUG	A programmer's tool used to create programs, modify memory, and, if you're careless, mess up a disk drive. Don't run this program. (If you do, press Q to quit.)
DELTREE	A hyper version of the DEL command that deletes all files in the current directory *and in all subdirectories*. This one command could wipe all information from your hard drive. Just don't use it.
FDISK	Could destroy all information on your hard drive if you use it improperly.
FORMAT C:	Should be used only with drives A and B to format floppy disks. Never format drive C, or any drive letter higher than C.
RECOVER	Sounds healthy but is dumb and deadly. If you type this command, it destroys all files on your disk and removes all your subdirectories, replacing them with garbage — all without a Y/N warning. Don't try it.

Chapter 27

Ten Favorite DOS Commands

● ●

In This Chapter
▶ CD
▶ CLS
▶ COPY
▶ DEL
▶ DIR
▶ DISKCOPY
▶ FORMAT
▶ MORE
▶ REN
▶ TYPE

● ●

A few DOS commands are mentioned more than once in this book. I've added a few more to round out the number to ten.

You probably use other DOS commands with as much frequency as some of these. They're listed in the reference section of this book, along with every other DOS command, whether you use them or not. This chapter lists the ones that most people find the most useful.

The CD Command

Purpose: To display the pathname of the current directory.

Sample: CD

Comments: Type **CD** and the name of the current drive and directory — the pathname — is displayed. That name tells you where you are in the maze of your hard drive structure.

Other purpose: To change to another directory.

Sample: `CD \WP51\DATA`

Comments: The CD command is followed by a space and the full name of the directory to which you're changing. The directory's pathname usually *starts* with a backslash but doesn't *end* with a backslash.

Where to look: Chapter 2, the section "Changing Directories"; almost all of Chapter 17; Chapter 19, the section "Finding a Lost Subdirectory."

A longer version of this command is CHDIR. Both CD and CHDIR do the same thing; CHDIR was just designed for large bureaucracies, where typing must take longer in order to occupy time that would otherwise be spent being efficient.

The CLS Command

Purpose: To clear the screen.

Sample: `CLS`

Comments: CLS clears the screen, erasing the display and any embarrassing error messages that may be glowing therein. Simple enough.

The COPY Command

Purpose: To make a copy or duplicate of a file.

Sample: `COPY C:FILE1 A:FILE2`

Where to look: Chapter 18, the sections "Duplicating a File," "Copying a Single File," "Copying a File to You," "Copying a Group of Files," and "Moving a File"; you may also want to check "What Is a Pathname?" in Chapter 17 and "Wildcards (Or Poker Was Never This Much Fun)" in Chapter 19.

The general rule: First comes the location and name of the file you're copying and then the location and name of the copy you're making. If you're already logged to the source or the destination, you can leave that location off; if that's confusing, however, just give the entire location (the *pathname*) for both halves of the command.

Give the entire pathname, as shown in this example:

```
C> COPY C:\WP51\DATA\FILE\ A:\FILE1
```

This command copies FILE1 from drive C to drive A. You *can* change the name of the copy — and if you're making a copy to the same place as the original, you *have to* change the name.

The DEL Command

Purpose: To delete one or more files, eliminating them from a disk and freeing up the space they used.

Sample: DEL USELESS.TXT

Or: DEL *.BAK

Comments: The DEL command totally zaps a single file (or a group of files if you use a wildcard). This practice is necessary to eliminate older files and to give your computer more disk space.

A handy trick to use with the DEL command is to tack on the /P (slash-P) switch:

```
DEL *.* /P
```

The following command directs DOS to prompt you, yes or no, for each file deleted:

```
C:\WIN.COM Delete (Y/N)?
```

Press **Y** to delete the file or **N** to save it from certain peril.

Where to look: Chapter 18, the sections "Deleting a File," "Deleting a Group of Files," and "Moving a File"; also in Chapter 18, you may want to peek at the section "Undeleting a File." Check out the sections "What Is a Pathname?" in Chapter 17 and "Wildcards (Or Poker Was Never This Much Fun)" in Chapter 19; also see the section "The Perils of DEL *.*," in Chapter 21.

DEL has a twin brother — ERASE. Both DEL and ERASE do the same thing: ruthlessly kill files. The ERASE command was implemented for certain south-paw extremist groups because you don't need the right hand to type it.

The DIR Command

Purpose: To display a list of files on disk.

Sample: DIR

Or: `DIR C:`

Or: `DIR C:\WP60`

Comments: DIR is probably the most common DOS command, and it's the only way to look at the files you have on disk. You can see a list of files on any drive or in any subdirectory by following the DIR command with the drive letter or subdirectory pathname.

Where to look: Chapter 2, the section "DIR Command"; Chapter 17, the section "That Funny <DIR> Thing"; and Chapter 19, the sections "Using the DIR Command," "The wide DIR command," and "Displaying a sorted directory."

The DISKCOPY Command

Purpose: To make an exact duplicate of a floppy disk.

Sample: `DISKCOPY A: B:`

Or: `DISKCOPY A: A:`

Comments: This command makes an *exact* copy of a disk. Both drives A and B have to be the same kind (physical size and capacity). If not (or if you have only one floppy drive), type **DISKCOPY A: A:**; DOS copies the disk in drive A and then prompts you to swap in a blank disk for the copy.

Where to look: Chapter 13, the section "Duplicating Disks (The DISKCOPY Command)."

The FORMAT Command

Purpose: To prepare floppy disks for use.

Sample: `FORMAT A:`

Comments: All disks must be formatted before you can use them. The FORMAT command must be followed by the drive letter (and a colon) of the floppy drive containing the disk to be formatted. *Never* use the FORMAT command with any drive letter higher than B.

Where to look: Chapter 13, the sections "Formatting a Disk" and "Formatting a Low-Capacity Disk in a High-Capacity Drive." Also look up the section "Reformatting Disks," in that chapter.

The MORE Command

Purpose: To view text files one screen at a time.

Sample: `MORE < FILENAME`

Comments: The `MORE` command is followed by a space, a less-than symbol (<), another space, and then the name of a text file you want to view. At the end of each screen, you see the *more* prompt; press the spacebar to see the next screen. Press Ctrl+C to cancel.

Where to look: Chapter 2, the section "Looking at Files"; in Chapter 17, the section "The Tree Structure" discusses another interesting use of the MORE command; also look at the section about the TYPE command, later in this chapter.

The REN Command

Purpose: To rename a file, giving it a new name without changing its contents.

Sample: `REN OLDNAME NEWNAME`

Comments: What's to comment? Just follow the DOS naming rules. DOS objects if you try to give the file the same name as another file in the same directory.

Where to look: Chapter 18, the section "Renaming a File"; also Chapter 19, the section "Name That File!"

If you think that REN is really the name of a cartoon character, you can use the longer version of this command, RENAME. Both REN and STIMP, er, RENAME do the same thing.

The TYPE Command

Purpose: To display a file on-screen, enabling you to read its contents.

Sample: `TYPE STUFF.DOC`

Comments: The TYPE command displays any file you name, though only files that contain readable text can be understood by humans. If the file displays as garbage, press Ctrl+C to cancel the TYPE command.

Where to look: Chapter 2, the section "Looking at Files."

DOS Command Reference

Here's the whole lot of DOS commands, including those mentioned in Chapter 27. I've discovered that really no one keeps a reference of DOS commands anywhere anymore. Especially if you're using Windows 95 or Windows 98, you'll discover that DOS references are hard to come by. This is your last hope!

You may want to use some of these commands from time to time. The rest of these commands others can use. They're useful, but they aren't covered in depth here because they are beyond the scope of the book.

Each command is briefly described. If necessary, a reference is made to the command elsewhere in this text. Otherwise, I just poke fun at it and leave it at that.

Some of these commands are no longer available in Windows 95 and Windows 98. If so, I mention that fact in the command's description. Otherwise, if the command isn't available for your version of DOS, then, well, it just isn't available. **Remember:** Microsoft tried to please everyone. And what it came up with was Windows. Sorry!

APPEND   Weird command. Like the PATH command, this command enables DOS to look in other subdirectories to find data files. It's not really as keen as it sounds and generally causes more trouble than it's worth. An older command best avoided. (Dead under Windows 95 and Windows 98.)

ASSIGN   Forces DOS to ignore one disk drive, replacing it with another. For example, if you don't have a drive B, yet some idiot program insists on saving stuff there, you can use the ASSIGN command to tell the program to look on drive A instead. Programs can be so dumb. (This command is no longer included with DOS 6 or later; you use the SUBST command instead.)

ATTRIB   Changes a file's attributes, which describe how DOS can treat a file. Refer to the section "The File! I Cannot Kill It!" in Chapter 18.

BACKUP   The old backup command for DOS versions earlier than 6.0. If you have DOS 6, use the MSBACKUP command instead; see Chapter 17. (Dead under Windows 95 and Windows 98.)

BREAK	Turns special Ctrl+C and Ctrl+Break testing on or off. With this command on, Ctrl+C may be a little more responsive; with it off, your computer runs faster.
CD	Either displays the name of the current directory or changes to another directory on the disk. See Chapter 2, almost all of Chapter 17, plus a wee bit of Chapter 19.
CHCP	The *change code page* command, which enables you to switch in an alternative character set for the screen. (Although it sounds like fun, setting up a PC to do that is complex and confusing.)
CHDIR	A longer version of the CD command.
CHKDSK	Reports the status of a disk, how many files are on it, and how much of the disk is used by what. It can also check to see whether a disk has lost file clusters, which you should destroy immediately. CHKDSK is covered in Chapter 17, in the sections "Checking the disk (the CHKDSK command)" and "CHKDSK Says That I Have Lost Files in Clusters or Something." (This command has been supplanted by ScanDisk with MS-DOS 6.2 and later.)
CLS	A handy and easy command that clears the screen!
COMMAND	Actually DOS, the program you use when you work on your PC (it's COMMAND.COM). Never delete this program.
COMP	Compares the contents of two files line by line and tells you whether they're identical. This command goes into detail beyond just comparing a file's name and its size by looking at it using the DIR command. (COMP is not included in DOS 6 and later; use the more cryptic FC command instead.)
COPY	A popular command that makes a copy or duplicate of a file. See Chapter 18 for your file-duplicating needs.
CTTY	Interesting command, although typing it can disconnect your keyboard and monitor, forcing you to reset the computer to regain control. It's more of a curiosity than a command you can get any mileage from.
DATE	Displays the current date (according to the computer, at least) and gives you the opportunity to enter a new one. See the section, "The Date and Time," in Chapter 7.
DEBUG	Really a secret snooper type of program, intended for use by programmers and not mere mortals such as you or me.
DEFRAG	Actually a disk tune-up program you should run every so often to ensure that your hard drive is up to snuff. (DOS 6 only.)

DEL	A popular command that deletes one or more files. Refer to Chapter 18 for more information.
DELTREE	A powerful and merciless version of the tamer DEL command. Don't tempt fate by messing with this command. Even the experts don't use it without a garlic wreath, silver bullet, or recent backup handy. (DOS 6 and later only.)
DIR	The number-one DOS command; displays a list of files on disk. Refer to the section, "DIR Command," in Chapter 2, and refer to Chapters 17 and 19.
DISKCOMP	Compares two disks to see whether they're identical. Because the DISKCOPY command is very reliable, this command is a colossal waste of time. (Dead under Windows 95 and Windows 98.)
DISKCOPY	Duplicates a floppy disk. Covered in Chapter 13, in the section "Duplicating Disks (The DISKCOPY Command)."
DOSKEY	Runs a special keyboard enhancer that gives you more editing power and control over the command line. Although this command can be a fun and useful tool, it's a little too advanced for this book.
DRVSPACE	A command (called DBLSpace in DOS 6.2) that runs your DOS Disk Compression Headquarters. Not recommended. (DOS 6 only; DOS 6.21 has no disk compression utility.)
EDIT	A "command" that runs the DOS Editor program, which you can use to create and edit text files on disk. Refer to Chapter 16 for your editing pleasure.
EDLIN	Yuck! It's DOS's old command-line editor. Refer to Chapter 1, where I make my real feelings clear about using this cruddy old program. (No longer included with DOS 6 and later.)
EMM386	Controls DOS's expanded memory manager for 386, 486, and other advanced microprocessors. There's no point in mess-ing with it, though official memory-management information is presented in this book in Chapter 8.
ERASE	The same thing as the DEL command.
EXE2BIN	A programmer's tool. (Dead under Windows 95 and Windows 98.)
EXIT	Used to quit DOS — actually, the COMMAND program that DOS runs (see COMMAND, earlier in this reference). Refer to the section "How Do I Get Back?" in Chapter 21.
EXPAND	A program covertly used by the Setup program when it installs MS-DOS. You have no need to bother with it.

FASTOPEN	A program used to speed up access to files on disk. I've heard about nothing but problems with it, especially with switching floppy disks. Do not use this command.
FC	Stands for *file compare*. Unlike the old COMP command, FC offers more detailed descriptions of the differences between two files, and it's not as chicken about looking at files as the COMP command was (and it's the only way to compare files under DOS 6).
FDISK	Used when you first set up a hard disk. It prepares the disk for formatting. Using this command after the disk has been prepared could damage your hard drive. Do not use this command; only let an expert play with FDISK.
FIND	Used to find text in a file, or it can be connived into searching for text in a DOS command. A sample of this feat is offered in Chapter 19, in the section "Finding a Lost Subdirectory."
FORMAT	A necessary command that prepares floppy disks for use. See the section "Formatting a Disk," in Chapter 13.
GRAFTBL	One of DOS's many *code page* commands. It loads a code page (foreign-language character set) into the memory on your computer's screen (graphics adapter). No longer included with DOS 6 and later.
GRAPHICS	Works with IBM and Hewlett-Packard printers, enabling them to print graphics accurately. (Dead under Windows 95 and Windows 98.)
HELP	The DOS 6 online help command, the one that lists the full details of all the commands covered in this and the preceding chapter. Refer to Chapter 22 for all you want to know about getting help.
INTERLNK	The InterLink programs, INTERLNK and INTERSVR, enable you to swap files between two PCs by using a simple cable you construct using loose hair strands and pieces of spaghetti. (DOS 5 and 6 only.)
JOIN	Used to fake DOS into thinking that one of your disk drives is really a subdirectory. Weird. Also dangerous. (Eliminated in DOS 6 and later.)
KEYB	Loads a foreign-language keyboard driver into memory, enabling you to type by using special foreign-language characters. (Ooo, la-la!)
LABEL	Used to add or change a disk's volume label. Refer to Chapter 13 for more information.
LH	A shorter name for the LOADHIGH command.

WARNING!

LOADFIX If you ever see the message Packed file corrupt when you try to run a program, don't panic. At the next DOS prompt, type **LOADFIX** and a space, and then type the name of the program again (plus any options or other doodads). That should fix the problem, and that's about all this command is good for. (Dead under Windows 95 and Windows 98.)

LOADHIGH A memory-management command, along with its shorter version, the LH command. Because the DOS 6 MemMaker command deftly handles this information, no need to dwell further.

LOCK Grants disk access rights and privileges to older DOS programs that may not want to run under Windows 95 and Windows 98. (Available with Windows 95 and Windows 98 only.)

MD The MD (also MKDIR) command is used to make a subdirectory. Refer to the section "How to Name a Directory (The MD Command)," in Chapter 19.

MEM Tells you about memory in your computer and how it's used. Refer to the section "Conventional Memory," in Chapter 8.

MEMMAKER DOS's memory-management command, painlessly covered in Chapter 8.

MKDIR A longer version of the MD command.

MODE Configures a variety of things on your computer: the screen, keyboard, serial ports, printer, and so on. Refer to the sections "Funky Text," in Chapter 9; "Controlling the Keyboard," in Chapter 10; and "Serial Connection," in Chapter 11.

MORE Used to view text files one screen at a time. Refer to the section "Looking at Files," in Chapter 2.

MOVE Moves a file or group of files from one place to another. It works like a combined COPY–DEL command; you first COPY files to another place, and then you thoughtlessly slaughter the originals. See the section "Moving a File," in Chapter 18.

MSAV The Microsoft Anti-Virus command. (DOS 6 only.)

MSBACKUP Used to archive files from your hard disk to several floppy disks. Its use is covered in Chapter 17. (DOS 6 only.)

MSD The Microsoft Diagnostic program — a true PC privacy peeker — discussed covertly in Chapter 22. (Dead under Windows 95 and Windows 98.)

NLSFUNC	Yet another *code page* program. It adds *natural language support* to DOS, enabling foreigners to type in their own native lingo.
PATH	The PATH command creates the DOS *search path,* which is a list of one or more subdirectories in which DOS looks for programs to run. It goes in your AUTOEXEC.BAT file that runs when you turn on the computer.
POWER	The laptop PC power-saving and -management program. (DOS 6 only.)
PRINT	Although a logical person such as yourself would assume that the PRINT command prints files — and it does — the illogical truth is that it does much more, additional unnecessary stuff. (Dead under Windows 95 and Windows 98.)
PROMPT	Changes the appearance of the DOS prompt. Refer to the section "Prompt Styles of the Rich and Famous," in Chapter 3.
QBASIC	More than a command — it's MS-DOS's free-of-charge Basic programming language interpreter. If you want to get into the Basic programming language, consider picking up a book about QBasic and teaching yourself to program. It's much more fun than playing with the DOS prompt. (Dead under Windows 95 and Windows 98.)
RECOVER	Not as pleasant as its name may suggest. RECOVER tries too hard. Using this command can permanently damage all files on disk and instantly rob you of your subdirectories. Under no circumstances should you ever use this command. In fact, delete it from your hard disk. Fortunately, RECOVER is not included with DOS 6 and later.
REN	Renames files and, with DOS 6 and later, directories. See the section "Renaming a File," in Chapter 18; see also the section "Name That File!" in Chapter 19.
RENAME	A longer version of the REN command.
REPLACE	Interesting command: Searches out and replaces all files on the hard disk with newer versions on a floppy disk. Because most programs come with their own INSTALL or SETUP program, you rarely need to use the REPLACE command. (Dead under Windows 95 and Windows 98.)
RESTORE	Used to copy files from a backup disk back to your hard drive — but only for the old BACKUP command. With MS-DOS 6.2, the MSBACKUP command handles this job. Refer to the sections "I Just Deleted an Entire Subdirectory!" and "Restoring from a Backup," in Chapter 21.
RMDIR	A longer version of the RD command.

WARNING!

RMDIR	(Also RD.) Used to delete a subdirectory. The subdirectory must be empty first.
SCANDISK	MS-DOS 6.2's ultrakeen disk check-up tool; finds and repairs any disk maladies you may have, hard or floppy disks, no problem. Refer to Chapter 17 for the full details.
SET	Used in two ways: First, by itself, SET displays the contents of the DOS *environment*. Second, SET can be used to place items in the environment or remove them. Yawn.
SETVER	Used to fool some old DOS programs into thinking that they're running under their favorite DOS versions. It's best that you leave this command alone.
SHARE	The "something to do with networks" command. When you or your guru installs your network, this command may tuck itself inside your PC's CONFIG.SYS or AUTOEXEC.BAT file. If so, grand. If not, eh. . . .
SORT	Used to sort the output of some other DOS command or text file.
START	Lets you start another program in another window on-screen. (Windows 95 and Windows 98 only.)
SUBST	Used to fake DOS into thinking that a subdirectory is actually a disk drive. Dangerous, too.
SYS	Used to make a disk bootable. It transfers the DOS system files to a disk so that the disk can be used thereafter.
TIME	Displays what DOS thinks is the current time and gives you the chance to enter a new time whenever you want. Refer to the section "The Date and Time," in Chapter 7.
TREE	Displays a "visual" representation of your hard drive's tree structure — a map of your subdirectories. Refer to Chapter 17 for an example. (Dead under Windows 95 and Windows 98.)
TYPE	Displays a file's content on-screen. Hopefully, it's a text file, which you can read. Refer to Chapter 2.
UNDELETE	Rescues files back from the brink, safely recovering stuff you deleted too quickly. Refer to Chapter 18. (Dead under Windows 95 and Windows 98.)
UNFORMAT	Another lifesaver; undoes whatever it is the FORMAT command does to a disk. (Of course, being careful with the FORMAT command in the first place always helps.) Refer to Chapter 21. (Dead under Windows 95 and Windows 98.)

UNLOCK	Opposite of the LOCK command. (Available only with Windows 95 and Windows 98.)
VER	Displays DOS's name and the version number. Refer to the section "Names and Versions," in Chapter 3.
VERIFY	Turns on double verification of all the information DOS writes to disk. With the command on, you're certain that the information is properly stored. On the down side, it slows down your computer. Normally, VERIFY is off.
VOL	Displays a disk's volume label. Refer to the section "Changing the Volume Label," in Chapter 13.
VSAFE	The lesser half of the MS-DOS 6 antivirus brigade; actually more of a pain than it's worth. Heed the rules offered in the section "More Than Bugs: Viruses," in Chapter 22, and you never have to bother with this meddlesome command. (Dead under Windows 95 and Windows 98.)
XCOPY	Like a super COPY command; much faster and smarter than the plain old COPY command. You can use XCOPY as a straight-across substitute for the COPY command if you like. It even copies subdirectories! Wow, this modern age.
XCOPY32	A hyper version of the XCOPY command with more switches and more power than a steam locomotive, able to leap tall disk drives in a single bound, and so on. (Available only with Windows 95 and Windows 98.)
ZED	Doesn't exist. I made it up. If you try to use the ZED command, you get a `Bad command or file name` error.

The 5th Wave   By Rich Tennant

"LET ME GUESS – NO SURGE PROTECTORS...RIGHT?"

Glossary

386

Number that refers to all computers that have an 80386 microprocessor, or brain.

80286

The number of a microprocessor, or brain, in an AT or 286 computer. It's one notch less than an 80386 and one notch greater than an 8086.

80386

Refers to the microprocessor, or brain, in all 80386 computers. There are two types: the 80386DX and the 80386SX. The SX is simply a cheaper version of the DX model, with all the caffeine but only half the calories.

80486

Refers to the brains found in an 80486 computer. It's a notch better than an 80386 system and puts a bigger dent in your wallet.

8086/8088

Refer to the first processors in the first line of PCs out the chute. Although many of these models were sold, and many are still up and running, few are sold today.

Alt-key

A key combination involving the Alt key plus some other key on the keyboard — a letter, number, or function key. When you see Alt+S, it means to press and hold the Alt key, type an S, and then release both keys. Note that Alt+S doesn't imply Alt+Shift+S; the S key by itself is fine.

applications

A term applying to computer programs, generally programs of a similar type. For example, you can have word-processing applications, spreadsheet applications, and so on. Several computer programs fit into each application category. Everything is generally referred to as *software,* which makes the computer do its thing.

arrow keys

Some keys on the keyboard that have directional arrows on them. Note that some keys, such as Shift, Tab, Backspace, and Enter, also have arrows on them. The traditional arrow keys are used to move the cursor. *See also* cursor keys.

ASCII

An acronym for American Standard Code for Information Interchange. ASCII (ASK-ee) uses code values from 0 to 127 to represent letters, numbers, and symbols used by a computer. In DOS, you often see ASCII used to refer to a plain text file, one that can be viewed by giving the TYPE command and read by a human.

backslash

The \ character, a backward-slanting slash. Under DOS, the backslash character is used as a symbol for the root directory, as well as a separator between several items in a pathname.

back up

A method of copying a whole gang of files from a hard drive to a series of floppy disks (though other devices, such as tape systems, can also be used). It could also refer to a duplicate of a single file — an unchanged original — used in case anything happens to the copy you're working on.

baud

Part of the old computer cliché "Byte my baud," it actually refers to a technical description of a *signal change*. With computers, people often use the term baud to refer to bits per second or bps, the speed of a modem. Baud comes from the 19th century French telegrapher J.M.E. Baudot. *See also* bps.

binary

A counting system involving only two numbers, which in a computer are one and zero. Humans, which includes most of you, use the decimal counting system, which consists of ten numbers, zero through nine.

BIOS

An acronym for Basic Input/Output System. The BIOS is actually some low-level instructions for the computer, providing basic control over the keyboard, monitor, disk drives, and other parts of the computer. When the computer is on and running, DOS is actually in charge. To use the computer, though, DOS uses the BIOS to "talk" with other parts of the PC.

bit

A contraction of a bit refers to a single tiny switch inside the computer, which contains the values one or zero. Millions of such switches — bits — are inside the typical PC. They form the basis of all the memory and disk storage.

block command

Blocks are chunks of text in a word processor: a word, sentence, paragraph, page, or several words that the word processor treats as a group or block. Block commands manipulate a block of text somehow. Typical block commands copy, cut, delete, or perform a variety of functions on a whole group of words at one time.

boot

The process of turning on a computer that, surprisingly enough, doesn't involve kicking it with any Western-style footwear. When you turn on a computer, you are *booting* it. When you reset a computer, you are *rebooting* it, or giving it a *warm boot* (which sounds kind of cozy, you must admit).

bps

An acronym for bits per second, it refers to the number of bits a modem can send over the phone line in one second. Typical values are 300, 1200, 2400, and 9600 bits per second. The higher the value, the faster information is sent. Note that this is the accurate term used to describe how fast a modem sends information; the term *baud* is often, though incorrectly, used interchangeably with *bps*.

byte

A group of eight *bits,* all clustered together to form one unit of information inside a computer. Conceptually speaking, a byte is one single character stored inside a com-puter. The word *byte* would require four bytes of storage inside your PC. Bytes are also used as a measure of capacity; *see also* kilobyte and megabyte.

capacity

The amount of stuff you can store, which is the total number of bytes that can be stored in memory or, more likely, on a disk. Some hard disks have a capacity of 100 megabytes. Floppy disks have storage capacities ranging from 360K on up through 2.8MB. Some closets have a capacity for 24 pairs of shoes, though many women find miraculous ways to put more shoes into that tiny space.

CD-ROM

An acronym for Compact Disc Read-Only Memory, a special optical storage device that contains millions of bytes of information. As with the musical CDs, you can use the appropriate CD-ROM hardware to have access to the volumes of information stored on a CD disc. And just like with a musical CD, you cannot record any new information on the disc; it's *read only.*

centronix port

See printer port.

CGA

An acronym for Color Graphics Adapter. The CGA was the first video system for the PC that offered both color text and graphics. The text was lousy and the graphics were good for only the chintzi-est of games. CGA was soon replaced by the *EGA* graphics standard.

circuit breaker

A safety device installed between a power source and delicate electronic equipment, such as a computer. If the power going through the line is too strong, the circuit breaker "blows." The breaker shuts off the power, but in the process stops nasty electrical things from invading your computer.

clock speed

The measure of how fast a computer's microprocessor, or brain, can think. It's measured in millions of cycles per second, or megahertz (*see also* MHz). The faster the clock speed, the faster the computer (and the more it costs).

clone

"Oh, give me a clone, yes a clone of my own, with the Y chromosome changed to the X. And when I'm alone, 'cause this clone is my own, she'll be thinking of nothing but ___." Actually, *clone* is a term used to describe an imitation of an original. The term doesn't appear much these days, although nearly all PCs are clones of the first IBM microcomputers, the original PC and PC/AT systems.

CMOS

Refers to special memory inside the computer. The CMOS memory stores information about your PC's configuration and hard drive and keeps track of the date and time. All this is maintained by a battery, so when the battery goes, the computer becomes terribly absentminded. CMOS. See MOS run. Run, MOS, run.

compatible

A term used to refer to a computer that can run DOS software. Although compatibility used to be an issue a few years ago, today nearly all PCs are completely compatible with DOS and all its software.

console device

Nerd talk for your screen and keyboard.

Ctrl+key

A key combination involving the Control (or Ctrl) key plus another key on the keyboard, typically a letter, number, or function key. When you see Ctrl+S, it means to press and hold the Control (Ctrl) key and type an S, after which you release both keys. Note that although Ctrl+S shows a capital S, you don't have to press Ctrl+Shift+S.

conventional memory

Memory that DOS uses to run programs. Most PCs have the full 640K of conventional memory, also called *DOS memory* or *low DOS memory*.

conventional memory

It's a common term, so I've listed it twice.

CPU

An acronym for central processing unit, CPU is another term for a computer's microprocessor, or brain. CPU. Don't step in the PU. *See also* microprocessor.

Ctrl

The name of the Ctrl key as it appears on the keyboard. *See* Ctrl+key.

cursor

The blinking underline on the screen. The cursor marks your position on the screen, showing you where any new text you type will appear. The word *cursor* comes from the Latin word for *runner*.

cursor keys

Special keys on the keyboard that are used to control the cursor on the screen. The four primary keys are the up-, down-, left-, and right-arrow keys. Also included in the cursor key tableau are the PgUp (page up) and PgDn (page down) keys and the Home and End keys.

data

Information or stuff. Data is what you create and manipulate using a computer. It can really be anything: a word-processing document, a spreadsheet, a database of bugs your daughter has collected, and so on.

default

A nasty term computer jockeys use to mean the standard choice, the option or selection automatically taken when you don't choose something else. They should really use the term *standard choice* instead. *Default* is a negative term, usually associated with mortgages and loans.

DIP switch

A tiny switch inside a computer, on the back of a computer, or on a printer. DIP switches are used to control the way a computer or printer automatically behaves, to tell the system about more memory, or to configure some doohickey to work properly. It needs to be set only once, or twice if you weren't paying attention the first time.

directory

A collection of files on disk. Every disk has one main directory, the *root directory*. The disk can also have other directories, or *subdirectories*. Files are saved to disk in the various directories. You view the files by using the DIR, or directory, command.

disk

A storage device for computer information. Disks are of two types: hard disks and floppy disks. The floppy disks are removable and come in two sizes: 3½-inch and 5¼-inch.

diskette

A term applied to a floppy disk, usually to distinguish between it and a hard disk (which isn't removable). Diskettes are often referred to as disks. *See also* disks.

display

The computer screen or monitor. The term *display* is rather specific, usually referring to what is displayed on-screen as opposed to the monitor (which is hardware).

document

A file created by a word processor. The term *document* means something you've saved with your word processor, usually a file that contains formatting information, various text styles, and so forth. This marks the line between a file created by a word processor (the document) and a plain text file, which lacks the formatting information (and can be viewed by giving the TYPE command).

DOS

An acronym for Disk Operating System. DOS is the main program that controls all of your PC, all the programs that run, and anything that saves information to or loads it from disk.

DOS memory

Another term for *conventional memory,* the basic 640K of memory in a PC. *See also* conventional memory.

dot matrix

A type of printer that uses a series of pins to create an image on paper. Dot-matrix printers are a cheap, quick, and noisy way to print computer information, not as slow as the old daisy-wheel printer and not as fast, expensive, or cool as a laser printer.

dump

A place where you take the computer after you're fed up with it. Actually, *dump* is an old computer term that means to wash out one thing and dump it into another. For example, a screen dump takes the information displayed on the screen and literally dumps it out to the printer. *See also* screen dump.

eek! eek!

The noise a computer mouse makes. *See also* mouse.

EGA

An acronym for Enhanced Graphics Adapter. The EGA was the second graphics standard for the PC, after CGA. It offers many more colors than CGA and has the benefit of easy-to-read text. EGA has since been superseded by the VGA standard. *See also* VGA.

EMS

An acronym for Expanded Memory Specification. The EMS, or more precisely, the LIM EMS (LIM for Lotus/Intel/Microsoft) is a standard for accessing extra memory on all types of PCs. This memory, *expanded memory,* is directly of use to DOS and most DOS applications. *See also* expanded memory.

escape

The name of a key on the keyboard, usually labeled "Esc." The Escape key is used by many programs as a cancel key.

expanded memory

Extra memory in a PC, useful to DOS and lots of DOS applications. To get expanded memory, you must add expanded memory hardware and software to your PC. (For a 386 system, you need only the software.) After the memory is installed, your computer will have access to lots of extra memory, which can be put to immediate use by many applications.

expansion card

A piece of hardware that attaches to your computer's innards. An expansion card expands the capabilities of your PC, enabling you to add new devices and goodies that your computer doesn't come with by itself. Expansion cards can add memory (such as *expanded memory*), a mouse, graphics, a hard disk, or external devices like CD-ROM drives, scanners, and plotters.

expansion slot

A special connector inside most PCs that enables you to plug in an expansion card

(see preceding entry). The typical PC has room for five to eight expansion cards, allowing you to add up to that many goodies.

extended memory

Extra memory in an 80286 or 386 computer; it's not *expanded memory.* Extended memory is primarily of use to operating systems other than DOS. On an 80286, it's better to have expanded memory. On a 386 system, you can add extended memory — as much as you like — and then convert it to the more usable expanded memory by using special software.

field

An area on the screen where you enter information. It's part of database-speak: A file is a collection of records; records contain fields; fields contain elements. For example, a folder full of employment applications is like a file; each application is a record; and the fill-in-the-blank items on each application are fields.

file

A collection of stuff on disk. DOS stores information on disk in a file. The contents of a file could be anything: a program for DOS, a word-processing document, a database, a spreadsheet, a graphics image of Claudia — you name it.

fixed disk

An old, IBM word for a hard disk. The word *fixed* refers to the fact that a hard disk cannot be removed, unlike the floppy disk. *See* hard disk.

floppy disk

A removable disk in a PC, usually fitting into a 3½-inch or 5¼-inch disk drive. *See also* disk or diskette.

font

A typesetting term used in computer desktop publishing or word processing. The term really should be *typeface,* or a specific style of text. For example, many books use the Cheltenham typeface, or font. Other fonts are usually available, depending on your printer or the software you're using. (The term *font* actually refers to a style of typeface: bold, italic, and so on.)

form factor

A heavy-duty term that really means the size of something. Typically, you see form factor used to describe a disk drive. Essentially, it means what size the disk drive is, what kind of disks it eats, and how much information you can store on the disks. When you see form factor, just replace it mentally with the word *dimensions.*

format

The process of preparing a disk for use by DOS. All disks come naked out of the box. For DOS to use them, they must be formatted and prepared for storing files or information. That's done under DOS by the FORMAT command.

free

Nothing is free.

function keys

Special keys on the keyboard, labeled F1 through F10 or F12. Function keys

perform special commands and functions, depending on which program you're using. Sometimes they're used in combination with other keys, such as Shift, Ctrl, or Alt. (WordPerfect takes it to the max, with as many as 42 combinations of function keys to carry out various actions in the program.)

geek

A nerd with yellow Chee-tos between his teeth. *See also* nerd.

gigabyte

A perilously huge number, typically one billion of something. (That's billion with a *b.*) A gigabyte is one billion bytes, or 1,000MB (megabytes).

graphics adapter

A piece of hardware that controls your monitor. Three common types of graphics adapters are on the PC: monochrome, EGA, and SVGA. The graphics adapter plugs into an expansion slot inside your PC.

hard disk

A high-speed, long-term storage device for a computer. Hard disks are much faster and store lots more information than floppy disks.

hardware

The physical side of computing, the nuts and bolts. In a computer, hardware is controlled by the software, in much the same way as an orchestra plays music; the orchestra is the hardware and the music is the software.

Hayes-compatible

A type of modem that works like the original Hayes Micromodem, or at least that shares similar commands. Getting a Hayes-compatible modem guarantees that your communications software will work with it.

Hewlett-Packard

HP makes calculators and special scientific devices, but it's the company's computer printers that make it popular with the PC crowd. A Hewlett-Packard laser printer is compatible with just about every piece of software out there. I say this for two reasons: I personally don't have an HP printer, and it's a real pain. And, I want to be nice to them so that they'll send me a freebie.

hexadecimal

A totally nerdy way to count: in base 16, where you have the numerals 0 through 9 and then the letters A through F to represent values 10 through 15. The numeral *10* in hexadecimal equals 16 in the good old base 10 system. Why bother? No reason, unless you're a programmer or know someone who speaks programmer lingo.

IBM

International Business Money or something like that. It made the first original IBM PC, which formed the platform on which the modern PC industry was launched. Some 60 million PCs later, IBM no longer plays a leading role in the industry, although it still makes quality computers (mostly for the Mercedes crowd).

I/O

An abbreviation for Input/Output, the way a computer works. Computers gobble up input and then spit out output. It's also what the Seven Dwarfs were singing when they went down into the mines.

icon

A religious symbol or painting. However, when you run Microsoft Windows, an icon is a teensy, tiny picture that represents a program. For example, Word for Windows has a pretty icon that looks like a big blue *W* stamped over a newspaper. That's how Windows presents programs to you: pretty pictures or icons. (DOS uses ugly text and — heck, the Phoenicians were doing that 7,000 years ago!)

i486

A common way of describing the Intel 80486 microprocessor. They write "i486" on top of the chips, so many folks write "i486" when they refer to that microprocessor. *See also* 80486.

K, KB

Abbreviations for *kilobyte. See* kilobyte.

keyboard

The thing you type on when you're using a computer. The keyboard has a standard typewriter-like part, plus function keys, cursor keys, a numeric keypad, and special computer keys.

kilobyte

One thousand bytes or, more accurately, 1,024 bytes. It's equal to about half a page of text. Note that kilobytes is abbreviated as K or KB, so 24K is about 24 thousand bytes (more or less).

laptop

A special, compact type of computer, usually running off batteries, that you can take with you. Laptops are popular additions to a desktop system, enabling you to compute on the road. They are, however, considerably more expensive than regular computers.

laser printer

A special type of printer that uses a laser beam to create the image on paper. Most laser printers work like a copying machine, except that they use a laser beam to help form the image rather than smoke and mirrors. Laser printers are fast and quiet, and they produce excellent graphics.

LCD

An acronym for liquid crystal display, a type of computer screen particular to laptop computers. Most LCDs are compatible with a desktop system's VGA display, though they're limited to displaying black and white or shades of gray.

load

To move information (a file) from disk into the computer's memory. Only after you've loaded something (a worksheet or document, for example) into memory can you work on it. *See also* save.

M, MB

An abbreviation for megabyte. *See also* megabyte.

macro

A program within a program, usually designed to carry out some complex function, automate a series or commands, or make life easier for anyone who doesn't want to hassle with a program's complexities. Macros exist in just about every application — even DOS — to make routine things easier. (Under DOS, the macros are called *batch files.*)

math processor

A special companion chip to a computer's microprocessor, specifically designed to perform complex arithmetic and to do it faster than the microprocessor can by itself. The math coprocessor chip is numbered similarly to the microprocessor, except that the last digit is a 7 rather than a 6. Note that the 80486 microprocessor has its math coprocessor built in.

megabyte

One million bytes, or 1,024K. A megabyte is a massive amount of storage. For example, *War and Peace* could fit into a megabyte with room to spare. Typically, hard drive storage capacity is measured in megabytes.

memory

Where the computer stores information as it's worked on. Memory is temporary storage, usually in the form of RAM chips. The microprocessor can only manipulate data in memory. After that's done, it can be saved on disk for long-term storage.

memory-resident program

A special type of program that stays in memory when it's done. Memory-resident programs do one of two things. First, a memory-resident program will add to or modify some function of DOS. Examples are a mouse driver, a printing program, and a program allowing you access to more memory. Second, memory-resident programs can be pop-up utilities; that is, programs activated by pressing special key combinations that then appear on the screen — as if by magic. These programs include pop-up editors, calculators, and printing-control programs. Borland's SideKick was probably the best example of a pop-up memory-resident program.

menu

A list of commands or options in a program. Some menus are displayed across the top or bottom of the screen, giving you one-word commands or choices. Some fill the screen, asking you "what next?" Some menus are graphical pull-down menus that display a hidden list of items or commands. Fun, fun, fun.

MHz

An abbreviation for megahertz. It refers to how fast a computer's microprocessor can compute. The typical PC zips along at 20 MHz. The typical human brain, scientists have discovered, works at about 35 MHz — or 40 MHz after six cups of coffee.

microprocessor

The computer's main brain, where all the calculations take place and the control center for the entire computer. Microprocessors are also called processors or CPUs. They're given numbers such as 80286, 80386, and so on. (Refer to the numbers at the beginning of this glossary.)

modem

A contraction of a modem is a device that takes electronic information from your computer and converts it into sounds that can be transmitted over the phone lines. Those sounds can be converted back into electronic information by the other computer's modem.

monitor

The computer's display or video system. The monitor is like a TV set, showing you information. It's actually only half of your computer's video system. The other half is the graphics adapter, plugged into an expansion slot inside your PC.

monochrome

A type of computer display that shows only two colors: black and white (or green and white). Some monochrome systems display shades of gray, substituting them for the various colors.

motherboard

The main circuitry board inside your computer. The motherboard contains the microprocessor, some memory, and expansion slots into which you can plug additional goodies.

mouse

A small, hand-held pointing device used primarily in graphics programs to manipulate stuff on the screen. A mouse has two parts: the hardware part, consisting of the mouse unit itself connected to a mouse card in your computer (or a serial port), and the software part, which is a program that controls the mouse and allows your applications access to it.

MS-DOS

The long, formal title for DOS, the Microsoft Disk Operating System.

nerd

Someone who enjoys using a computer. No one reading this book should be a nerd, though one day you may become one. There is no cure.

network

Several computers hooked together. When your computer is on a network, you can share printers with other computers, easily send files back and forth, or run programs or access files on other computers. It sounds neat, but in practice a network can be a hassle to set up and a pain to maintain.

online

To be on and ready to go. When a printer is online, it's turned on, contains paper, and is all ready to print.

option

An item typed after a DOS command and that isn't required. You type an option after a command to control the way the command performs. Most options typed after a DOS command are in the form of *switches,* which are slash characters typically followed by a letter of the alphabet.

parallel port

See also printer port.

pathname

The full, exact name of a file or directory on a disk. The pathname includes the drive letter, a colon, and all directories up to and including the directory in question and a filename. Pathnames are an extremely specific way of listing a file on disk.

PC

An acronym for personal computer. Before the first IBM PC, personal computers were called *microcomputers,* after the *microprocessor* — the computer's brain. The *PC* in IBM PC means personal computer, and since the time the IBM PC was introduced, all microcomputers — even non-DOS computers — have been called PCs.

PC-DOS

The IBM-specific brand of DOS, the Personal Computer Disk Operating System. The differences between this brand of DOS and MS-DOS are slight, and you can run PC-DOS on non-IBM computers.

Pentium

The official name Intel gave to the "586" microprocessor. The reason was to keep all the knock-off goofs from calling their chips the 586 (but they'll do it anyway), because Intel can't copyright numbers.

peripheral

Any item attached to the outside of the computer, such as a printer, a modem, or even a monitor or keyboard.

pixel

An individual dot on the computer's display, used to show graphics. A graphics image on a computer is made up of hundreds of dots or pixels. Each pixel can be a different color or in a different position, which creates the image you see on the screen. The number of pixels horizontally and vertically on the display give you the graphics *resolution*.

pixel dust

That thin layer of dust that coats your monitor. It's deposited there nightly by the pixel fairy.

port

Essentially, a connection on the back of the computer to which you attach various external items (*peripherals*). Two primary ports are on each PC, a *serial port* and a *printer port,* though what the keyboard and monitor plug into could also be considered ports.

printer

A device that attaches to your computer and prints information. A printer is necessary to give you *hard copy,* which is printed output of the information inside your computer.

printer port

The connection on the back of the PC into which you plug a printer cable, thereby attaching a printer to your computer. Most PCs have the capability to handle several printers, though you need to add special hardware to give your system the extra ports. The printer port is also known as the *parallel port* or sometimes you'll hear some dweeb call it a *Centronics port.*

program

A special file on disk that contains instructions for the computer. Under DOS, all programs are stored in files with their second part named either COM, EXE, or BAT. To run a program, you need to type in only the first part of the filename.

prompt

The ugly C> thing you see when you use DOS, telling you to "type that ridiculous command line here." The DOS prompt is the most familiar of all the prompts. Other programs may use their own prompts, each of which is designed to show you where information is to be entered on the screen. Handy.

RAM

An acronym for random access memory, the primary type of memory storage in a PC. RAM = memory.

redundant

See also redundant.

resolution

Refers to the number of dots (*pixels*) on the screen. The higher the resolution, the greater the number of dots vertically and horizontally, and the finer the graphics image your computer can display.

RGB

An acronym for red-green-blue. These colors are used in all computer displays to show you all colors of the rainbow and from which graphics are created. In the old CGA days of computing, RGB also referred to a type of monitor for use with a PC.

ROM

An acronym for read-only memory. These special chips on the computer contain instructions or information. For example, the computer's BIOS is stored on a ROM chip. ROM chips are accessed just like regular RAM memory, but unlike RAM they cannot be changed; they're read-only.

root directory

The primary directory on every DOS disk. Other directories, or subdirectories, branch off the root directory. The symbol for the root directory is the single backslash (\).

RS-232

A technical term used to describe a serial port. *See also* serial port.

save

The process of transferring information from memory to a file on disk for permanent, long-term storage.

screen dump

An ugly term for taking the information on the screen and sending a copy of it to your printer. A screen dump is performed on a PC by pressing the Print Screen key, which may be labeled Print Scrn, PrtSc, or something along those lines. Note that the screen dump does not include graphics screens. If your printer can't handle the special IBM characters, then who-knows-what will happen.

SCSI

An acronym for small computer system interface, it's like a very fast and versatile serial port. I mention it here only because it's pronounced "scuzzy" and I think that's cool.

serial port

A special type of port into which a variety of interesting devices can be plugged. The most common item plugged into a serial port is a modem (which leads some to call it a modem port). You can also plug a computer mouse, a printer, a scanner, or a number of interesting devices into the serial port. Most PCs have one or two serial ports.

shareware

A category of software that's not free, yet it's stuff you don't have to buy before you try it. Generally, shareware consists of programs written by individuals and distributed hand to hand through user groups, national software clearinghouses, or via modem. You try the software and, if you like it, send the author the required donation.

slide rule

Whoever is on top of the ladder gets to go down the slide first.

software

What makes a computer worth having. It's the vast collection of programs that control the hardware and enable you to get your work done. Software controls computer hardware.

source

The original from which a copy is made. When you copy a file or duplicate a disk, the original is called the source. The source drive is the drive from which you're copying. The destination, or the location to which you're copying, is referred to as the target.

string

In computer lingo, any group of characters. A string of text is a line of text, a command you type, or any other non-numeric information. Don't let the term throw you or force you to insert twine or yarn into the disk drive.

subdirectory

A term for a directory in relation to another directory. All directories on a disk are subdirectories of the root.

SVGA

An acronym for Super Video Graphics Array; the nex-generation VGA. Turn the computer off and you get mild-mannered Clark Kent VGA.

syntax

The format of a DOS command, the things you must type, the options, what order they go in, and what they do. When you goof up and specify something out of order, DOS tosses you back a Syntax Error. It's not fatal; it just means that you need to find the proper syntax and retype the command.

tab shooter

Someone you employ to make a tab stop real fast, or a wimpy drink made with tequila and a popular diet drink.

tab stop

Just like on a typewriter, a tab stop on a computer is the location where characters appear after you press the Tab key.

Sometimes, the Tab key simply produces eight spaces. In most word processors, you can set tab stops at specific positions on a line of text.

target

The location of a copy or duplicate of an original file. A target can be a filename, a subdirectory, or a disk drive — the final destination of the file. Copying things on a computer is a lot like archery.

text editor

A special type of word processor that creates or edits only text files, often called ASCII, unformatted, or nondocument files. A text editor lacks most of the fancy formatting features of a word processor. Oh, you might want to look up *ASCII* since I mention it here. (Not that it helps much.)

toggle

Something that can be on or off; a single switch that's pressed once to turn something on and again to turn it off. This term appears when describing something you can do in a program that turns a function on and then doing it again turns it off.

TSR

An acronym for terminate-and-stay-resident. Believe it or not, that's an MS-DOS programmer's function, not anything any human being will use. Yet it's a quick-and-dirty term that can be used to describe a *memory-resident program*, also described in this glossary.

user

The person who operates a computer or runs a program. The computer is then the usee.

V20

A special, faster type of 8088 chip, usually found in some of the cheaper laptop computers. *See also* 8088/8086.

V30

A special, faster type of 8086 chip, found in some lightweight laptop computers. *See also* 8088/8086.

VGA

An acronym for Video Graphics Array, the current top-of-the-line in PC graphics systems. VGA offers you stunning color graphics, great resolution, and crisp text, much better than its predecessor, EGA. A SuperVGA (also known as *SVGA*) is available that extends the powers and capabilities of VGA.

window

An area on the screen where special information appears. It can be a graphics window, à la the Microsoft Windows program, or it can be a text window, outlined with special graphical text characters.

word wrap

The capability of a word processor to move a word from the end of one line to the beginning of the next while you're typing. Word wrap enables you to type an entire paragraph of text without having to press Enter at the end of each line.

write protect

A method of protecting information on disk from being accidentally changed or erased. You do this by putting a write-protect tab on a 5¼-inch disk or by sliding the little tile off the hole of a 3½-inch disk. After that's done, the disk is write protected and you cannot change, rename, delete, or reformat it.

WYSIWYG

An acronym for what-you-see-is-what-you-get. It refers to a program's capability to display information on the screen in exactly the same format in which it will be printed. Sometimes it works, sometimes it doesn't. Generally speaking, if a program is WYSIWYG, what you see on the screen is close enough to what you get when it's printed.

Index

Dummies Books™
Bestsellers on Every Topic!

GENERAL INTEREST TITLES

SINESS & PERSONAL FINANCE

Title	Author	ISBN	Price
...ating For Dummies®	John A. Tracy, CPA	0-7645-5014-4	$19.99 US/$27.99 CAN
...ss Plans For Dummies®	Paul Tiffany, Ph.D. & Steven D. Peterson, Ph.D.	1-56884-868-4	$21.99 US/$29.99 CAN
...ss Writing For Dummies®	Sheryl Lindsell-Roberts	0-7645-5134-5	$16.99 US/$27.99 CAN
...ting For Dummies®	Bob Nelson & Peter Economy	0-7645-5034-9	$21.99 US/$29.99 CAN
...ner Service For Dummies®, 2nd Edition	Karen Leland & Keith Bailey	0-7645-5209-0	$21.99 US/$29.99 CAN
...ising For Dummies®	Dave Thomas & Michael Seid	0-7645-5160-4	$19.99 US/$27.99 CAN
...g Results For Dummies®	Mark H. McCormack	0-7645-5205-8	$19.99 US/$27.99 CAN
...Buying For Dummies®	Eric Tyson, MBA & Ray Brown	1-56884-385-2	$16.99 US/$24.99 CAN
...Selling For Dummies®	Eric Tyson, MBA & Ray Brown	0-7645-5038-1	$19.99 US/$29.99 CAN
...Resources Kit For Dummies®	Max Messmer	0-7645-5131-0	$29.99 US/$44.99 CAN
...ing For Dummies®, 2nd Edition	Eric Tyson, MBA	0-7645-5162-0	$21.99 US/$29.99 CAN
...r Dummies®	John Ventura	1-56884-860-9	$21.99 US/$29.99 CAN
...rship For Dummies®	Marshall Loeb & Steven Kindel	0-7645-5176-0	$19.99 US/$27.99 CAN
...ging For Dummies®	Bob Nelson & Peter Economy	1-56884-858-7	$21.99 US/$29.99 CAN
...ting For Dummies®	Alexander Hiam	1-56884-699-1	$21.99 US/$29.99 CAN
...l Funds For Dummies®, 2nd Edition	Eric Tyson, MBA	0-7645-5112-4	$19.99 US/$27.99 CAN
...iating For Dummies®	Michael C. Donaldson & Mimi Donaldson	1-56884-867-6	$19.99 US/$27.99 CAN
...al Finance For Dummies®, 3rd Edition	Eric Tyson, MBA	0-7645-5231-7	$21.99 US/$28.99 CAN
...al Finance For Dummies® For Canadians, 2nd Edition	Eric Tyson, MBA & Tony Martin	0-7645-5123-X	$19.99 US/$27.99 CAN
...Speaking For Dummies®	Malcolm Kushner	0-7645-5159-0	$21.99 US/$29.99 CAN
...Closing For Dummies®	Tom Hopkins	0-7645-5063-2	$16.99 US/$25.99 CAN
...Prospecting For Dummies®	Tom Hopkins	0-7645-5066-7	$16.99 US/$25.99 CAN
...g For Dummies®	Tom Hopkins	1-56884-389-5	$16.99 US/$24.99 CAN
...Business For Dummies®	Eric Tyson, MBA & Jim Schell	0-7645-5094-2	$21.99 US/$29.99 CAN
...Business Kit For Dummies®	Richard D. Harroch	0-7645-5093-4	$29.99 US/$44.99 CAN
...2001 For Dummies®	Eric Tyson & David J. Silverman	0-7645-5306-2	$15.99 US/$23.99 CAN
...Management For Dummies®, 2nd Edition	Jeffrey J. Mayer	0-7645-5145-0	$21.99 US/$29.99 CAN
...g Business Letters For Dummies®	Sheryl Lindsell-Roberts	0-7645-5207-4	$21.99 US/$29.99 CAN

TECHNOLOGY TITLES

TERNET/ONLINE

Title	Author	ISBN	Price
...ica Online For Dummies®, 6th Edition	John Kaufeld	0-7645-0670-6	$19.99 US/$27.99 CAN
...ng Online Dummies®	Paul Murphy	0-7645-0458-4	$24.99 US/$34.99 CAN
...™ For Dummies®, 2nd Edition	Marcia Collier, Roland Woerner, & Stephanie Becker	0-7645-0761-3	$21.99 US/$32.99 CAN
...l For Dummies®, 2nd Edition	John R. Levine, Carol Baroudi, & Arnold Reinhold	0-7645-0131-3	$24.99 US/$34.99 CAN
...alogy Online For Dummies®, 2nd Edition	Matthew L. Helm & April Leah Helm	0-7645-0543-2	$24.99 US/$34.99 CAN
...net Directory For Dummies®, 3rd Edition	Brad Hill	0-7645-0558-2	$24.99 US/$34.99 CAN
...net Auctions For Dummies®	Greg Holden	0-7645-0578-9	$24.99 US/$34.99 CAN
...net Explorer 5.5 For Windows® For Dummies®	Doug Lowe	0-7645-0738-9	$19.99 US/$29.99 CAN
...arching Online For Dummies®, 2nd Edition	Mary Ellen Bates & Reva Basch	0-7645-0546-7	$24.99 US/$37.99 CAN
...earching Online For Dummies®	Pam Dixon	0-7645-0673-0	$24.99 US/$34.99 CAN
...ting Online For Dummies®, 3rd Edition	Kathleen Sindell, Ph.D.	0-7645-0725-7	$24.99 US/$37.99 CAN
...l Planning Online For Dummies®, 2nd Edition	Noah Vadnai	0-7645-0438-X	$24.99 US/$34.99 CAN
...net Searching For Dummies®	Brad Hill	0-7645-0478-9	$24.99 US/$34.99 CAN
...o!® For Dummies®, 2nd Edition	Brad Hill	0-7645-0762-1	$19.99 US/$29.99 CAN
...nternet For Dummies®, 7th Edition	John R. Levine, Carol Baroudi, & Arnold Reinhold	0-7645-0674-9	$21.99 US/$32.99 CAN

PERATING SYSTEMS

Title	Author	ISBN	Price
...For Dummies®, 3rd Edition	Dan Gookin	0-7645-0361-8	$21.99 US/$32.99 CAN
...ME For Linux® For Dummies®	David B. Busch	0-7645-0650-1	$24.99 US/$37.99 CAN
...X® For Dummies®, 2nd Edition	John Hall, Craig Witherspoon, & Coletta Witherspoon	0-7645-0421-5	$24.99 US/$34.99 CAN
...® OS 9 For Dummies®	Bob LeVitus	0-7645-0652-8	$21.99 US/$32.99 CAN
...Hat® Linux® For Dummies®	Jon "maddog" Hall, Paul Sery	0-7645-0663-3	$24.99 US/$37.99 CAN
...ll Business Windows® 98 For Dummies®	Stephen Nelson	0-7645-0425-8	$24.99 US/$34.99 CAN
...x® For Dummies®, 4th Edition	John R. Levine & Margaret Levine Young	0-7645-0419-3	$21.99 US/$32.99 CAN
...lows® 95 For Dummies®, 2nd Edition	Andy Rathbone	0-7645-0180-1	$19.99 US/$27.99 CAN
...lows® 98 For Dummies®	Andy Rathbone	0-7645-0261-1	$21.99 US/$32.99 CAN
...lows® 2000 For Dummies®	Andy Rathbone	0-7645-0641-2	$21.99 US/$32.99 CAN
...lows® 2000 Server For Dummies®	Ed Tittel	0-7645-0341-3	$24.99 US/$37.99 CAN
...lows® ME Millennium Edition For Dummies®	Andy Rathbone	0-7645-0735-4	$21.99 US/$32.99 CAN

Dummies Books™
Bestsellers on Every Topic!

GENERAL INTEREST TITLES

FOOD & BEVERAGE/ENTERTAINING

Title	Author	ISBN	Price
Bartending For Dummies®	Ray Foley	0-7645-5051-9	$15.99 US/$23.99 CAN
Cooking For Dummies®, 2nd Edition	Bryan Miller & Marie Rama	0-7645-5250-3	$21.99 US/$32.99 CAN
Entertaining For Dummies®	Suzanne Williamson with Linda Smith	0-7645-5027-6	$19.99 US/$27.99 CAN
Gourmet Cooking For Dummies®	Charlie Trotter	0-7645-5029-2	$19.99 US/$27.99 CAN
Grilling For Dummies®	Marie Rama & John Mariani	0-7645-5076-4	$19.99 US/$27.99 CAN
Italian Cooking For Dummies®	Cesare Casella & Jack Bishop	0-7645-5098-5	$19.99 US/$27.99 CAN
Mexican Cooking For Dummies®	Mary Sue Miliken & Susan Feniger	0-7645-5169-8	$21.99 US/$29.99 CAN
Quick & Healthy Cooking For Dummies®	Lynn Fischer	0-7645-5214-7	$19.99 US/$27.99 CAN
Wine For Dummies®, 2nd Edition	Ed McCarthy & Mary Ewing-Mulligan	0-7645-5114-0	$21.99 US/$29.99 CAN
Chinese Cooking For Dummies®	Martin Yan	0-7645-5247-3	$21.99 US/$29.99 CAN
Etiquette For Dummies®	Sue Fox	0-7645-5170-1	$21.99 US/$29.99 CAN

SPORTS

Title	Author	ISBN	Price
Baseball For Dummies®, 2nd Edition	Joe Morgan with Richard Lally	0-7645-5234-1	$19.99 US/$27.99 CAN
Golf For Dummies®, 2nd Edition	Gary McCord	0-7645-5146-9	$21.99 US/$29.99 CAN
Fly Fishing For Dummies®	Peter Kaminsky	0-7645-5073-X	$21.99 US/$29.99 CAN
Football For Dummies®	Howie Long with John Czarnecki	0-7645-5054-3	$19.99 US/$27.99 CAN
Hockey For Dummies®	John Davidson with John Steinbreder	0-7645-5045-4	$19.99 US/$27.99 CAN
NASCAR For Dummies®	Mark Martin	0-7645-5219-8	$21.99 US/$29.99 CAN
Tennis For Dummies®	Patrick McEnroe with Peter Bodo	0-7645-5087-X	$21.99 US/$29.99 CAN
Soccer For Dummies®	U.S. Soccer Federation & Michael Lewiss	0-7645-5229-5	$21.99 US/$29.99 CAN

HOME & GARDEN

Title	Author	ISBN	Price
Annuals For Dummies®	Bill Marken & NGA	0-7645-5056-X	$16.99 US/$24.99 CAN
Container Gardening For Dummies®	Bill Marken & NGA	0-7645-5057-8	$16.99 US/$24.99 CAN
Decks & Patios For Dummies®	Robert J. Beckstrom & NGA	0-7645-5075-6	$16.99 US/$24.99 CAN
Flowering Bulbs For Dummies®	Judy Glattstein & NGA	0-7645-5103-5	$16.99 US/$24.99 CAN
Gardening For Dummies®, 2nd Edition	Michael MacCaskey & NGA	0-7645-5130-2	$19.99 US/$29.99 CAN
Herb Gardening For Dummies®	NGA	0-7645-5200-7	$16.99 US/$24.99 CAN
Home Improvement For Dummies®	Gene & Katie Hamilton & the Editors of HouseNet, Inc.	0-7645-5005-5	$19.99 US/$26.99 CAN
Houseplants For Dummies®	Larry Hodgson & NGA	0-7645-5102-7	$16.99 US/$24.99 CAN
Painting and Wallpapering For Dummies®	Gene Hamilton	0-7645-5150-7	$16.99 US/$24.99 CAN
Perennials For Dummies®	Marcia Tatroe & NGA	0-7645-5030-6	$19.99 US/$29.99 CAN
Roses For Dummies®, 2nd Edition	Lance Walheim	0-7645-5202-3	$21.99 US/$32.99 CAN
Trees and Shrubs For Dummies®	Ann Whitman & NGA	0-7645-5203-1	$16.99 US/$24.99 CAN
Vegetable Gardening For Dummies®	Charlie Nardozzi & NGA	0-7645-5129-9	$16.99 US/$24.99 CAN
Home Cooking For Dummies®	Patricia Hart McMillan & Katharine Kaye McMillan	0-7645-5107-8	$21.99 US/$27.99 CAN

TECHNOLOGY TITLES

WEB DESIGN & PUBLISHING

Title	Author	ISBN	Price
Active Server Pages For Dummies®, 2nd Edition	Bill Hatfield	0-7645-0603-X	$24.99 US/$37.99 CAN
Cold Fusion 4 For Dummies®	Alexis Gutzman	0-7645-0604-8	$24.99 US/$37.99 CAN
Creating Web Pages For Dummies®, 5th Edition	Bud Smith & Arthur Bebak	0-7645-0733-8	$24.99 US/$37.99 CAN
Dreamweaver™ 3 For Dummies®	Janine Warner & Paul Vachier	0-7645-0669-2	$24.99 US/$37.99 CAN
FrontPage® 2000 For Dummies®	Asha Dornfest	0-7645-0423-1	$24.99 US/$34.99 CAN
HTML 4 For Dummies®, 3rd Edition	Ed Tittel & Natanya Dits	0-7645-0572-6	$24.99 US/$34.99 CAN
Java™ For Dummies®, 3rd Edition	Aaron E. Walsh	0-7645-0417-7	$24.99 US/$34.99 CAN
PageMill™ 2 For Dummies®	Deke McClelland & John San Filippo	0-7645-0028-7	$24.99 US/$34.99 CAN
XML™ For Dummies®	Ed Tittel	0-7645-0692-7	$24.99 US/$37.99 CAN
Javascript For Dummies®, 3rd Edition	Emily Vander Veer	0-7645-0633-1	$24.99 US/$37.99 CAN

DESKTOP PUBLISHING GRAPHICS/MULTIMEDIA

Title	Author	ISBN	Price
Adobe® In Design™ For Dummies®	Deke McClelland	0-7645-0599-8	$19.99 US/$27.99 CAN
CorelDRAW™ 9 For Dummies®	Deke McClelland	0-7645-0523-8	$19.99 US/$27.99 CAN
Desktop Publishing and Design For Dummies®	Roger C. Parker	1-56884-234-1	$19.99 US/$27.99 CAN
Digital Photography For Dummies®, 3rd Edition	Julie Adair King	0-7645-0646-3	$24.99 US/$32.99 CAN
Microsoft® Publisher 98 For Dummies®	Jim McCarter	0-7645-0395-2	$19.99 US/$27.99 CAN
Visio 2000 For Dummies®	Debbie Walkowski	0-7645-0635-8	$21.99 US/$32.99 CAN
Microsoft® Publisher 2000 For Dummies®	Jim McCarter	0-7645-0525-4	$19.99 US/$27.99 CAN
Windows® Movie Maker For Dummies®	Keith Underdahl	0-7645-0749-1	$19.99 US/$27.99 CAN

Notes

Notes

Notes

Notes